Caribbean Perspectives on Criminology and Criminal Justice

Volume 1

CARIBBEAN
PERSPECTIVES
ON CRIMINOLOGY AND
CRIMINAL JUSTICE

VOLUME I

Edited by

WENDELL C. WALLACE Ph.D.

Westphalia Press
An Imprint of the Policy Studies Organization
Washington, DC
2019

CARIBBEAN PERSPECTIVES ON CRIMINOLOGY
AND CRIMINAL JUSTICE, VOLUME 1

All Rights Reserved © 2019 by Policy Studies Organization

Westphalia Press
An imprint of Policy Studies Organization
1527 New Hampshire Ave., NW
Washington, D.C. 20036
info@ipsonet.org

ISBN: 978-1-63391-494-0

Cover and interior design by Jeffrey Barnes
jbarnesbook.design

Daniel Gutierrez-Sandoval, Executive Director
PSO and Westphalia Press

Updated material and comments on this edition
can be found at the Westphalia Press website:
www.westphaliapress.org

"Poverty is no excuse for crime and self-deprivation but a surmountable hurdle in the journey to the top."

—Wendell C. Wallace

DEDICATION

There is no doubt that the Caribbean is heavily influenced by Western dicta on criminology and criminal justice; however, there is a need to (re)write the Caribbean's criminology and criminal justice through Caribbean lens. With that said, this book is dedicated to those early Caribbean scholars who laid the foundation for generations of Caribbean criminologists to follow. Despite the challenges they faced in having their works recognized and published, their indomitable spirit lives on in the multiplicity of Caribbean criminologists who are now endeared to conduct scholarly research so that we can understand crime in the Caribbean through Caribbean perspectives. In sum, this book is dedicated to those individuals who believe that the Caribbean's legacy, whether criminological, economic, social, political, historical, legal, or otherwise, must be conceptualized and preserved through Caribbean lens. This book is especially dedicated to the late Ken Pryce for his call for a Caribbean Criminology in 1976.

CONTENTS

FOREWORD

C rime continues to be one of the major social problems facing the Caribbean today—it pervades every aspect of society and every individual is affected, either directly, indirectly or through a culture of hypervigilance. In addition to having direct effects on victims, crime can also generate a climate of fear among citizens, threaten public safety, impose widespread costs and diminish economic growth and development, while creating unsafe and inhospitable spaces for investment. Crime is a complex social issue that cannot be examined in isolation and we must be cognisant of the boundaries of the criminal justice system in the region. As the future of those convicted and the need for closure for victims and their families lie in the hands of the criminal justice system, it is important for this system to be robust and capable of protecting the rights of all citizens.

Because of the Caribbean's unique history and colonial legacy, crime, like many other social problems, is deeply embedded in our sociohistorical and colonial past. The location of the region, its porous borders and economic situation increase the Caribbean's vulnerability to crime. It is no secret that a large percentage of the Caribbean's resources is invested in developing long term plans, programmes and policies to reduce the high rates of crime and its damaging effects. However, the very nature of these plans and intervention strategies are wedged within a Eurocentric dogma and as such, they have been mostly reactive and ineffective. This is why, more than forty years ago, Ken Pryce (1976) called for the development of a new Caribbean Criminology. Adding to the seminal ideas of Ken Pryce, Jones (1981, 166) proposed *"... any of the approach to better understanding of this problem ... must be looked at from the viewpoint of the developing country. Ideas are often exported as manufactured goods and the result is often a disastrous to third world countries"*. In light of this recommendation, many Caribbean criminologists have taken heed, and refrained from using first world criminological theories and ideas and applying them wholesale in spaces that require more grounding and new understandings. Today, attempts have been made to create Caribbean spaces and an identity for evidence-based criminological research.

This ongoing search for a Caribbean Criminology, is by no means an easy feat, as necessitated by the process of building the body of research. Caribbean criminologists must therefore take control of the growing crime situation and through their research, offer the ideas, plans and strategies that can bring about the systemic change that is needed to address crime and the issues that plague a weak and overwhelmed criminal justice system. Therefore, Caribbean criminologists have a duty to acknowledge and act upon the recommendations made by the earlier scholars, in line with ethical practice.

Without fear of criticism and recognising the need to contribute meaningfully to the Caribbean society, the author of this book has carefully put together a rich compilation of research on criminological issues, which provides a comprehensive understanding of the cross-cultural boundaries of crime and the criminal justice system, as well as, evidence-based solutions and recommendations. The chapters cover a wide range of areas that include, the socio-legal system, policing and police corruption, community crime and gang violence, migration, drug trafficking and money laundering, and the sociolinguistic analysis of communication in the court. The chapters also capture some of the key areas in Criminology that have been underexplored and have now been given credence to be part of a holistic approach to understanding crime. This edited volume is a true reflection of some of the work that has already started. Additionally, this volume features both the single and co-authored work of regional and international researchers and policy makers who saw the need to share their experiences and findings within an empirically and theoretically oriented framework. This book represents a true masterpiece of Caribbean scholarship and the thrust towards making the region a safer and more secure place for all citizens. It not only represents a shift in research perspectives on crime and criminal justice but gives a pragmatic understanding of crime from a postcolonial and sociohistorical Caribbean context. It offers a true representation of the main challenges which we now face as academics, criminal justice professionals, practitioners and policy makers.

As you begin your journey through the various chapters of this book, I promise you an exciting indulgence of connecting research, theory and practice. This book communicates the excitement of research and conveys the latest developments and trends in crime and criminal justice. It also provides the impetus research for driving the evidence-based polices on crime and presents you with the ways in which the criminal justice system in the Caribbean can be further strengthened. This book is intended to serve future researchers, students, policy makers and practitioners in the field of criminology and criminal justice. As a prequel to the next volume, this book sets the foundation for building and advancing Caribbean Criminology. If we are to continue along these trends, a look towards the future for Caribbean Criminology is promising.

Dr. Christine Descartes

Lecturer in Psychology, The University of the West Indies, St. Augustine

PREFACE

Caribbean Perspectives on Criminology and Criminal Justice provides an insight into the multiplicity of socio-legal challenges and criminological issues facing Caribbean societies. These challenges are both traditional and emerging and are worthy of explication. The book examines a range of challenges and concerns facing Caribbean societies and their criminal justice systems as it has been argued that there is a multiplicity of factors that impinge on Caribbean criminal justice systems and by extension, the people who utilize those services. In fact, the challenges facing Caribbean societies and their governments were deemed to be so monumental that in order to effectively present them, it was decided that a two-volume book would be the medium for publishing the research findings. This book (Volume 1) examines topics including, but not limited to, homicides, the Judiciary, sex workers, drug trafficking, money laundering, police corruption, crime prevention, and language usage in Caribbean criminal justice systems.

This book has several objectives. The first objective is to cast light upon the challenges, issues, and factors that plague Caribbean communities and their criminal justice systems. The second objective is to highlight research undertaken by Caribbean-based scholars, Caribbean scholars in the diaspora, as well as international scholars who focus on social and others issues facing the region. The third objective is to proffer effective strategies aimed at alleviating the identified concerns. The final objective is to build upon the extant criminological literature that exists in the Caribbean and in doing so answer Ken Pryce's (1976) call for the development of a Caribbean Criminology.

This genesis of this book is my time as a Master of Science student in Criminology and Criminal Justice at The University of the West Indies, St. Augustine campus between 2005 and 2006. I was constantly bothered by the fact that almost all of the reading materials, theoretical frameworks, and concepts emanated from the Western world and that there appeared to be a dearth of Caribbean literature on criminology and criminal justice. Added to this, in one of my late night sojourns, I came across the readings of Ken Pryce (1976) and soon realized that the aforementioned lacuna was a pre-existing condition, taking into consideration that Pryce's call for a Caribbean Criminology was made since 1976.

After surviving the defense of my Doctoral dissertation, I attended and presented at several international conferences and realized that apart from the relatively limited criminological literature emanating from the Caribbean, that there was a genuine interest by non-Caribbean scholars in scholarly Caribbean literature on criminology and criminal justice. Thereafter, I continued attending international conferences and expanding my network of scholars in the Caribbean, United States, UK, Africa, Europe, Asia, and Latin America. Subsequently, I deliberated with several established scholars and lecturers in the Caribbean, esteemed criminologists in the Global North as well as Caribbean scholars in the diaspora, relative to conducting research aimed at highlighting the plethora of issues facing criminal justice systems in the Caribbean. Instructively, one of my mentors advised me that due to the multifaceted nature of criminological issues facing Caribbean criminal justice systems, that I should author an edited book and allow other scholars to contribute perspectives from and on different Caribbean islands. I duly accepted the challenge and this book is therefore the culmination of a challenge that began in 2005–2006 when I was a postgraduate student.

Though I willingly accepted the challenge to author and edit this book, the journey was not always a smooth one as several trials and tribulations were encountered along the way; however, much was learnt and I am now in a better position to continue similar sojourns after this learning experience. As indicated above, the journey to completion of Volume 1 of this book was not without its rocky moments and at times, I felt like giving up. As an individual, I am keen on meeting deadlines and being dependent on authors and reviewers to ascribe to those standards was a difficult task. Indeed, many of the book chapters were submitted late and in some instances, both reviewers and book chapter authors were the recipient of numerous reminders that their deadlines had elapsed. In a few instances, I did not receive the courtesy of a reply and this dampened my desire to continue; however, I often recalled my father Codrington Wallace extolling to me certain virtues and one of his oft-repeated saying was "nothing ventured, nothing gained." This served to strengthen my resolve to continue the book to completion. The aforementioned is a snapshot of some of the problems that came up during the editing process and how these trials and tribulations were managed. Instructively, as an individual, the process of editing this book has allowed me to become more patient and not see the world only through my timelines. In sum, I have gained invaluable experiences and expanded my knowledge base through the editing process and I have certainly changed as an author.

The purpose of this book is to shed light on the many pervasive issues that impact upon Caribbean societies and their criminal justice systems from criminological and criminal justice perspectives. In reading this book, it is hoped that readers will become enlightened about these issues, research conducted, and recommendations aimed at alleviating them. *Caribbean Perspectives on Criminology and Criminal Justice* (Volume 1) is directed to students, government officials, policymakers, security professional, and individuals who are interested in the development of a Caribbean criminology. Specifically, for these readers, the book details the views of Caribbean and international academicians on several socially bothersome criminological and criminal justice issues in the Caribbean.

In closing, it was always my intention to personally research some of the topics contained in this book and to publish them, however, due to the guidance received from one of my mentors as well as from my observations on criminal justice systems throughout the Caribbean, I was literally guided, or maybe it was divine intervention that led me to edit this book and to share the research with the world at large and thus put the spotlight on *Caribbean Perspectives on Criminology and Criminal Justice*. For the reading audience, I thank you for accessing this book; however, I humbly request that in reading the book, that you do so in the context of attempting to understand the criminological and criminal justice challenges that nation states in the Caribbean currently face. Do enjoy your reading and as you flip through these pages, do remember that Volume 2 offers further elucidation of the criminological and criminal justice challenges facing the Caribbean.

Dr. Wendell C. Wallace

ACKNOWLEDGMENTS

This book could not have been completed without the support and assistance of a number of individuals and agencies. First, I would like to recognize and thank the many hardworking and dedicated educators at Bishop's High School, Tobago, The University of the West Indies, St. Augustine, Beckles and Associates Law Tutors, and Northumbria University (Northumbria Law School) whose hard work, dedication, and commitment to quality education engendered in me the desire to achieve beyond my wildest dreams.

I must extend my heartfelt gratitude to the authors of the book chapters who willingly accepted the challenge to become a part of this book and who conducted their mandated tasks with aplomb and professionalism. Without this dedicated team of authors, it would have been impossible to shed light on the criminological and criminal justice challenges that are operational in the region and to provide possible solutions to these issues. A special thank you is dedicated to the following book chapter authors: Dr. Keron King, Dr. Nathan W. Pino, Miss Nirmala Sookoo, Dr. Charles M. Katz, Dr. Andrew M. Fox, Miss Lexi Gill, Dr. Suzette A. Haughton, Dr. Trevor Smith, Dr. Wendy-Ann P. Isaac, Professor Wayne G. Ganpat, Dr. Marlene Attzs, Mr. Thomas E. Isaac, Dr. Avekadavie Parasramsingh Mano, Dr. Ashaki Dore, Dr. R. Sandra Evans, and Mr. Kevin Sean Peters.

On a more personal note, I would like to recognize my family and close friends for their faith in my ability to complete this project and the support that they gave to make it happen. Especially to my parents Codrington and Ann Eastman-Wallace and my deceased grandparents Josey and Miriam Eastman, for starting me on the path that has brought me to this point, developing in me the determination to follow it, and providing me with the resources to do so.

Special thanks must be approximated to my siblings Sandra, Roger (deceased but not forgotten), Dale, and Merville Wallace who assisted me in numerous ways and provided moral support throughout the duration of this project. Merville, the first copy of this book that comes off the press belongs to you. To my uncles, aunts, children, nephews, nieces, cousins, friends, and academic colleagues (Cecil, Ashton, Dariq, Elisha, Abigail, DeJuan, Malique, Janae and Toni-Lisa Wallace, Kurt, Brent and Oswald

Eastman, Shaneika Joseph, Tyrelle Taylor, Akeem Adams, Antoinette Knights, Ayinka Nurse-Carrington, Brian Caesar, Cedric Neptune, Dr. Dianne Williams, and Dr. Allan Patenaude), thank you for your unwavering support.

I also owe a huge debt of gratitude to the reviewers of this book. Though many of the reviewers of the articles contained in this book would prefer to remain faceless, it would be remiss of me to not extend my profound gratitude to these reviewers who took time away from their busy academic, professional, and family lives to review the many articles that were received in response to the Call for Papers for this book. Not only did the reviewers review the articles in a timely and professional manner, but they performed the task "*pro bono*" and for this, I am extremely grateful.

I also wish to extend a heartfelt thank you to the many researchers who submitted research articles for the two volumes of this book. Though over 60% of the book chapters that were initially submitted for publication consideration in Caribbean Perspectives on Criminology and Criminal Justice were not accepted due to constraints of space, it was these invaluable submissions that ensured that the Chapters that were eventually selected for publication were of the highest caliber. Though many book chapter authors may be disappointed that their book chapters were not selected, I salute every author who submitted a book chapter for review and wish them the best with those submissions that were returned for revision and submission to international Journals.

I owe a special debt of gratitude to my academic colleague Dr. Christine Descartes for always lending a critical eye, a listening ear to my never-ending proposals, for providing pastoral care when I needed to vent, and who is forever supportive of my research efforts. Christine, I must also thank you for authoring the foreword of this book. On behalf of the Book Chapter authors, thank you Dr. Rahima Schwenkbeck for persevering with this book project, for your oversight and edits to the respective chapters and to Westphalia Press for publishing this book.

Finally, and most importantly, thank you God for the divine inspiration and strength which you gave to me to attempt and complete this book which hopefully would provide insightful literature to a wide range of individuals and serve to assist policymakers in the Caribbean. To every individual who assisted in the production of this book, even in the most miniscule manner, though your names may not be mentioned, thank you for your support and assistance.

Dr. Wendell C. Wallace

August 2019

Notes on Contributors

ATTZS, MARLENE

Dr. Marlene Attzs currently serves as Advisor to the Pro Vice Chancellor and Campus Principal of The University of the West Indies, St. Augustine campus (with responsibility for Institutional Effectiveness and Strategy). She is a development economist with her main research interests being the Economics of Disaster Risk Management and Climate Change Adaptation; Gender Mainstreaming in Disaster Risk Management and Climate Change Adaptation; and in Sustainable Tourism Development, all with particular reference to Small and Island Developing States (SIDS). Substantively, Dr. Attzs is a Lecturer in Economics and has served as Head of the Department of Economics and Deputy Dean of the Faculty of Social Sciences. She has provided consulting advice nationally, regionally, and internationally, in the above-mentioned areas and was a review editor for the IPCC's Fifth Assessment Report (Chapter 3, Social, Economic, and Ethical Concepts and Methods). Dr. Attzs has consulted with regional institutions such as the Caribbean Disaster and Emergency Management Agency (CDEMA), the Caribbean Development Bank (CDB), and internationally with the Inter-American Development Bank (IDB), the World Bank (Washington, DC), and the Department for International Development (DFID) (UK).

DORE, ASHAKI L.

Dr. Ashaki L. Dore is a Corporal in the Trinidad and Tobago Regiment (TTR) and has 15 years of military service. Dr. Dore is currently attached to the Military Community Support System Task Force (MCSS). She has conducted field research in El Salvador and Trinidad and Tobago and has presented papers on her postgraduate work at the International Studies Association (ISA), the Graduate School of Policy and Global Studies at the University of Massachusetts Boston, the Centre for Citizenship Studies at Wayne State University, SALISES, and Caribbean Studies Association (CSA). Her previous publications include "Human Security: A New Regionalism for the Caribbean," "Tracking the Perfect Storm: Subsistence Piracy and Illegal Immigration in Trinidad and Tobago" (Forthcoming), and "Leveraging the Asylum System to Overcome Immigration Barriers in Small Island States" to be published in "Selected Essays on Contemporary Caribbean Issues" (Forthcoming).

EVANS, R. SANDRA

Dr. R. Sandra Evans is a lecturer in linguistics in the Department of Modern Languages and Linguistics, at The University of the West Indies, St. Augustine, Trinidad and Tobago. She is also the coordinator of the postgraduate program in linguistics. She holds a Ph.D. in linguistics and her doctoral research explored the language use patterns and practices of legal system in St. Lucia to determine how they operate to provide proper access to justice to French-lexicon Creole (Kwéyòl) speakers. Dr. Evans specializes in forensic linguistics/language and the law and her research interests also include creole linguistics, language education, language policy, and language rights in the creole-speaking Caribbean.

FOX, ANDREW M.

Dr. Andrew M. Fox is the Research and Policy Senior Manager for Juvenile Rehabilitation in Washington State. His research interests include social network analysis, delinquency, gangs, crime prevention, program evaluation, and communities. Fox has served as the research partner on a number of federal initiatives, including Strategies for Policing Innovation, Innovative Prosecution Solutions, and the Police–Prosecution Partnership Initiative. He was previously an assistant professor at the University of Missouri-Kansas City and California State University, Fresno. He received his Ph.D. and M.S. from Arizona State University in Criminology and Criminal Justice. Some of his work has been published in Crime and Delinquency, Justice Quarterly, Police Quarterly, and the American Sociological Review. Andrew can be reached at foxam@dhsh.wa.gov.

GANPAT, WAYNE G.

Professor Wayne G. Ganpat is an internationally recognized Agricultural Extension expert. Professor Ganpat spent a significant part of his career providing public and consultancy services in the field of Agricultural Extension and Communications before coming to full-time academia. His academic career began in 1998 as a part-time Lecturer at The University of the West Indies, St. Augustine, before assuming a full-time post in

2010. Professor Ganpat served as Head of the Department of Agricultural Economics and Extension (2015–2016) and is currently the Dean of the Faculty of Food and Agriculture at The University of the West Indies, St. Augustine Campus.

Professor Ganpat has collaborated with highly respected international researchers and has published 7 books, 45 refereed journal articles, 9 book chapters, 9 technical reports, as well as 4 reports prepared for regional governments. He serves as the Chair of the Editorial Board for Tropical Agriculture, the Journal of the Faculty of Food and Agriculture, The University of the West Indies, St. Augustine, and is a reviewer for several journals in the field of Extension and Communications. Professor Ganpat's work has been widely recognized with awards including an Outstanding Contribution and Service Excellence Award (2002) from the Government of the Republic of Trinidad and Tobago Government, for innovative work in Agricultural Extension. He was also recognized as Most Outstanding Researcher 2014–2016 at the UWI/NGC's Research Awards in 2016. Professor Ganpat is also Senior Fellow and President of the Association for International Agricultural and Extension Education (AIAEE).

HAUGHTON, SUZETTE A.

Dr. Suzette A. Haughton is a Senior Lecturer at the Department of Government, The University of the West Indies, Mona Campus, Kingston, Jamaica. She lectures on International Security Issues and Public International Law. She was a Commonwealth Scholar and obtained her Ph.D. from the Department of War Studies, King's College, London. Her research spans security threats affecting the Americas. Dr. Haughton has published extensively on drug trafficking, border security, border disputes, and their impacts on the nation-state and on the lived experiences of citizens.

ISAAC, WENDY-ANN P.

Wendy-Ann P. Isaac is a Senior Lecturer in Crop Science in the Department of Food Production, Faculty of Food and Agriculture, The University of the West Indies, St Augustine campus. Her research and teaching revolve around her area of experience: sustainable vegetable production, integrated weed management, and innovative farming technologies, including protected agriculture and controlled environmental agriculture.

She also has interest in Participatory action research techniques and small farmers. She has worked with Fairtrade banana small farmers in St. Vincent and the Grenadines using the Participatory Research methods as part of her Ph.D. Studies. She has authored and co-authored papers and chapters on these topics, which have been published in both regional and international peer-reviewed journals and has also co-edited books on Sustainable Food Production Practices in the Caribbean Agricultural Development and Impacts of climate change on food production in Small Island Developing States (SIDS).

ISAAC, THOMAS E.

Thomas E. Isaac is a part-time lecturer at the University of the Southern Caribbean where he lectures in World Religions, God and Human Life and History and Sociology. He holds an M.A. in Education and is a Ph.D. candidate in cultural studies at The University of the West Indies, St Augustine. His thesis is entitled "De-constructing the Trinidad Carnival; in search of the Trinidad psyche." He has spent several years as an educator where he served as a Secondary School Principal and later as a School Supervisor III with the Ministry of Education in Trinidad and Tobago.

KATZ, CHARLES M.

Professor Charles M. Katz is the Watts Family Director of the Center for Violence Prevention and Community Safety and is a Professor in the School of Criminology and Criminal Justice at Arizona State University. His work focuses on police transformation and strategic responses to crime. He has worked under contract with the Ministry of National Security of the Republic of Trinidad and Tobago to develop a comprehensive strategic plan to reform the Trinidad and Tobago Police Services. Since then he has completed a project funded by the UNDP to assess citizen insecurity throughout the Caribbean; and worked for the Eastern Caribbean's Regional Security System to diagnose the gang problem in nine Caribbean nations and develop a regional approach to responding to gangs. He has also completed several research projects for the U.S. Department of Homeland Security and USAID in El Salvador and Honduras on issues involving the police and an evaluation of a violence prevention and intervention program. He is currently working on the Community, Family, and Youth Resilience project and CariSECURE, both sponsored by USAID.

KING, KERON

Dr. Keron King is a Senior Lecturer in Criminal Justice at the College of Science, Technology and Applied Arts of Trinidad and Tobago. His research interests include community-oriented policing, democratic policing, police legitimacy, procedural justice, crime prevention, police reform, restorative justice, and prisoner reintegration. Dr. King adopts a postcolonial theoretical framework to examine the issues of crime and justice where the philosophy of Peacemaking Criminology is often prominent. His doctoral dissertation explored how residents of an urban community in Trinidad and Tobago constructed their experiences with the police.

PARASRAMSINGH MANO, AVEKADAVIE (AVEKA)

Dr. Avekadavie Parasramsingh Mano holds a Ph.D. in Criminology and Criminal Justice from The University of the West Indies, St. Augustine. Her doctoral research focused on the Belizean sex trade, particularly on the aspect of migratory sex work, and involved the methodological innovation of Attride-Stirling's thematic network analysis technique. This innovative research was published in the International Annals of Criminology in 2018. Her current research examines the collapse of Venezuela's economy and its consequential impact on Trinidad and Tobago's sex industry. Her research interests include victims of crime, penology, human trafficking, sex trafficking, qualitative research methods, and criminological theories.

PETERS, KEVIN SEAN

Mr. Kevin Peters holds degrees in Agribusiness Management and Sociology (undergraduate) and Criminology and Criminal Justice (Master's) from The University of the West Indies, St. Augustine. He is currently a Ph.D. candidate Criminology and Criminal Justice at The University of the West Indies, St. Augustine. Mr. Peters is a lecturer in the Department of Criminal Justice and Legal Studies at the College of Science Technology and Applied Arts of Trinidad and Tobago (COSTAATT). He is also a part-time teacher at the St. Jude's School for Girls where he prepares girls under the care of the state for the Caribbean Secondary Education Certificate (CSEC) in Social Studies and Principles of Business. His research interests include the juvenile justice system (with an emphasis on the rehabilitation of girls), prisoner re-entry and reintegration, penology, and migration and crime. Mr. Peters most notable publication titled "Faith Based Programmes as a Means to Combat the Revolving Door Syndrome in Trinidad and Tobago" has been published with the Caribbean Journal of Criminology and Public Safety.

PINO, NATHAN W.

Dr. Nathan W. Pino is a professor of sociology and honorary professor of international studies at Texas State University. Professor Pino has published 4 books and over 30 articles and book chapters on the relationships between globalization, development, crime, and crime control; policing and police reform in an international context; sexual and other forms of extreme violence; and the attitudes and behaviors of college students. In 2009, Dr. Pino served as a Fulbright scholar in Trinidad and Tobago at The University of the West Indies, St. Augustine, teaching courses in criminology and crime policy and conducting research on police–community relations and police reform efforts. He is the co-author (with Graham Ellison) of Globalization, Police Reform, and Development: Doing it the Western Way? (Palgrave, 2012), and (with Robert Shanafelt) Rethinking Serial Murder, Spree Killing, and Atrocities: Beyond the Usual Distinctions (Routledge, 2015).

SOOKOO, NIRMALA

Miss Nirmala Sookoo is currently a research consultant and Ph.D. candidate in Criminology and Criminal Justice at The University of the West Indies, St. Augustine, Trinidad and Tobago. She has previous publications entitled "White Collar Crime in Trinidad", "Perceptions of Injustice and Alienation", and "Exploring the Link between Corruption and Rule of Law in Five Caribbean Nations". Her research specialisations include policing, white collar crime, corruption and alienation studies. The main goal, that drives her research is building knowledge about crime as well its consequences within the Caribbean region.

SMITH, TREVOR A.

Dr. Trevor Smith is a Senior Lecturer in Marketing and Research Methods at Mona School of Business and Management (MSBM), The University of the West Indies, Mona Campus. He is the Academic Director of the M.Sc. National Security and Strategic Studies and Unit Head for MIBES (Marketing, International Business, Entrepreneurship and Strategy) at the School. Dr. Smith has published in a number of rated international Journals in two streams or research—Marketing Psychology and Management and utilizes structural equation modeling (SEM) in most of his work.

WALLACE, WENDELL C.

Dr. Wendell C. Wallace is a Lecturer in Criminology and Criminal Justice at The University of the West Indies, St. Augustine. He is also a certified Mediator with the Mediation Board of Trinidad and Tobago as well as an Attorney-at-Law who has been called to the Bar in both England and Wales and Trinidad and Tobago. In 2014, he was awarded the best Doctoral paper by the Academy of Criminal Justice Sciences (ACJS), Juvenile Justice Section, in the United States for his research paper "Addressing the unmet educational needs of children and youth in detention in Trinidad and Tobago." In 2017, he received the Frederic Milton Thrasher Award for Superior Accomplishments in Gang Research from the National Gang Crime Research Center (NGCRC) in the United States. Dr. Wallace's research interests include policing, security, organized crime, violence, gangs, and the tourism/crime nexus. He is an active member of the Accreditation Council of Trinidad and Tobago, The Honourable Society of Gray's Inn, London, and the Caribbean Child Research Conference Network.

INTRODUCTION

Without a doubt, crime and criminal activities are uppermost on the minds of Caribbean residents. This is the result of increased crime and deviance in most Caribbean islands as evidenced by increased crimes against tourists, increasing serious crimes and the proliferation of radicalized Caribbean residents who have left the region as overseas jihadists to fight on behalf of ISIS. According to Harriott (2002), Hill (2012), Wallace (2018), and other scholars, the crime rates in almost all Caribbean islands have been on the increase for the past two decades and this is noticeable in all islands for which data is available.

This increase in crime has been attributed to a host of factors including, but not limited to, development, technological advances, gang proliferation, globalization, drug trafficking, human trafficking, and the deportation of criminals from Canada, United States, and the UK to the Caribbean. Added to this, it is argued that the location of Caribbean islands on the direct trade routes between North and South America (consumers and producers of drugs) facilitates increased criminal activities. Further, that the porous borders and large budgets of Transnational Organized Crime groups which are, in some instances, larger than the national budgets of some small Caribbean states serves to facilitate the corruption of state officials.

When the aforementioned are juxtaposed against Caribbean countries with fragile economies, a chronic lack of resources and a dependency syndrome on the Global North for training of law enforcement personal and other forms of aid, these inter-related and interwoven factors contribute to the toxicity that is increasing crime in the region. As a result of the increase in crime and deviance across the region, Caribbean social scientists are now arguing for a Caribbean dictum in seeking to understand the rationale for the increase in crime as well as to identify and implement intervention strategies that are non-Western in their orientation.

As a region, the Caribbean, has been deeply affected by 'colonial exploitation' (Nixon, 2015) as well as the yolk of colonialism. This yolk appears to be ever present, even in the post-independence period and appears to be indelibly etched on the psyche of some Caribbean criminal justice practitioners, legislators and policy makers, deeply embedded in the criminal justice systems of many Caribbean islands and entrenched in the mind of many Western scholars. Unfortunately, many of these Western scholars insist upon resisting notions of a Caribbean criminology and refuse to submit themselves to Caribbean understandings of crime, deviance, criminality and non-Western interventions in relation to a Caribbean sense of self. It is against this background that Agozino (2017, p. i) submits "There is an urban and western bias in criminology.........", however, contemporary Caribbean academicians are increasingly calling for Caribbean-based understandings of crime and deviance and thus move away (though not totally) from Western concepts, theories, and explanations of crime, deviance, and criminality. For some researchers, this desire for local conceptualizations in seeking to understand crime in the region represents a paradigm shift; however, for others, this is a mere continuation of Ken Pryce's call for a Caribbean criminology in 1976, a call that will be explored in the following paragraphs.

Instructively, in 1976, the late Ken Pryce called specifically for a Caribbean criminology as he pointed out that the "one-size fits all approach" to understanding crime from a Western perspective is a convoluted idea. According to Cain (1996, p. v), Pryce, in 1976, argued that "first world theories do not fit, that in the Caribbean, the global context and the colonial past provide better explanations of criminality than accounts focusing on the negotiation of face to face encounters, and also that not all macro theories make equal sense of the problem." In the words of Cain (1996, p. v), "Pryce thus raised the key issue, and in so doing left complex and challenging dilemmas for the rest of us."

The continued call for a Caribbean criminology as well as the premise of this book is built upon the works, not only of Pryce (1976), but also to a lesser extent on the works of scholars such as Sumner (1980) and Jones (1981) who both have criticized modernization theories of "third world" criminality and who have opposed the predominantly Western dicta that crime is an inevitable outcome of urbanization and an unescapable consequence of development. Sumner (1980) and Jones (1981) also cogitate that former colonies must not follow the same trajectory which the West followed during the industrial revolution (Clinard & Abbott, 1973) as the economic context in these former colonies, for example, is radically different. From a Caribbean perspective, Jones (1981) quite succinctly sums up the issue as he submits that when discussing crime, violence, causation, and solutions to crime and violence, these issues must be examined from the viewpoint of the developing country. In sum, this book is a direct response to the call by Ken Pryce in 1976 for a subdiscipline that focuses on the Caribbean as a unique area of study in criminology.

In the aftermath of Pryce's (1976) call for a Caribbean Criminology, several regional and international scholars have accepted Pryce's challenge, whether knowingly or unknowingly, and have conducted research aimed at creating this subdiscipline (a Caribbean criminology). For example, there have been research on aspects of criminology in the Caribbean including, but not limited to, Deosaran (2003), Griffith (2000), Harriott (2002), Hill (2012), Katz, Maguire, and Choate (2011), Lancaster-Ellis (2013), Levy (2012), Maguire, Willis, Snipes, and Gantley (2008), Mars (2009), Meeks (2011), Moncrieffe (2008), Morris and Graycar (2011), Pino (2016), Wallace (2018), Wallace et al. (2019), and Williams (2009). Importantly, Caribbean Perspectives on Criminology and Criminal Justice builds on these previous works by collating research into a book format that is easier to access than journals that are spread over wider distances.

While Caribbean Perspectives on Criminology and Criminal Justice (Volume 1) may appear to be regional in its orientation (and rightfully so due to its focus), the book is certainly not limited by its title due to the regional and international repute of the book chapter authors. In fact, the authors of the book chapters represent emerging, early career, mid-career, established, Caribbean, as well as international scholars in their respective fields. In this regard, the book is a true representation of the diverse nature that is now indicative of contemporary academia. For example, Drs. Charles M. Katz, Andrew M. Fox, and Nathan W. Pino are U.S. scholars who have researched and published extensively on the Caribbean. On the other hand, Caribbean Perspectives on Criminology and Criminal Justice (Volume 1) contains articles written by established Caribbean-based scholars including, but not limited to, Professor Wayne G. Ganpat and Dr. Suzette Haughton, emerging scholars and Ph.D. candidates Kevin Sean Peters and Nirmala Sookoo, as well as early career scholar Dr. Avekadavie Parasramsingh Mano. In sum, based on the foregoing, the book transcends the Caribbean.

Issues of criminology and criminal justice were hotly contested topics in the Caribbean 40–50 years ago as most of the Caribbean countries had recently severed their past colonial attachment to England and had become independent nation states, though still attached to England as the Queen in England remained the Head of State in several instances. The continuing dependence is also evident in many Caribbean jurisdictions as their final Court of Appeal remain the Judicial Committee of the Privy Council that was based in England. Importantly, issues surrounding criminology and criminal justice in the Caribbean have had time to settle over time; however, some remain in a state of flux, for example, the death penalty. Today, issues of criminology and criminal justice are again at the crossroads as several issues have resurfaced in the contemporary Caribbean. This is partly due to emergent issues such as police brutality, human trafficking, money laundering, crimes by and against tourists, and increased crime in general.

This book contains several chapters examining aspects of criminology and criminal justice in the Caribbean and this ranges from migratory sex workers, drug trafficking, money laundering, and crime prevention to homicides, the Judiciary, the criminological dimensions of agriculture, and language usage within the criminal justice system. Contributors to Volume 1 of *Caribbean Perspectives on Criminology and Criminal Justice* addresses the multiplicity of social and criminological issues plaguing the region through qualitative and quantitative approaches and proffer suggestions and recommendations aimed at alleviating these concerns for the greater good of the region. These suggestions, recommendations, and answers are presented against a backdrop of technological advances, revolutions in the teaching of tertiary education, increased protection of the rights of offenders, deportation (the new method of the age old transportation), and limited resources for justice officials.

Instructively, the authors of the respective book chapters have discussed some traditional criminal justice system challenges facing the Caribbean region as well as some contemporary and emergent ones. This is done on the premise that some of the emergent issues (as well as some traditional ones) often fall prey to limited to nonexistent research and literature or research conducted through non-Caribbean lens. Importantly, the book chapter authors took cognizance of this and whether by accident or by design gravitated toward researching these issues. By way of reflexivity, my considered view is that "these issues are now critical for the development of a Caribbean criminology as well as for the development of appropriate responses to the social issues facing the region."

ORGANIZATION OF THE BOOK

Caribbean Perspectives on Criminology and Criminal Justice (Volume 1) is organized into an introductory chapter and 10 book chapters. A brief description of each of the chapters follows.

The first chapter is authored by Keron King (College of Science, Technology and Applied Arts of Trinidad and Tobago) and Nathan W. Pino (Texas State University, USA) and focuses on policing in the Caribbean. In this chapter the authors adopt a broad framework for elucidating their ideas and seek to frame policing in a Caribbean context. King and Pino present a historical and contextual discussion of formal policing in the Caribbean from its colonial moorings to the present day. Instructively, the authors place special focus on Trinidad and Tobago as a case study in an effort to illustrate larger trends in the Caribbean. King and Pino delve into contemporary police culture throughout the Caribbean by making some astute observations of policing as foisted upon the Caribbean by the English colonials.

The second chapter, by Nirmala Sookoo (The University of the West Indies, St. Augustine) represents another chapter on policing in the Caribbean. Quite distinct from chapter 1, the author examines the Influence of Organizational Justice on police corruption in Trinidad and Tobago by gathering and analyzing data from members of the Trinidad and Tobago Police Service (TTPS). This research is quite timely and topical as within the past three decades there have been numerous allegations emanating from members of the public as well as from the media regarding rampant corruption within the TTPS. These allegations portray police officers on the island as symbols of unfettered corruption and the author sought to test the influences of organizational justice on police officers and police corruption within the TTPS.

In Chapter 3, Katz (Arizona State University), Fox (Department of Children, Youth, and Families, State of Washington), and Gill (University of Missouri-Kansas City) utilize a gang expert survey, census data, and official homicide data to illustrate how gangs and community social structure are related to homicide in Trinidad and Tobago. The information contained in this article, never examined conjunctively before, provides a clear understanding of gang-penetrated communities in Trinidad and Tobago and seeks to answer the question of whether the presence of gangs and gang members in gang-penetrated communities will lead to higher levels of homicides. This article is invaluable as it gives readers a glance into the causes and correlates of violence on the island.

Suzette A. Haughton and Trevor Smith (The University of the West Indies, Mona) provides a comprehensive analysis of Jamaica's transnational crime problems of drug trafficking and money laundering in Chapter 4. The authors utilize secondary data and desk-based reviews of governmental documents and laws to elucidate the twin evils of drug trafficking and money laundering that consecutive Jamaican government has been grappling with. In doing so, they bring into the fold academic perspectives of Jamaica's drug trafficking and money laundering problems. This article serves to enhance our knowledge base and understanding of contemporary criminological and criminal justice issues in Jamaica.

Following this analysis, Wendy-Ann P. Isaac, Wayne G. Ganpat, Marlene Attzs, and Thomas E. Isaac (The University of the West Indies, St Augustine) present their work on the criminological dimensions of agriculture in the Caribbean. The authors provide a cogent and well-articulated review of the security threats posed by criminals to the livelihood of Caribbean farmers. The information contained in this article has never been consolidated in a criminological dimension and provides a clear understanding of a range of challenges facing small farmers in the Caribbean. The authors of this chapter explore specific security measures for the agricultural community and contend that investing in particular mechanisms will ensure the highest level of protection for Caribbean farmers against the wide range of security threats.

I am honored to have facilitated the publication of Chapter 6 by early career scholar Dr. Avekadavie "Aveka" Parasramsingh Mano (The University of the West Indies, St Augustine) as she examined the lives and work of migratory sex workers in Belize and sought to challenge the stigmas and stereotypes that are typically associated with their job. In the midst of generally negative literature on sex work as well as on migratory sex workers, Dr. Mano sought to proffer a different and more nuanced manner of understanding the rationales for women who are involved in sex work by using Belize as the proxy for her study. On this later point, the author is successful in challenging the stigmas and stereotypical views that are associated with female migrants who are involved in sex work.

In her research, Mano interviewed a wide range of persons involved in the sex work industry in Belize and placed herself in the midst of the industry in order to have a firsthand view of its operations. For an emerging scholar, Dr. Mano must be commended for her effort.

Chapter 7 presents the work of Ashaki Dore who adopts a philosophical orientation in the analysis of citizen participation in crime prevention in Trinidad and Tobago and the nuances that are associated with the provision of incentives for achieving this noble goal. Dore's work, "Incentivizing Crime Prevention through Citizen Participation in Trinidad and Tobago," analyzes a plethora of strategies ranging from the imposition of harsher penalties to providing incentives to deter individuals from engaging in criminal activities. She argues that incentivizing crime prevention in Trinidad and Tobago is appealing to the criminal element on the island and argues for a new focus, one which engages law-abiding citizens of Trinidad and Tobago rather than rewarding those citizens who engage in criminal activities.

R. Sandra Evans (The University of the West Indies, St Augustine) explores the language component of the criminal justice system in St. Lucia and provides evidence of a particular language bias. This bias is premised on the notion that due to St. Lucia dual connection to both English and French colonialist, the language used on the island is both English and Kwéyòl (a mixture of English and French). However, she argues that the criminal justice system on the island is inherently biased against speakers of Kwéyòl. This crimino-linguistic masterpiece, aptly entitled "We reduce it in writing: Exploring the status of Kwéyòl in the criminal justice system in St. Lucia" skillfully examines the use of language within the criminal justice system in St. Lucia and must be contextualized from the perspective of moral issues pertaining to the predominance of one language over the other in a dual-language state.

In Chapter 9, Wendell C. Wallace (The University of the West Indies, St Augustine) takes a different route to the study of issues and challenges facing an "overburdened Judiciary" in Trinidad and Tobago. The author takes a philosophical orientation in debating the rights and wrongs that have been associated with Trinidad and Tobago's Judiciary. Dr. Wallace utilizes a qualitative approach (a semi-structured interview and narrative analysis), together with practitioner observations and a desk-review of documents to shed light on the challenges, loopholes, weaknesses, and the possible ways to improve the Trinidad and Tobago's Judiciary. As a component of his research, the author utilizes data from a two-part interview with Senior Counsel Mrs. Pamela Elder, who shares her experiences with the judicial system on the island.

Chapter 10 discusses some important considerations concerning female juveniles who are in care of the state in Trinidad and Tobago. Written by Kevin Sean Peters, a lecturer at the College of Science, Technology and Applied Arts of Trinidad and Tobago and a Doctoral candidate in Criminology and Criminal Justice at The University of the West Indies, St Augustine, this chapter is both timely and topical as it addresses the plethora of issues facing these young female juveniles who are placed in the state care for a variety of reasons. The author expertly attempts to create a profile of the females and thus send a message to policymakers on the island in terms of possible proactive interventions.

The Editor of *Caribbean Perspectives on Criminology and Criminal Justice (Volume I)*, Wendell C. Wallace, authors the conclusion to this captivating, inspiring, and dynamic book. In concluding the book, Wallace succinctly summarizes the work of the book chapter authors.

Wallace also extends his gratitude to those individuals who served as reviewers and to all persons who contributed to moving this book from a mere idea to a reality. Further, Wallace issues a challenge to prospective readers to make a determination of the book's value and contribution to the development of new knowledge from a Caribbean perspective.

The book chapters in this volume were selected in order to proffer a balanced perspective that focuses on regional, cross Caribbean, historical, as well as current perspectives on criminology and criminal justice issues in the Caribbean. The topics elucidated in Volume one of this two volume book provides comprehensive coverage of a wide range of timely, topical and relevant subject matter. The book is unique and its uniqueness is premised on its transdisciplinary approach to criminology and criminal justice issues in the Caribbean by integrating scholarly contributions from an international team of prominent scholars with a team of regional scholars in the fields of criminology and criminal justice, law, and linguistics. Caribbean Perspectives on Criminology and Criminal Justice is therefore a much-needed resource material for researchers, students, and practitioners in the fields of criminology and criminal justice, law, security studies, sociology, social work, psychology, and for anyone seeking cogent information of criminology and criminal justice literature on the Caribbean.

In sum, the authors who contributed their articles to this book make a significant contribution to the advancement of knowledge as well as the development of critical thought on criminological and criminal justice issues in the Caribbean. Added to this, these authors have contributed to the development of a Caribbean Criminology and in doing so have responded to Ken Pryce's (1976) call for a criminology in the Caribbean through localized research and localized research lens.

Figure 1: The Caribbean Region

Source: Kmusser. https://en.wikipedia.org/wiki/Caribbean_Sea

RESEARCH CONTEXT—THE CARIBBEAN

The Caribbean has been conceptualized in a variety of ways by different authors, for instance, English-Caribbean, Dutch-Caribbean, and French-Caribbean. However, in order to ensure that the term "Caribbean" is neither mysterious nor esoteric for the readership of this book, it is important that the term is clarified. Instructively, the Caribbean is comprised of a variety of countries (see Figure 1) with differing social, economic, ethnic, and cultural identities (Wallace, 2018). Wallace (2018) also points out that in spite of the differences, there are also many commonalities inclusive of, but not limited to crime, criminal justice systems, culture, history, politics, colonialism, and language. He cogitates that though some of the islands are small islands; there are larger continent-bound states.

Some of the countries are also independent island states; however, Guyana is located on the continental mainland close to the Caribbean Sea, but has close cultural and historical ties to the Caribbean. Quite importantly, many of these countries have been independent nation states for over 40 years, some are still colonial dependents; some possess middle to high-level incomes; and some are the poorest states in the Western hemisphere. Others have extremely high rates of violent crime which position them among the highest in the world, while others are still idyllic with crime almost nonexistent (Wallace, 2018).

Reference to the Caribbean refers to a set of English-speaking island states located in the Caribbean Sea consisting of the independent nations of Antigua and Barbuda ("Antigua"), the Commonwealth of the Bahamas ("Bahamas"), Barbados, Belize, the Commonwealth of Dominica ("Dominica"), Grenada, the Cooperative Republic of Guyana ("Guyana"), Jamaica, the Federation of St. Kitts and Nevis ("St. Kitts"), St. Lucia, St. Vincent, and the Grenadines ("St. Vincent"), and the Republic of Trinidad and Tobago ("Trinidad and Tobago") (Fraser, 2006, p. 208). For this purpose of this book, several of the chapters focused on the Caribbean in a broad context, while others concentrated specifically on Belize, Jamaica, St. Lucia, and Trinidad and Tobago. The book is therefore a representation of the views from a wide range of member states of the regional Caribbean Community and Common Market (CARICOM).

CONCLUSION

Crime is ubiquitous and poses a real danger to modern societies in the Caribbean. Apart from posing a clear and present danger to Caribbean communities, crime also negatively impact the overall economic viability of many countries in the region (Bennett & Lynch, 1996). With this in mind, it is argued that research and solutions to crime in the Caribbean should adopt a localized approach based on global best practices as the "one size fit all approach" is an expensive failure. This book set out to examine and shed light upon criminological and criminal justice issues that plague contemporary Caribbean societies. Without a doubt, these issues are quite pervasive and in need of elucidation. To a large extent, Volume

1 of Caribbean perspectives on Criminology and Criminal Justice has addressed most of these issues; however, Volume 2 will continue addressing similar issues as one book certainly could not proffer an all-inclusive response to such wide-ranging challenges.

From the chapters contained in Volume 1 of this book, it is quite evident that there are exciting times ahead for Caribbean criminologists and social scientists. As researchers, we often struggle for solutions to serious social issues; however, we are never daunted in the quest for knowledge, solutions, and possible best practices aimed at alleviating a range of painful situations. This book is testament to our fortitude, not only as academicians, but also as human beings seeking an end to pain, suffering, and misery. Although negative attitudes may remain about solutions to crime and deviance in the Caribbean, barriers are constantly being removed by the engagement of pracademics (practitioners and academics) with broad visions for a safe and secure Caribbean.

Instructively, the qualitative and quantitative research approaches utilized by the researchers who submitted their work to this book offer exciting opportunities to observe how the researchers engaged with their research across a broad spectrum of disciplines. In no uncertain terms, the authors of the book chapters contained in Volume 1 have made significant contributions to academia via their insightful and impactful research of traditional and contemporary issues. Further, in some instances, they have also contributed new knowledge to academia via their critical thoughts and writings on the range of topics in espoused in this book.

It is hoped that Caribbean students of criminology and criminal justice, national security studies, safety and security studies, risk management and security, and criminal justice will not face the same challenges that students in the late 1990s and early 2000s faced in the context of the limited availability of Caribbean criminological literature. In fact, this exciting book should enhance student's understanding of the criminological and criminal justice issues facing the Caribbean. At this point, it must be confessed that I am thrilled to have edited this book and look forward to working on Volume 2. Finally, wherever and whenever this book is read, it is most definitely a step in the right direction toward the establishment of a Caribbean criminology and thus reverse the traditionalist snobbery of Caribbean criminology.

References

Agozino, B. (2017). Critical perspectives on deviance and social control in rural Africa. *African Journal of Criminology and Justice Studies, 10*(1), 1-21.

Bennett, R. R., & Lynch, J. P. (1996). Towards a Caribbean criminology: Prospects and problems. *Caribbean Journal of Criminology and Social Psychology, 1*(1), 8–37.

Cain, M. (1996). Crime and criminology in the Caribbean—an introduction. *Caribbean Quarterly, 42*(2/3), v–xx.

Clinard, M., & Abbott, D. (1973). *Crime in developing countries: A comparative perspective.* New York: Wiley.

Deosaran, R. (2003). *Prison recidivism: Towards reduction, rehabilitation and reform. Research and policy report.* Trinidad: University of the West Indies, St. Augustine Campus, Centre for Criminology and Criminal Justice.

Fraser, A. (2006). From forgotten through friction to the future: The evolving relationship of the Anglophone Caribbean and the Inter-American system of human rights. *Revista Instituto Interamericano de Derechos Humanos, 43,* 207–237.

Griffith, I. L. (2000). *The political economy of drugs in the Caribbean.* New York: St. Martin's Press.

Harriott, A. (2002). *Crime trends in the Caribbean and response.* Kingston, Jamaica: The University of West Indies Press/UN Office of Drugs and Crime.

Hill, S. M. (2012). Bridging the gap in data collection, research and analysis in crime control in the Caribbean. *United Against Crime, Association of Caribbean Commissioners of Police (ACCP), 9,* 41–43.

Jones, H. (1981). *Crime, race and, and culture.* New York: Wiley.

Katz, C. M., Maguire, E. R., & Choate, D. (2011). A cross national comparison of gangs in the United States and Trinidad and Tobago. *International Criminal Justice Review, 21*(3), 243–262.

Lancaster-Ellis, K. (2013). Personal perspectives: Challenges for women in policing within the Caribbean. *Pakistan Journal of Criminology, 5*(1), 1–36.

Levy, H. (2012). *Youth violence and organized crime in Jamaica: causes and counter-measures: An examination of the Linkages and Disconnections.* Ottawa, ON: International Development Research Centre.

Maguire, E. R., Willis, J. A., Snipes, J., & Gantley, M. (2008). Spatial concentrations of violence in Trinidad and Tobago. *Caribbean Journal of Criminology and Public Safety, 13*(1&2), 44–83.

Mars, J. (2009). Ethnic diversity and police community relations in Guyana. *Commonwealth and Comparative Politics, 47*(4), 506–616.

Meeks, B. (2011). The Dudus events in Jamaica and the future of Caribbean politics. *Social and Economic Studies, 60*(3/4), 183–202.

Moncrieffe, J. (2008). *Making and unmaking the young "Shotta"[Shooter]: Boundaries and (Counter)—actions in the "Garrisons".* IDS Working Paper 297. Brighton, UK: Institute of Development Studies, University of Sussex.

Morris, P. K., & Graycar, A. (2011). Homicide through a different lens. *British Journal of Criminology, 51*(5), 823–838.

Nixon, A. V. (2015). Resisting Paradise: Tourism, Diaspora, and Sexuality in Caribbean Culture. Jackson: University Press of Mississippi.

Pino, N. (2016). Trinidad and Tobago: Crime, police corruption and police reforms. In K. R. Hope (Ed.), *Police corruption and reform in developing societies* (pp. 207–228). Boca Raton, FL: CRC Press.

Pryce, K. (1976). Towards a Caribbean criminology. *Caribbean Issues, 11*(2), 3–19.

Sumner, C. (1980). Crime, justice, and underdevelopment: Beyond modernisation theory. In: Colin Sumner (Ed.), *Crime, justice, and underdevelopment* (pp. 1–39). London: Heinemann.

Wallace, W. C. (2018). The importance of Caribbean police leaders' perspectives on the death penalty. In W. C. Wallace (Ed.), *The death penalty in the Caribbean: Perspectives from the police* (pp. 1–16). Washington, DC, USA: Westphalia Press.

Wallace, W. C., Gibson, C., Gordon, N., Lakhan, R., Mahabir, J., & Seetahal, C. (2019). Domestic violence: Intimate partner violence victimization non-reporting to the police in Trinidad and Tobago. *Justice Policy Journal, 16*(1), 1–30.

Williams, D. (2009). Conceptualizing restorative justice in the Caribbean: The philosophy, the policy and the practice. *Caribbean Journal of Criminology and Public Safety, 14*, 259–284.

CHAPTER I

POLICING IN THE CARIBBEAN FROM COLONIALISM TO TODAY

Keron King and Nathan W. Pino

College of Science, Technology and Applied Arts of Trinidad and Tobago, Trinidad and Tobago/Texas State University, TX, USA

ABSTRACT

This chapter will present a historical and contextual discussion of formal policing in the Caribbean from colonialism to the present day. Modern policing in the Caribbean cannot be divorced from its early colonial roots, so we discuss the history of colonial policing in the Caribbean, followed by a discussion of how policing changed, and did not change, after independence was gained across different countries in the region. We present research by international and local groups, academics, and local NGOs with regard to police behavior, effectiveness, and related issues. In addition, drawing on our own research experiences, we place special focus on the country of Trinidad and Tobago as a case study to illustrate larger trends in the region, examining the country's history of policing and the prospects for and challenges to developing more democratic forms of policing in Trinidad and Tobago and the rest of the Caribbean.

Keywords: Policing; Caribbean; police brutality; police corruption; colonialism; peacemaking

INTRODUCTION

This chapter presents a historical and contextual discussion of formal policing in the Caribbean from colonialism to the present day. In this chapter, drawing on our own research experiences,[1]

---

1 Original research conducted by the second author is cited throughout this chapter.

we place special focus on Trinidad and Tobago as a case study to illustrate larger trends in the region, examining the country's history of policing—including various reform efforts over the years—and the prospects for and challenges to developing more democratic forms of policing in Trinidad and Tobago and the rest of the Caribbean. In what follows, we present a history of policing in the Caribbean before and after Caribbean countries gained independence; critical issues in policing in the present day such as poor governance, police deviance, police reform, and the militarization and privatization of security; and end with an assessment of the possibilities for more democratic and effective policing in the future.

POLICING IN THE COLONIAL ERA

Modern policing in the Caribbean cannot be divorced from its colonial roots. The history of policing in the Caribbean and most, if not all, former British colonies has been characterized as bearing the "undesirable" feature of paramilitarism (Ahire, 1991; Danns, 1982; Harriott, 2000; Hills, 1995; Killingray & Anderson, 1991; Mars, 2009). This is because Britain's task, as colonizer, was to impose "alien law" onto the "indigenous population" of her colonies (Jefferies, 1952, p. 25). The Deputy Under-Secretary of State for the Colonies, Sir Charles Jefferies, stated in his 1952 book, aptly titled *The Colonial Police*, that Britain had a different role for the police in the colonies. He explained that "in such conditions the function of the police [was] closer to that of the Roman than to that of the Anglo-Saxon tradition..." (Jefferies, 1952, p. 25). Nineteenth-century policing emphasized excessive force and arbitrary and unjust attempts at social control of a subjugated population. This approach, as opposed to the Peelian model, was thought to be more effective to preserve social order in the "period of social and economic readjustment" that followed the abolition of slavery in 1834 (Jefferies, 1952, p. 27).

Jefferies (1952) provides the details of a harrowing account of policing in Jamaica in 1836, just 2 years after the abolition of slavery. He gives voice to the first Inspector General for the Jamaican police, Mr. Williams Ramsay, who reports that he "got into trouble" with the ruling oligarchy

---

Most of these publications (Pino, 2016, 2009; Pino & Johnson, 2011; Ellison & Pino, 2012) were informed by field work in TRINIDAD AND TOBAGO conducted by the second author, with the first author acting as a research assistant.

for not dispersing "a perfectly ordered meeting" by force. What Ramsay meant by "not dispersing" was explained in his appeal to England for his subsequent dismissal. Ramsay refused to "turn the guns and bayonets under his command against the bosoms of his fellow-citizens and gratify the insatiable thirst of a faction for the people's blood" (Jefferies, 1952, p. 27). Indeed, oppression of the subjugated populations by the colonial power, England, was not restricted to Jamaica, but was also conducted throughout the Caribbean. For instance, residents of Grand Bay, Dominica, who according to St. Jean (2007), lived "hand to mouth" and in financial debt with few having any emergency savings, had similar views of the police. Instructively, the residents of Grand Bay, Dominica, viewed policing as "state oppression and an interruption of poor people's informal livelihood and recreation" (St. Jean, 2007, p. 15).

This tumultuous relationship with the State and by extension the police pre-dates independence in the Caribbean and goes back as far as the 1690s when the police burnt the property of a European Catholic because he "insisted on erecting a large wooden cross on land he purchased from the Caribs" (St. Jean, 2007, p. 14). This form of police oppression led to rebellions, slave revolts, land uprisings, Maroon wars, and census riots. However, it was the police, holding the state's monopoly on force, who were called upon to quell these uprisings, sometimes resorting to using "brutal tactics" (St. Jean, 2007, p. 15). It is this history that led one Grand Bay resident to retort, *"young people seems to have a pride in saying that they do not like the police ... it is like a fashion, a kind of patriotism to Grand Bay to not like the police"* (St. Jean, 2007, p. 15).

In Guyana, an ethnically diverse society, policing and its use of lethal force reflected the diversity of the society and strengthened the divide and rule ethos of the British Crown. Mars (2009) explains that during the 1823 and 1856 riots, "Amerindian or East Indian elements of the population were used to reinforce White troops in the capture, incarceration, mutilation, or execution of Black rebels" (p. 508). Similarly, in the 1905 Georgetown riots for better wages and working conditions, "a predominantly White officer contingent of the colonial police force ordered the use of deadly force against unarmed Black workers" (Mars, 2009, p. 508). In the Enmore riots of 1948, the authorities used mainly "Black police officers to help suppress rebellious East Indian strikers on the sugar plantation" killing five of the strikers (Mars, 2009, p. 508). This divide and rule policy along with the excessive use of force by the police exacerbated existing racial tensions within the society and between the black-majority police and the East-Indian community.

The approach to policing in the British Caribbean colonies was modeled after the Royal Irish Constabulary, which was reportedly preferred over the Anglo-Saxon tradition because the colonial government needed an "organized force at its disposal to keep order and maintain the law" (Jefferies, 1952, p. 25). Jefferies (1952) best explains below:

> "... it is clear enough that from the point of view of the Colonies there was much attraction in an arrangement which provided what we should now call a paramilitary organisation or gendarmerie, armed, and trained to operate as an agent of the central government in a country where the population was predominantly rural, communications were poor, social conditions were largely primitive and the recourse to violence by members of the public who were agin [against] the government was not infrequent. It was natural that such a force, rather than one organized on the lines of the purely civilian and localized forces of Great Britain should have been taken as a suitable model for adaptation to Colonial conditions."
> (p. 31)

In a formal sense, policing in Trinidad and Tobago began during the Spanish occupation of Trinidad and Tobago starting in 1592, where six officers served under the management of the mayor in the capitol Port of Spain, and in country districts on other parts of the island a ward watch system was established (De Verteuil, 1986; Ottley, 1964). This arrangement lasted for two centuries until the expansion of sugar, coffee, and cocoa plantations increased the island's population and the British took control in 1797 (Ottley, 1964). At that point, Governor Picton mandated compulsory enlistment of "colored men" to serve in the police force, leading many to assume that service in the police force was a form of punishment (De Verteuil, 1986, p. 29; Ottley, 1964). Because few individuals wanted to join the police, men from Ireland arrived to fill the ranks, and a comprehensive set of rules to govern the police was then issued in 1835 (De Verteuil, 1986). By 1850, the Trinidadian police consisted of an inspector commandant, 2 subinspectors (one each in Port of Spain and San Fernando), 10 sergeants, and 100 constables consisting largely of lower-class Whites from Barbados (De Verteuil, 1986; Ottley, 1964).

Interestingly, the British continued using both Spanish and British law books for 50 years after they took over, but by 1844, they instituted English law, including trial by jury (Ottley, 1964). Justice reform occurred only after things were considered to be out of control. In 1874, five members of the Royal Ulster Constabulary (RUC) were appointed to reorganize and strengthen a plainclothes Inspector branch that was started in 1862, and by 1884, the Police Force in Trinidad numbered 435, mostly Irish men (De Verteuil, 1986; Ottley, 1964) and pay for the police was increased as well. A little later, in the 1890s, the local Senior Inspector, a former RUC officer, modeled the local Police Force after the RUC, laying out San Fernando and Port of Spain into beats for purposes of crime prevention and detection (De Verteuil, 1986; Ottley, 1964). The police were tasked with quelling riots in the late 1800s, such as the Carnival riots of 1881 and the Hosay Riots of 1884. The police were provided with firearms after a riotous crowd assaulted policemen in Arouca in 1891 (De Verteuil, 1986; Ottley, 1964). The water riots of 1903 led to protests against police brutality, but only one officer was put on trial and he was acquitted (Ottley, 1964).

Changes in 1905 to the Police Force provided the basis for how the police would function until the end of the colonial period. The Constabulary Ordinance of 1905 changed the police into an armed constabulary charged with paramilitary duties, detecting crime, repressing internal disturbances, and defending the colony "against external aggression" (Ottley, 1964, p. 115). By 1932, there were around 900 officers in the Police Force, most all of them from Trinidad or Tobago, housed in 58 stations (4 of which were in Tobago) (Ottley, 1964). The police continued to suppress riots and feuds between religious groups, in addition to controlling steel band activity, and 15 men were formed into a local commando unit (Ottley, 1964). By the 1950s, there were approximately 2,000 officers in the Police Force in Trinidad and Tobago. At this time, the police started the 999 emergency call system, a police association was authorized, female officers were hired, and new systems for recording crime were instituted (Ottley, 1964).

CARIBBEAN POLICING AFTER INDEPENDENCE

Police Deviance and Ineffectiveness

Throughout Latin America and the Caribbean, residents perceive the police to be ineffective at controlling serious crime, abusive to lawful and unlawful citizens, in collusion with criminals, untrustworthy, and to be feared and bribed (Chevigny, 1990; Harriott, 1998; Paes-Machado & Noronha, 2002). Police deviance and repressive actions, in particular, are an echo from the colonial policing era where police were highly responsive to social and political power (Harriot, 1998). In Guyana, for instance, Danns (1982) describes a police force that was more about controlling a segment of the population than protecting all citizens from a criminal minority. For Danns (1982), the police's role was to maintain the order that existed in slavery and colonialism. Danns (1982, p. 173) pointed out that the police "functioned not for the good of all citizens, but purely and exclusively to exercise the will of the colonial state and the economically dominant class in the society." Danns (1882) analysis of Guyana's police officers is instructive as he describes them as an "instrument of the political directorate and [hence the reason why it is] distinguished by its militarist nature and intimate involvement in an overall militarist experimentation in nation building and economic development" (Danns, 1982, p. 177).

Police brutality continues to be a challenge in the Caribbean perhaps, most notably in Jamaica. For instance, the Jamaican Constabulary Force (JCF) has been accused of numerous extra-judicial killings. A unit within the JCF, the Crime Management Unit, was disbanded 30 months after its establishment in 2000 because it had been involved in 40 fatal shootings. McDavid, Clayton, and Cowell (2011, p. 52) even suggested that "key actors in the institutional environment may well have felt that the extra-judicial killings were a positive development ...." In Guyana, police–community relations continue to deteriorate along racial and political lines. For instance, Mars (2009) reports that in the 2000s, the police have been accused of targeting various segments of the Black population in response to the agenda of the predominantly East Indian ruling political party. Whereas, the East Indian business class claimed the police has not protected them from "economically motivated crime and violence" (Mars, 2009, p. 511). Needless to say, distrust and dissatisfaction with the police is at an all-time high.

The United Nations Development Programme (UNDP) 2012 Caribbean Human Development Report identifies three challenges facing the police agencies of the region. The first, a capacity challenge: regional police departments, although on average having higher police density than Latin America and the world, still underperform in areas on service delivery and protection of the population. The report suggests that the effective use of human resources may be the issue. Secondly, issues of corruption continue to negatively impact police effectiveness, efficiency, and legitimacy. A 2010 UNDP Citizen Security Survey illustrated that 89% of Suriname and 94% of Jamaican residents believed that corruption and crime are linked and that the government should invest more in reducing corruption. The last challenge deals with citizen rights. The UNDP (2010) report highlights that Caribbean police departments vary in the area of abuse of force and points out that countries with higher homicide rates tend to have higher frequencies of civil rights abuses and extra-judicial killings.

The (UNDP) 2012 Caribbean Human Development Report revealed some poignant results regarding Caribbean residents' perceptions of the police. For instance, on average, only 32.9% of victims of domestic violence believed the police treated them with respect, whereas 20.7% of all citizens believed the police respected the rights of all citizens; and only 1 in 10% or 11.9% had a great deal of confidence in the police to control crime. Caribbean police forces in the main, with the exception of possibly Barbados, continue to be seen as ineffective and continually struggle to meet the needs of the public. This is generally premised on the notions that most police organizations in the Caribbean have unreformed police structures with no real accountability or meaningful community participation (Gomes, 2007; UNDP, 2012).

Policing after independence in Trinidad and Tobago remained in the traditional, colonial style, and was beset by numerous systemic problems, many of which to this day have never been overcome. Numerous reports over time revealed these problems. For example, the Committee on the Restructuring of the Police Service (CRPS) (1984) reported that relations within the police service were poor and that morale was low. Police leadership was ineffective to say the least: senior officers were not communicating with each other, leading to managerial inefficiencies uneven and unclear officer workloads, and ineffective disciplinary procedures.

As a result, junior officers did not respect the leadership (CRPS, 1984). According to the same report, the police were seen by the public as "a repressive force ready to harass people at every opportunity" (CRPS, 1984, p. 138). A lack of vehicles and manpower lead to ignored urgent calls for assistance. The public viewed the police as indifferent, unresponsive, and unsympathetic; overly harsh in their treatment of suspects; engaging in arbitrary search and arrest; ignoring serious crimes while attending to minor offenses; destroying the homes of squatters; not conducting internal investigations of police misconduct; and failing to engage in foot patrols (CRPS, 1984). O'Dowd (1991) wrote a separate report for the Trinidad and Tobago Police Service (TTPS) and found similar problems 7 years later, including weak leadership, lack of internal investigations of misconduct, widespread accusations of corruption, lack of response by the police after receiving calls for service, and the like.

In 1987, a few years before O'Dowd's 1991 report, the government of Trinidad and Tobago published a report of the Commission on Enquiry into the extent of the problem of drug abuse in Trinidad and Tobago. The Commission was chaired by Garvin Scott and has become infamously known in Trinidad and Tobago as the Scott Drug Report. Its findings revealed systemic corruption in the TTPS regarding the organization's involvement in the illegal drug trade. The Commission reported that police officers of all ranks were involved in illicit drug use and drug trafficking, and were close associates of drug dealers and traffickers (Scott, 1987, p. 30). It was also found that police officers recycled seized drugs onto the illegal market (Scott, 1987, p. 49). The Commission concluded that:

> "there is not the slightest doubt that many members of the Police Service in every one of its divisions, including some of its most senior personnel are engaged in the illegal drug trade in one way or another" (p. 49).

The next decade witnessed another report on policing in Trinidad and Tobago and this report produced similar findings to that Scott's (1987) report. In a similar vein to Scott (1987), Seaby (1993) found that corruption was endemic and widespread across all ranks of the TTPS. The findings indicated that some senior police officers lived beyond their legitimate means thanks to the embezzlement of police service monies and the protecting of drug dealers, routes, and supplies. Police officers would also steal from each other and from the canteen, and some officers, working across different ranks, were found to have committed murders and rapes, transport cocaine, grow marijuana, and sell drugs. Officers would also promote those under them in the chain of command that engaged in corruption with them (Seaby, 1993). Additionally, citizens had to pay officers for service, and officers would blackmail people as a means to not arrest them or to hide evidence of a crime (Seaby, 1993).

Seaby (1993) reported that the colonial style of policing was still present in Trinidad and Tobago that local commanders had too much control over their own areas, the police lacked investigative skills, and there was no sense of community service among members of the TTPS. In addition, problems in other areas of the criminal justice system, such as long court delays, allowed for more corruption and unlawful activities such as the destruction of records and evidence, and police only showing up at court if they felt like it (Seaby, 1993). Drugs and other evidence must be exhibited during a trial in Trinidad and Tobago, and due to the long windows between an arrest and the trial, this made evidence tampering all too easy. Officers developed a fatalistic attitude, promoting the status quo, finding ways to avoid engaging in patrols (such as taking a desk job), and using knowledge of other officers' corruption as a way to keep their jobs (Seaby, 1993).

The state of policing in Trinidad and Tobago did not improve as the country moved into the new century. Job (2004) noted that previous calls for reform were never acted upon, and accused political leaders and their parties as well as the business community for politicizing the issue, benefitting from racial and ethnic divides, and failing to take no action. Amnesty International (2006) issued a document on unlawful killings by police and deaths in police custody in Trinidad and Tobago. The report documents numerous instances of police deviance such as excessive use of force including summary executions, deaths of persons in police custody, kidnappings, various forms of police harassment, and the failure of authorities to properly carry out investigations or sanction officers' misconduct (Amnesty International, 2006). Also reported were major flaws in both internal and external police complaints mechanisms, such as lengthy delays in judicial investigations into police shootings and deaths in custody. Official investigations were not made available to the public, data on police shootings and deaths in custody are not sufficiently available, and suspected officers were allowed to remain on active duty. On rare occasions, civil awards were provided to victims when officers are held criminally liable (Amnesty International, 2006).

Clearly, the legacies of the colonial system of policing are still present in the Caribbean in the twenty-first century (Harriott, 2000; King, 2009; Mars, 2009; Mastrofski & Lum, 2008; Pino & Johnson, 2011). In Trinidad and Tobago, for example, police recruit training still centers on riot suppression, and citizens still have to solicit police services because the police do not engage in proactive policing (Johnson, 2006; Parks & Mastrofski, 2008). Some police stations are dirty and decrepit, members of the TTPS suffer from poor remuneration packages, and inadequate staffing and equipment are prevalent, for example, few usable vehicles (Parks & Mastrofski, 2008). There are also continued problems of corruption, high turnover, and poor officer recruitment, management, and supervision (Mastrofski & Lum, 2008; Miller & Hendrix, 2007; Parks & Mastrofski, 2008; Police Service Commission, 2004). Owing to these problems, the police lack legitimacy in the eyes of the media and the public, who have a high fear of crime (Bennett & Morabito, 2006; Deosaran, 2002). As Bennett and Morabito state (2006, p. 243), "…this has evolved in Trinidad into a culture of alienation from the public. The police are demoralized, socially isolated, and antagonistic toward the public, and they provide little in the way of unsolicited police services."

Reform Efforts in Caribbean Policing

It must be acknowledged that there have been numerous attempts at police reform in the Caribbean. For instance, in 2002, police in St. Lucia partnered with the University of Central Florida (UCF) and the Orange County Sheriff's Office Tourist Oriented Police Sector of Florida to train its officers in tourism-oriented policing, a proactive approach to policing that focuses on fear reduction in tourists (Wolf, 2008). This training included a wide cross-section of law enforcement agencies: police officers, marine and beach patrol officers, customs and immigration officers, the rapid response unit, and private hotel security officers. However, because of "lack of supervisor involvement," the instructors from UCF felt that implementation was questionable (Wolf, 2008, p. 242).

The Barbadian police department has achieved some level of legitimacy in that members of the public are more willing to offer support as they see the police officers as more competent and fair when compared with law enforcement agents in Trinidad and Tobago and Jamaica (Bennett & Morabito, 2006; Bailey, 2007). In Jamaica, in response to the problems associated with the JCF mentioned above, a strategic review recommended that all constables be trained in graduated use of force, that it emphasizes community policing, and that it institutes a name change[2] from the JCF to Jamaica Police Service, by all accounts in an effort to highlight the service-oriented focus of policing (McDavid, Clayton, & Cowell, 2011). However, if any successes were to be derived from this strategic change, there would need to have been a decisive break from its past culture of force and coercion and a genuine commitment to community partnership.

Harriott (1997), referred to the 1993–1996 police reform efforts led by the appointment of an ex-Army officer, Colonel Trevor MacMillan to the position of Commissioner of Police (COP) in Jamaica as a "case of successful failure" (p. 11). The reforms were "fragile and reversible" (p. 11) and although they did increase some confidence in the JCF and professionalized aspects of their work it brought about little change in the system of accountability. The organizational change did little to challenge the deep-rooted paramilitarism of the JCF and any gains in police–community relations did not accompany any change to the "style of policing that generates the conflicts with the community" (Harriott, 1997, p. 9).

Fourteen years later, in 2010, the Jamaican government continued their reform efforts by strengthening police oversight. They repealed the Police Public Complaints Act which established the Police Complaints Authority (PCA): a civilian agency to probe allegations against members of the JCF. They also established the Independent Commission of Investigations (INDECOM) which has the authority to undertake investigations. According to the INDECOM website, this occurred on the backdrop of "prolonged public complaints of the conduct of investigations of alleged misconduct by the security forces" (INDECOM, n.d.). Although the JCF had three tiers of civilian oversight, external control was mostly ineffective (Gomes, 2007).

These examples, though scarcely researched and documented, should be highlighted as bona fide attempts of police reform in the Caribbean. One

---

2   The law enforcement body in Jamaica is still named the Jamaican Constabulary Force.

should note that Caribbean policing has two heads. On the one hand, the post-independence era has been characterized by various efforts of police reform, while on the other, there has been community policing, increasing use of technology, growing recruitment of women, and sustained commitment to continuing education among the ranks. That being said, it appears that the Achilles heel of Caribbean policing continues to be its reactive, traditional, para-militaristic approach of the colonial period that alienates the public and in the worst-case scenario violates their human rights.

There have been two areas in which Caribbean policing has made drastic changes in the post-independence era: training and networking. Prior to the independence movement of the 1960s, most senior police officers were educated and trained in Britain (Bowling, 2010, p. 70). Supposedly, as a result of this common training, Bowling (2010, p. 71) explains that the region experienced "extensive networking" among Caribbean police officers of senior rank. This, however, slowed at the end of colonial rule. The previously formed networks weakened, "regional training schools went out of favor and regional police leadership was fragmented" (Bowling, 2010, p. 72).

In 1987, however, there was a re-birth of sorts in Caribbean policing with the formation of the Association of Caribbean Commissioners of Police (ACCP) that aimed to rekindle the regionalism that was evident in policing during the colonial era. Thirteen members passed a resolution that committed the ACCP to the following objectives:

- Regional cooperation in the suppression of criminal activities in areas such as narcotics, terrorism, and organized crime,

- The exchange of information in criminal investigations,

- The sharing of common services which may include training, forensic analysis, and research, and

- The effective management of law enforcement agencies.

One result of this collaboration was seen in 1993 when the ACCP adopted community policing as the policy for its member states (Deosaran, 2002). With regard to training, presently all Caribbean police jurisdictions have the capacity to and offer basic recruit training. However, only Trinidad and Tobago, Jamaica, and Barbados offer management-level training. Many regional officers at the senior levels pursue advanced level training at Bramshill College in the UK, the Royal Canadian Mounted Police Academy, Canada or the Federal Bureau of Investigation (FBI) Academy in the USA (Jones & Satchell, 2009).

Police reform efforts in Trinidad and Tobago have been well documented. With Western assistance, Trinidad and Tobago has engaged in numerous police reform efforts since the early 1990s, starting with the decision in 1993 to implement community policing after the ACCP collectively decided to implement it (Deosaran, 2002). There were concerns with poor police capacity and lack of citizen support, but police leaders traveled abroad to the UK and United States to receive training and education on community policing in order to implement it back home. By 2002, however, support for community policing collapsed among the police owing to general officer resistance and poor recruitment and hiring of officers for the program (Pino, 2009). Officer resistance stemmed from poor police–community relations, and officers seeing community policing activities as social work instead of police work (Pino, 2009). Deosaran (2002) also found that while a majority of citizens were willing to work with the police, there was a lack of awareness of the community policing initiative among the public.

In 2006, Western consultants made another major attempt to reform the TTPS based in part on policing reforms deemed as successful in Northern Ireland. Reforms included giving the police commissioner more authority in terms of hiring, promoting, training, and discipline; and improving civilian oversight via the Civilian Complaints Authority (Mastrofski & Lum, 2008). In addition, officer review procedures were updated, some poor managers were removed, and various attempts were made to make the police more service-oriented utilizing Mastrofski's (1999) managerialist Policing for People model. As part of the service-oriented reforms, a model station program was instituted the next year. These stations were in high-crime areas in different parts of the country, and the stations got structural improvements, and more resources and equipment that were meant to enhance police capacity to prevent crime proactively (Mastrofski & Lum, 2008). Officers trained for these model stations were expected to engage in foot patrols, spend time with community residents, and manage victim assistance units (Wilson, Parks, & Mastrofski, 2011).

However, these reforms did not result in sustainable, systemic improvements in police behavior or police–community relations. Training started after the model stations were already opened, trainees did not show up for training or used it to be able to transfer elsewhere, managers were not sufficiently committed, and turnover among managers was high (Wilson et al., 2011). In addition, victim assistance staff members were not trained by the end of the first year of model station implementation. Pino (2009, 2016) also found few positive impacts of the reform efforts overall, in part because commitment to the reforms among important stakeholders was limited, the reforms did not fit the local context adequately, and civil society groups were not sufficiently involved in the process (also see Wallace, 2012). Civil society group members also disapproved of the reform efforts (Pino, 2009; Pino & Johnson, 2011). In addition to lacking awareness and involvement in the initiatives, they thought that police corruption, collusion with criminals, violence, incompetence, and other forms of police deviance were not reduced after the reforms were implemented (Pino & Johnson, 2011). Finally, Wallace (2012) found that police officers also see citizens as part of the problem, viewing citizens as fractured, criminal, and against the police. Watson, Boateng, Pino, and Morgan (2018) also recently reported that policy cynicism and fatalism is rampant in the police service, with police leaders feeling powerless to stop crime, lack faith in officers under their command, and refer to citizens as monsters and criminals.

Several years ago, after the community policing reforms based on Policing for People described above were implemented, officers from Scotland Yard had come to assist the TTPS, but according to the Trinidad and Tobago Minister of National Security, those officers did very little training work while receiving large salaries (roughly $150,000 U.S. per month) (Clark, 2014). In addition to hiring and training, almost 300 new officers, half of which were women, former New York Mayor Rudy Giuliani and New York City Police Commissioner William Bratton, both known for implementing draconian zero-tolerance policing schemes in New York City, arrived in January 2015 to conduct an audit of the TTPS geared toward improving investigation methods and forensic testing, as well as to improve the low crime detection rate (Clark, 2014).

Police reform efforts in Trinidad and Tobago have been hampered by high violent crime rates and gang activity. The murder rate peaked in 2008 at 42 per 100,000, but in recent years, the murder rate has been approaching the 2008 peak, with the 2018 murder rate approaching just under 40 per 100,000 (see TT Crime, 2019). Gang activity and the drug trade in particular are thought to be the primary driver of murders and other violent crimes in the country, including domestic violence, child abuse, and governmental corruption (Adams, Morris, & Maguire, 2018). The major gang leaders in the country, who parade themselves as community leaders, appear to be above the law as they are central figures within highest levels of society, the economy, and government, fighting over and securing lucrative labor-intensive work contracts meant to benefit the unemployed (Adams, Morris, & Maguire, 2018).

In 2006, it was reported that the then Prime Minister of Trinidad and Tobago, Mr. Patrick Manning, negotiated a peace treaty with the major gang leaders in the country (most of whom have since been murdered) and the government has since been criticized for awarding those and future gang leaders, work contracts, including one for $2 million that was given to a "community leader" so that a public housing development could be converted into a police station (Baboolal, 2013).

There have also been some recent restrictions on civil liberties in Trinidad and Tobago in response to gang violence. For example, in late August 2011, the government imposed a state of emergency after 11 murders occurred on one weekend (Gabbatt, 2011). The then People's Partnership government oversaw the mass arrests of hundreds of suspected gang members, instituted roadblocks, and established curfews for all citizens between 11 pm and 4 am. In early September 2011, the government extended the state of emergency for 3 months, justifying the policy on security concerns and threats stemming from gangs and crime while claiming the curfew had thus far prevented a mass criminal uprising (Associated Press, 2011).

In 2012, Mr. Austin "Jack" Warner was appointed as the new Minister of National Security, even though he was being investigated on corruption-related issues in 2011 when he was the President of CONCACAF (the governing body for association football/soccer in North America, Central America, and the Caribbean). Subsequently, Mr. Warner had to resign as the Vice President of FIFA (the International Federation for association football/soccer) (Trinidad and Tobago Guardian, 2013). While in the capacity of Minister of National Security in Trinidad and Tobago, Mr. Warner instructed the police to suppress the number of murders and other Trinidad and Tobago crime statistics because he thought that the opposition political party (the People's National Movement) would use the statistics to "create more mischief" in a way that would lead to further crimes (Kowlessar, 2012). In 2013, the official FIFA report on the bribery allegations against Mr. Warner was released, forcing him to resign as the Minister of National Security (Trinidad and Tobago Guardian, 2013).

One promising development in Trinidad and Tobago was the strengthening of the PCA, which was created by an act of Parliament in 1993 to act as an independent body to compile citizen complaints against the police (Deosaran, 2002). The PCA did not have any real authority to conduct investigations or have any other substantive powers: it was merely a recording device, and one member of the Ministry of National Security claimed that the PCA was "largely defunct," and that there was no independent oversight body in Trinidad and Tobago hold officers accountable for police deviance (Pino, 2009). However, the PCA was reconstituted in late 2010 (Pino, 2016). The PCA is now able to engage in independent investigations of police misconduct (including corruption and criminal offenses by officers) so that the police are not solely investigating themselves. The PCA (2013) recommended various reforms including improved record keeping, legal awareness training for officers, the installation of closed caption television cameras in police stations, digitally stored on a remote server, and other policies that help preserve scenes where police shootings occur. As one might expect, some members of TTPS resisted external oversight with officers refusing to comply with PCA directives to assist in police shooting investigations and this caused numerous delays in the police informing the PCA of police shootings, hampering the investigations (Kowlessar, 2014).

Paramilitarization

One definite recent change in policing in the Caribbean is that the police have embraced paramilitarization even more than before, in part due to the heavy influence of Western donors (see Bowling, 2010; Gomes, 2007). For example, the United States and Trinidad and Tobago have signed ship rider agreements that allow U.S. law enforcement personnel to engage in hot pursuit and board ships suspected of transporting drugs in Trinidad and Tobago's territorial waters, in the name of the wars on drugs and terrorism (Griffith, 2000). In addition, Trinidad and Tobago has signed extradition and mutual legal assistance treaties with various

Western countries. In a tweet dated May 26, 2018, and posted by the U.S. Embassy in Trinidad and Tobago, the contents were as follows:

> 'Lecturers at the [TTPS] Training Academy are now more empowered to create change and influence, following the completion of a 4-day Subject Matter Expert Exchange (SMEE) on Psychological Operations. The training was facilitated by the Embassy's Military Liaison Office'.

According to the website of the U.S. Embassy in Trinidad and Tobago, the Embassy has also engaged in SMEEs on disaster management with the assistance of the Delaware National Guard, and another on "public affairs and strategic communication" with Trinidad and Tobago Ministry of National Security staff in attendance. These mutual assistance treaties result in further paramilitarization, blurring the distinction between police and military roles, and in the name of fighting transnational crime and terrorism justifies extra-judicial actions that deny civil liberties (McCulloch, 2007). Police shootings of civilians have increased in the 2010s (Kowlessar, 2014; Trinidad Express, 2015), and some of those shot have been mentally ill, demonstrating the well-known fact that the police are not sufficiently trained to contend with the mentally ill (Kowlessar, 2017).

In 2004, the Special Anti-Crime Unit of Trinidad and Tobago (SAUTT) was established. SAUTT was a paramilitary and investigative unit comprised of previous members of the Coast Guard, TTPS, and Defence Force and was tasked with alleviating gang-related homicides in Trinidad and Tobago. Unfortunately, SAUTT was disbanded by the People's Partnership government during its tenure in office between 2010 and 2015. Another state paramilitary group that exists is the Interagency Task Force (IATF), which combines military and police personnel and has been used to manage high-crime neighborhoods on the island. According to civil society leaders who were interviewed by Pino (2009), the IATF is known to maraude through these neighborhoods utilizing offensive tactics that harass and abuse suspects. Paramilitarization is not just relegated to these special units, however. The TTPS and special units such as SAUTT maintained aggressive paramilitary tactics during the model station reform period mentioned above, occasionally utilizing model stations and their staff for various operations (Wilson et al., 2011).

Privatization of Security

Rising crime in select countries in the region has led to increased spending by private firms on private security. Both the poor and the wealthy increasingly rely on private security. In Kingston, Jamaica, the formal police are not seen as effective, so many affluent residents live in gated communities and rely on private security companies (Jaffe, 2012). The city's poor, in contrast, must rely on criminal "Dons" to provide security and resolve disputes. According to Jaffe (2012), poor residents view the Dons as more effective security providers than the formal police, even though the Dons cause crime in addition to engaging in activities to prevent it. Sutton (2017) reports that 70% of firms in the Caribbean reported spending money on security in 2013/2014. This included equipment, insurance, personnel, professional security services, alarm systems, security cameras, and gates. The number of firms utilizing private security was as low as 44% in St. Lucia to a high of 85% in Trinidad and Tobago.

The private security sector in Trinidad and Tobago is extensive and appears to be expanding. The sector includes prisoner transport companies, private security for businesses, and gated communities for wealthier residents (Miller & Hendrix, 2007; Mycoo, 2004). High crime rates and lack of trust in government institutions have led to increases in the use of private security in Trinidad and Tobago. Upper and middle-class residents of Trinidad and Tobago have been moving to gated communities and have walled themselves off from the rest of the population in part due to high crime rates and a lack of trust in government institutions (Mycoo, 2004). Cain (2007) identified 57 firms in the local yellow pages, but Ellison and Pino (2012) found one website (www.tntisland. com/securityservices.html) that lists over 90 private security firms, including Amalgamated Security Services Ltd., which Pino (2009) had observed transporting prisoners in Port of Spain (note that prisoners are transported by private companies all over Trinidad and Tobago) for the government, and the American company Wackenhut. These firms pay low wages and managers of the firms justify it by claiming that there are many illegitimate companies with which they must compete (Cain, 2007).

DEVELOPING A MORE DEMOCRATIC POLICING
IN THE CARIBBEAN

Based on the above, including recent developments and trends, we assess the possibility for more democratic and more effective policing in the Caribbean. The policing challenge facing the region is a difficult one: it calls for nothing short of a re-imagination of policing. The task before the Caribbean does not require a mere changing of uniforms, gadgets, or names. Rather, the region needs to embark on a transformational change in our thinking about policing, one that recognizes its colonial past and the "us versus them" philosophy of policing that was inherited. One that "calls-out" the control freak (Agozino, 2010) and war making (Barak, 2005) nature of criminology that has dominated much of the discussion on crime and justice in the region. One that focuses on police legitimacy and procedure justice and the role of situational contexts in residents perceived legitimacy of the police (Johnson, Maguire, & Kuhns, 2014). Such a transformational change could come from the emerging literature on transformational justice. According to Gready and Robins (2014, p. 340):

> "Transformative justice is defined as transformative change that emphasizes local agency and resources, the prioritization of process rather than preconceived outcomes and the challenging of unequal and intersecting power relationships and structures of exclusion at both the local and the global level."

This implies the need for local actors leading sustainable, long-term structural reforms in a democratic way that emphasizes social capital, capacity, and genuine inclusion (Gready & Robbins, 2014; Lambourne, 2009). Components of transformative justice include emancipatory peacebuilding among everyday citizens; a rights-based approach; inclusive conflict transformation that utilizes local resources and seeks to remedy immediate problems as well as underlying causes; and an emphasis on contending gendered inequities, violence, and exclusion (Gready & Robbins, 2014). This approach dovetails well with many of the recommendations for sustainable police reform efforts offered by Ellison and Pino (2012), which, among other things, include accountability and transparency; local involvement and ownership; equal emphasis on both security and human rights; effective coordination among different countries, agencies, and other actors involved; and an emphasis on the long-term process, rather than short-term goals. In fact, the rhetoric of security sector assistance in general has shifted in a more transformative direction to emphasize participatory strategies, local ownership, and local capacity building, with less overt emphasis on security rhetoric (see Donais, 2009).

A peacemaking approach to policing can also be part of a transformational process. This approach comes from a perspective on crime, punishment, and justice that is known in Criminology as "peacemaking" (Pepinksy & Quinney, 1991). The advocates of this approach suggest that its core task is to "eliminate all forms of violence ..." and to do so we must "understand the workings of power, for power resides at the base of all forms of violence" (Sullivan & Tift, 1998, p. 6). Sullivan (cited in Wozniak, 2000, p. 271) further elucidates that:

> "peacemaking criminology offers a conception of justice defined in terms of equal well-being for all, where the needs for all are met equally but differentially, that is according to the unique needs of each. Hence peacemaking criminologists talk of justice defined as equal well-being and of creating social arrangements in which all are treated equally not only in terms of results achieved but also in terms of the means. All are encouraged to enjoy full participation in the design of the social arrangements that affect one's life, in the definition of one's needs, in the production of goods and services to satisfy those needs, and in the evaluation of the satisfaction of those needs."

A critical approach to policing, crime, and justice, such as this, may see the region experience a more relevant, genuine, effective, and democratic approach to policing. Further, a transformational approach must deal with the remnants of policing from the colonial past. As mentioned earlier, most, if not all jurisdictions are hampered by its colonial past, but while some argue that the community is willing to work with the police (Deosaran, 2002; Wallace, 2012), others have noted a significant strain on the police–community relationship (Bailey, 2007; Bennett & Morbaito, 2006; Pino & Johnson, 2011; St. Jean, 2007). Issues of corruption and police deviance have also been highlighted (Harriott, 2000; Pfaff & Bennett, 2008; Pino, 2009).

As such, an approach that locates power as the basis of interpersonal conflict and suggests a needs-based alternative will address three things that can serve as a foundation of any police reform effort. First, it will give the community an enriched voice into the policing process. It will require of the community full participation in designing the policing service that would best meet the needs of the community. The community's role would evolve from being the ears and eyes of the police to being a co-partner with the police in their peace and safety. This would lead to an increased role of the community as another accountability mechanism specifically to local police station districts. Second, with both the police and the community working together to meet the needs of all, the "us versus them" orientation will find little room to influence police and community relations. Third, another aim of policing, increased quality of life, has a greater chance of being realized as the police would have freed themselves of the means over ends syndrome (Goldstein, 1979).

It is likely that systemic and sustainable reform of policing in Caribbean countries will not occur without local ownership of reform efforts. The latest "best practices" provided by Western powers alone will not be able to transform policing, particularly if donors are providing aid largely for their own interests rather than in the interests of the recipients (e.g. the wars on drugs and terrorism). The Western-led reforms that included the model station program in Trinidad and Tobago mentioned above were not rooted in transformational justice principles to any significant extent. Rather, they were modeled on U.S. service-oriented community policing schemes as well as the police reforms in Northern Ireland, under the assumption that the sectarian divide in Northern Ireland was similar to the ethnic divides in Trinidad and Tobago. As Ellison and Pino (2012) point out, however, the ethnic divisions between Afro-Trinidadians and Indo-Trinidadians are not at all similar to the Unionist–Nationalist divide in Northern Ireland; the countries are in much different positions within the global economic and geopolitical arenas; and they differ dramatically in terms of rates of crime, the drug trade, and the extent of political and police corruption.

Members of NGOs and individuals within the Police Service and Ministry of National Security in Trinidad and Tobago thought that foreign consultants could assist and facilitate reform efforts, particularly with technical assistance, but they also as a group wanted to have local actors lead reform efforts (Pino, 2009). However, we must be mindful that who is considered a legitimate part of the "local" is contested (Harblinger & Simons, 2015). We contend that if reforms are to be effective and sustainable, it is imperative that Trinidad and Tobago and other Caribbean countries tap into their underutilized local capacity and civil society strength, the very groups that were ignored in previous reform efforts because they did not fit various restrictive governmental requirements (see Pino, 2009).

CONCLUSION

The rich and complicated history of policing in the Caribbean continues to impact policing today. Based on the foregoing paragraphs, it is observed that while numerous police reform efforts have been attempted in the post-colonial period, the police are still perceived to be violent, corrupt, incompetent, and resistant to change. Local and global economic and political barriers, coupled with historical and colonial legacies and high violent crime rates, inhibit systemic change further, and an eager and robust civil society has not been empowered to assist in top-down reform efforts or to help sustain them in any significant way. Foreign consultants are brought in on a regular basis, but the same policing problems remain after they leave, which brings forth further calls for foreign assistance as a way to show that something is being done. Locally devised and led approaches rooted in transformational justice might have a higher chance of succeeding than repeating past mistakes, but while these kinds of alternative approaches have been called for in the past numerous times, they have rarely if ever been implemented.

REFERENCES

Adams, E. B., Morris, P. K., & Maguire, E. (2018). The Impact of gangs on community life in Trinidad. *Race and Justice,* Advanced Online Publication. DOI 10.1177/2153368718820577.

Agozino, B. (2010). Editorial: What is criminology? A control-freak discipline! *African Journal of Criminology and Justice Studies, 4*(1), i–xx.

Ahire, P. (1991). *Imperial policing: The emergence and role of the police in colonial Nigeria 1860–1960.* Buckingham: Open University Press.

Amnesty International. (2006). Trinidad and Tobago: End police immunity for unlawful killings and deaths in custody. Retrieved from: https://www.amnesty.org/en/documents/amr49/001/2006/en/

Associated Press. (2011, September 5). Trinidad extends state of emergency for 3 months. *The Guardian*. Retrieved from https://japantoday.com/category/world/trinidad-extends-state-of-emergency-by-3-months.

Baboolal, Y. (2013, October 8). Doomed Strategy. Trinidad and Tobago Guardian. Retrieved from http://www.guardian.co.tt/article-6.2.408968.95993e9772.

Bailey, C. (2007). Fear and policing violent inner-city communities. *Wadabagei: A Journal of the Caribbean & Its Diasporas, 10*(1), 24–43.

Barak, G. (2005). A reciprocal approach to peacemaking criminology: Between adversarialism and mutualism. *Theoretical Criminology, 9*(2), 131–152.

Bennett, R., & Morabito, M. (2006). Determinants of constables' perceptions of community support in three developing nations. *Police Quarterly, 9*(2), 234–265.

Bowling, B. (2010). *Policing the Caribbean: Transnational security cooperation in practice.* Oxford: Oxford University Press.

Cain, M. (2007). Globality, glocalization, and private policing: A Caribbean case study. In C. Summer (Ed.), *The Blackwell Companion to Criminology* (pp. 417–436). Malden, MA: Blackwell.

Chevigny, P. (1990). Police deadly force as social control: Jamaica, Argentina, and Brazil. *Criminal Law Forum, 1*(2), 389–425.

Clark, C. (2014). Giuliani, Bratton Back Next Month—Griffith. *Trinidad Guardian.* Retrieved from http://www.guardian.co.tt/news/2014-12-13/giuliani-bratton-back-next-month—griffith.

Committee on the Restructuring of the Police Service. (1984). *Report of the committee on the restructuring of the police service.* Port of Spain: Republic of Trinidad and Tobago.

Danns, G. (1982). *Domination and power in Guyana: A study of the police in a third world context.* New Brunswick, NJ: Transaction Books.

De Verteuil, A. (1986). *Sylvester Devenish and the Irish in nineteenth century Trinidad.* Port-of-Spain, Trinidad and Tobago: Paria.

Deosaran, R. (2002). Community policing in the Caribbean: Context, community, and police capability. *Policing: An International Journal of Police Strategies and Management, 25*(1), 125–146.

Donais, T. (2009). *Local ownership and security sector reform.* Zurich: Lit Verlag.

Ellison, G., & Pino, N. W. (2012). *Globalization, police reform, and development: Doing it the Western way?* New York: Palgrave-Macmillan.

Gabbatt, A. (2011). 100 held in Trinidad and Tobago's state of emergency.' *The Guardian.* http://www.guardian.co.uk/world/2011/aug/25/trinidad-and-tobago-state-emergency.

Goldstein, H. (1979). Improving policing: A problem-oriented approach. *Crime & Delinquency, 25*(2), 236–258.

Gomes, C. (2007). *Police accountability in the Caribbean: Where are the people?* Paper presented at the workshop on Police Accountability at the Civicus World Assembly, Glasgow, Scotland, 23–27 May 2007.

Gready, P., & Robins, S. (2014). From transitional to transformative justice: A new agenda for practice. *The International Journal of Transitional Justice, 8*(3), 339–361.

Griffith, I. L. (2000). *The Political Economy of Drugs in the Caribbean.* New York: St. Martin's Press.

Harblinger, A. T., & Simons, C. (2015). The good, the bad, and the powerful: Representations of the "local" in peacebuilding. *Security Dialogue, 46*(5), 422–439.

Harriott, A. (1997). Reforming the Jamaica constabulary force: From political to professional policing? *Caribbean Quarterly, 43*(3), 1–-12.

Harriott, A. (1998). Policing styles in the commonwealth Caribbean: The Jamaican case. *Caribbean Journal of Criminology and Social Psychology, 3*(1–-2), 60–-82.

Harriott, A. (2000). *Police and crime control in Jamaica: Problems of re-*

forming ex-colonial constabularies. Jamaica: University of the West Indies Press.

Hills, A. (1995). Militant tendencies. *British Journal of Criminology,* 35(3), 450–458.

INDECOM Jamaica. (n.d.). Frequently asked questions. Retrieved from https://www.indecom.gov.jm/frequently-asked-questions/faq-commission.

Jaffe, R. (2012). Criminal dons and extralegal security privatization in downtown Kingston, Jamaica. *Singapore Journal of Tropical Geography,* 33(2), 184–197.

Jefferies, C. (1952). *The colonial police.* London: Max Parish.

Job, M. (2004). *Police reform and performance management: Crime, the Darby report, and history.* Trinidad: Alkebu Industries Company Limited.

Johnson, D. (2006). *Perceived legitimacy and willingness to assist the police in Trinidad and Tobago.* Paper presented at the 58th Annual Meeting of the American Society of Criminology, Los Angeles, California, 1–4 November 2006.

Johnson, D., Maguire, E. & Kuhns, J. (2014). Public perceptions of the legitimacy of the law and legal authorities: Evidence from the Caribbean. *Law and Society Review,* 43(40), 947–977.

Jones, M., & Satchell, N. (2009). Data gathering on police officers and civil service training courses in the Caribbean region. Washington, DC: Organization of American States.

King, K. (2009). *Policing your brother as the other: An analysis of policing in Trinidad and Tobago, "measuring paramilitarism."* Paper presented at the SALISES Tenth Annual Conference, The University of the West Indies, Cave Hill Campus, Barbados, 25–27 March 2009.

Killingray, D., & Anderson, D. (1991). Consent, coercion and colonial control: Policing the empire, 1830–1940. In D. Killingray & D. Anderson (Eds.), *Policing the empire: government, authority and colonial control, 1830–1940* (pp. 1–17). Manchester: Manchester University Press.

Kowlessar, G. (2012). 'Warner instructs police: Don't reveal crime statistics.' *Trinidad and Tobago Guardian*. Retrieved from http://www.guardian.co.tt/news/2012-10-10/warner-instructs-police-don't-reveal-crime-statistics.

Kowlessar, G. (2014). Cops not taking PCA seriously.' *Trinidad and Tobago Guardian*. Retrieved from http://www.guardian.co.tt/news/2014-06-12/cops-not-taking-pca-seriously.

Kowlessar, G. (2017). Cops not trained to deal with mental patients. *Trinidad and Tobago Guardian*. Retrieved from http://www.guardian.co.tt/news/2017-05-17/cops-not-trained-deal-mental-patients.

Lambourne, W. (2009). Transitional justice and peacebuilding after mass violence. *International Journal of Transitional Justice, 3*(1), 28–48.

Mars, J. (2009). Ethnic diversity and police community relations in Guyana. *Commonwealth and Comparative Politics, 47*(4), 506–616.

Mastrofski, S. (1999). *Policing for People*. Washington, DC: Police Foundation.

Mastrofski, S., & Lum, C. (2008). Meeting the challenges of police governance in Trinidad and Tobago. *Policing, 2*(4), 481–496.

McCulloch, J. (2007). Transnational crime as productive fiction. *Social Justice, 34*(2), 19–32.

McDavid, H., Clayton, A., & Cowell, N. (2011). The difference between the constabulary force and the military: An analysis of the differing roles and functions in the context of the current security environment in the Caribbean (The case of Jamaica). *Journal of Eastern Caribbean Studies, 36*(3), 40–71.

Miller, J., & Hendrix, N. (2007). Applying the problem solving model to the developing world context: The case of murder in Trinidad and Tobago. *Crime Prevention and Community Safety, 9*(4), 275–290.

Mycoo, M. (2004). The retreat of the upper and middle classes to gated communities in the post-structural adjustment era: The case of Trinidad. *Environment and Planning A, 38*(1), 131–148.

O'Dowd, D. J. (1991). *Review of the Trinidad and Tobago Police Service*.

Port-of-Spain: Republic of Trinidad and Tobago.

Ottley, C. R. (1964). *A historical account of the Trinidad and Tobago Police Force from the earliest times*. Trinidad.

Paes-Machado, E., & Noronha, C. V. (2002). Policing the Brazilian poor: Resistance to and acceptance of police brutality in urban popular classes (Salbador, Brazil). *International Criminal Justice Review, 12*(1), 53–76.

Parks, R., & Mastrofski, S. (2008). *Introducing service-oriented policing to Trinidad and Tobago*. Paper presented at the American Society of Criminology Annual Meeting, St. Louis Adam's Mark, St. Louis, Missouri on 30th November 2014.

Pepinsky, H., & Quinney, R. (1991). *Criminology as Peacemaking*. Bloomington: Indiana University Press.

Pfaff, D., & Bennett, R. (2008). Excessive use of force in Trinidad and Tobago: Investigating its determinants across time. *Caribbean Journal of Criminology and Public Safety, 13*(1&2), 1–47.

Police Complaints Authority of Trinidad and Tobago. (2013). *2013 Annual Report*. Retrieved from http://www.pca.org.tt/wp-content/uploads/2014/09/PCA-Annual-Report-2013-FAW-small.pdf.

Police Service Commission. (2004). *Annual Report of the Police Service Commission*. Port-of-Spain: Republic of Trinidad and Tobago.

Pino, N. (2009). Developing democratic policing in the Caribbean: The case of Trinidad and Tobago. *Caribbean Journal of Criminology and Public Safety, 14*(1&2), 214–-258.

Pino, N. (2016). Trinidad and Tobago: Crime, police corruption and police reforms." In K. R. Hope (Ed.), *Police corruption and reform in developing societies* (pp. 207–228). Boca Raton, FL: CRC Press.

Pino, N., & Johnson, L. M. (2011). Police deviance and community relations in Trinidad and Tobago. *Policing: An International Journal of Police Strategies and Management, 34*(3), 454–478.

Scott, G. (1987). *Report of the commission of enquiry into the extent of the problem of drug abuse in Trinidad and Tobago*. Trinidad and Tobago: Government Printery

Seaby, G. (1993). *Final report for the government of Trinidad and Tobago on investigations carried out by officers from new Scotland yard in respect of allegations made by Rodwell Murray and others about corruption in the Trinidad and Tobago Police Service.* London: Metropolitan Police Office.

St. Jean, P. K. B. (2007). Explaining strained community-police relations in a racially and ethnically homogenous community: Grand Bay, Dominica. *Journal of Ethnicity in Criminal Justice, 5*(2/3), 1–27.

Sutton, H. (2017). Unpacking the high cost of crime in the Caribbean: Violent crime, the private sector, and the government response." In L. Jaitman (Ed.), *The costs of crime and violence: New evidence and insights in Latin America and the Caribbean* (pp. 79–92). New York: Inter-American Development Bank.

Sullivan, D., & Tift, R. (1998). Criminology as peacemaking: A peace-oriented perspective on crime, punishment, and justice that takes into account the needs of all. *The Justice Professional, 11*(1–2) 5–34.

Trinidad Express. (2015). 46 killed by cops. Retrieved from: https://www.trinidadexpress.com/news/local/killed-by-cops/article_61 8b99b6-44d9-500b-b038-d39e1966bf70.html.

Trinidad and Tobago Guardian. (2013, July 23). Warner's rise and fall in PP'. *Trinidad and Tobago Guardian.* Retrieved from http://www.guardian.co.tt/news/2013-07-22/warner's-rise-and-fall-pp.

TT Crime. (2019). *Trinidad and Tobago crime statistics.* Retrieved from https://www.ttcrime.com/stats.php.

United Nations Development Programme (UNDP). 2010. Citizen security survey in support of the Caribbean human development report: Human development and the shift to better citizen security. New York: UNDP.

United Nations Development Programme. (UNDP). (2012). *Caribbean human development report 2012: Human development and the shift to better citizen security.* New York: UNDP. Retrieved from http://www.undp.org/content/dam/undp/library/corporate/HDR/Latin%20 America%20and%20Caribbean%20HDR/C_bean_HDR_ Jan25_2012_3MB.pdf

Wallace, W. C. (2012). Findings from a concurrent study on the level of community involvement in the policing process in Trinidad and Tobago. *The Police Journal, 85*(1), 61–83.

Watson, D., Boateng, F. D., Pino, N. W., & Morgan, P. (2018). The interface between exercise of state power and personal powerlessness: A study of police perceptions of factors impacting professional practices. *Police Practice and Research, 19*(5), 458–471.

Wilson, D. B., Parks, R. B., & Mastrofski, S. (2011). "The impact of police reform on communities of Trinidad and Tobago." *Journal of Experimental Criminology, 7*(4), 375–405.

Wolf, R. (2008). "Tourism oriented policing: An examination of a Florida/Caribbean partnership for police training. *International Journal of Police Science and Management, 10*(4), 402-416.

Wozniak, J. (2000). The voices of peacemaking criminology: Insights into a perspective with an eye to teaching. *Contemporary Justice Review, 3*(3), 267–289.

CHAPTER II

THE INFLUENCE OF ORGANIZATIONAL JUSTICE ON POLICE CORRUPTION IN TRINIDAD AND TOBAGO

Nirmala Sookoo

The University of the West Indies, St. Augustine, Trinidad and Tobago

ABSTRACT

Although police corruption has been of interest for many years, empirical investigations of the influencing role of organizational justice have ignored the phenomenon within Trinidad and Tobago. This study uses data from a random sample of 774 police officers from all nine policing divisions in Trinidad and Tobago to estimate the effect that organizational justice has on police corruption in Trinidad and Tobago. The results showed that officers who perceive the police service as fair and just in the allocation of rewards, such as salaries, promotion, and other work incentives, and who believed there was a systematic allocation of rewards were less likely to have values that support corruption. Furthermore, police officers who felt alienated from their jobs due to organizational injustice were more likely to have values that support corruption. Further, the alienation of police officers from their jobs was a significant mediator variable. The results from this study suggest that organizational justice and police alienation comprise a significant theoretical framework in investigating police corruption and integrity. Additionally, the results of this study may guide policymaking in the design of a work environment committed to just, unbiased, and systematic allocation of work-related rewards.

Keywords: Organizational justice, alienation, corruption, Trinidad and Tobago Police Service

INTRODUCTION

The police serve indispensable roles in society. They are the guardians of law and order and are entrusted to protect the fundamental rights of citizens. To accomplish their duties as sworn guardians, they wear many hats. Their duties may include mediating a domestic disturbance, transporting drunks, providing medical aid, apprehending offenders, investigating crime, and counseling juveniles. To accomplish such roles, the police are entrusted with extraordinary powers that set him apart from others (Pfaff, 2010). As keepers of the law and of a social contract, the police must display higher levels of integrity and moral character than others. Police officers must be humane and ethical and have qualities of human excellence (Prasanna, 2013). However, allegations, investigations, and media headlines outlining abuse and rampant corruption within the Trinidad and Tobago Police Service (TTPS) portray police officers (on the island) as symbols of unfettered corruption. The question posed is why do those entrusted with the power and authority to protect exploit that authority for their personal advantage (Wolfe & Piquero, 2011). This paper seeks to answer this question by initially describing the state of corruption within a police service in a post-colonial nation and testing the influences of organizational justice and alienation in determining levels of integrity or corruption.

"Police officers act corruptly when, in exercising or failing to exercise their authority, they act with the primary intention of furthering private or departmental/divisional advantage" Kleinig's (1996, p. 166). Narrowly defined, police corruption refers to officers who exploit their position and influence for personal rather than public gain (Bayley, 2011). It refers to any infringement of rules, such as physical abuse of prisoners, sexual misconduct, perjury, racial profiling, human trafficking, or selling narcotics. There are many paths to these corrupt activities. These paths include communal and political tolerance for corruption, a lack of quality of management, and opportunities for corruption and governance (Newburn, 2015).

Another path to corruption found in many developing societies is colonialism. According to Ezeanya (2012), the history of policing can be traced to the protection of citizens. However, in post-colonial nations, policing was established to promulgate colonial rule. For example, Mars (2004) noted that policing was employed to promote the colonist agenda

of an uninterrupted supply of labor. The police functioned like slave patrols, returning runaways and quelling rebellions by engaging in violent
and brutal force. Post-slavery, the police was again charged with protecting the labor supply of freed and indentured laborers. In present times,
the paramilitary culture of the police pervades, as they continue to en-
vision their role as protecting the island's elite from the rebellious public
(Trotman, 1986). This colonization process bequeathed its legacy to the
continual practice of citizen abuse and oppression, which increases tolerance for unethical practices, misconduct, and the abuse of authority.

POLICE CORRUPTION IN TRINIDAD AND TOBAGO

The earliest official reports investigating the extent of police corruption
came from the Scott Drug Reports in 1986 and 1993. The Scott Drug Report (1986) publicly revealed that police officers were deeply integrated
into the criminal underworld, as illustrated by their protection of drug
dealers, smuggling drugs, counterfeiting money, and possibly even committing murder. Corruption existed in all ranks, and the Commissioner of
Police, Randolph Burroughs, was identified as being linked to prominent
drug kingpins, such as Dole Chadee, Rudolph Mills, and Naim Naya Ali.
The Commissioner and his elite policemen, known as the "Flying Squad,"
were accused of being a law unto themselves (Griffith, 2015). Such detailed reports of corruption led to 53 officers being suspended based on
allegations of narcotic involvement in 1987. Shortly after the report was
released, constable Phillip Salvary suspiciously disappeared and was murdered in 1987 during a drug bust operation, which led to 16 police officers being suspended (Griffith, 1995). Even after the Scott Drug Report
of 1986, corruption among the rank and file of police continued, and in
1993, corruption was described as endemic and so dominant that it tar-
nished the entire police service (Seaby, 1993) More recent research by
Ryan, Rampersad, Bernard, Mohammed, and Thorpe (2013) revealed
that police officers were still active in the criminal underbelly, with participation in the drug economy. Ryan et al. (2013) estimated that the percentage of rogue cops could be as high as 40% and that members of the
police service were described as "invisible members of associates of gangs
or controller of their activities" (Ryan et al., 2013).

Gomes (2007) described the police services as being steeped in corruption and tainted by low accountability and professionalism. She blamed

high corruption levels, the excessive use of force, and excessive judicial executions on the unreformed police structures handed down from colonial times. Gomes (2007) further described the state of corruption within the TTPS, stating that in 2006, police officers were detained for the alleged possession of illegal drugs and firearms, kidnapping, and other illegal activities. Furthermore, in 2006, 11 people died in police custody. Data taken from the Police Complaint Authority (2017) in Trinidad and Tobago showed that complaints about the police increased by 95% from 2010/2011 to 2013/2014. The chief allegations made against the police were neglect of duty, misconduct, unnecessary use of authority, and corrupt practices. From October 1, 2016 to September 30, 2017, there were a total of 538 allegations made against police officers in Trinidad and Tobago. Thirteen allegations were made about police corruption: 241 about police misconduct and 197 allegations about criminal offences committed by the police. In 2017, the Police Manpower Audit Committee (2017) highlighted the problem of corruption within the service. In a survey conducted by the Police Manpower Audit Committee, 75% of the police officers agreed that corruption is present within the TTPS. The report confirmed the idea of corruption in police "ran deep and wide" (Police Manpower Audit Committee, 2017, p. 93) Additionally, 307 officers were suspended as of February 2017. Additionally, the audit committee asserted that complaints about police mistreatment and corruption dragged on for years without resolution. The report provided a glimpse into police corruption; however, there was a lack of statistics about the number of police officers charged, disciplined, and/or convicted for wrongdoings.

CONSEQUENCES OF CORRUPTION

The consequences of corruption are far reaching, as it impacts not only individual offenders, but also their victims, the police as an institution, and the wider community. The phenomenon has pervasive criminal, political, national, and international consequences. Corruption erodes public trust in the police and police legitimacy, which is paramount to preventing and detecting crime. The rapport between the public and the police is destroyed with reports of corruption and police misbehavior. Citizens may no longer distinguish the police as watchmen of justice, but instead view them as criminals. As a result, legitimacy is compromised. A report by the Latin American Opinion Poll illustrated that a mere 3% of the local populace trusted the police a lot, while 33% had an absolute lack of trust in the police (Kirton, Anatol, & Braithwaite, 2010). According to Ryan et al. (2013, p. 254), Dwayne Gibbs, a former Commissioner of Police in Trinidad and Tobago, asserted that corruption "causes citizens to doubt the integrity of the Police Service and dampens their willingness to cooperate with law enforcement officials to fight crime."

Police corruption also adversely influences the national trust and confidence in the government. Loree (2006) claimed that when persons cease respecting the police, the government's capability to act as a public agent worsens. Furthermore, police corruption sets limits in national development by challenging the country's economic and political stability (Pfaff, 2010). Nations that possess more excessive levels of perceived corruption also have reduced economic development (Nazario, 2007). A corrupt police service and the inability of the political body to govern means that crime would persist in multiplying, thereby reducing foreign investment and tourism. Although there have been multiple reports of corruption within the TTPS and the consequences of such corruption pose a threat to the community, political, economic and national development, there has been a lack of empirical driven research in investigating the influences of the phenomenon within Trinidad and Tobago. Therefore, this study seeks to fills this knowledge gap.

STATEMENT OF THE PROBLEM

Police officers are the entrusted gatekeepers for social control. They are not only responsible for maintaining law and order, but they are also charged with representing justice (Wolfe & Piquero, 2011). As such, reports, complaints, and allegations of police corruption taint the image of service, reduce legitimacy and community support, and limit nation building. There have been numerous local accounts and descriptions of police corruption. Yet, there are gaps in our understanding about what correlates with the phenomenon. Without empirical knowledge of such correlates, recommendations and policies would not reflect the reforms needed.

The literature has identified many factors related to corruption. The popular variables are based at the organizational level, including organizational policy, recruitment, and training (Ivković, 2005; Skolnick & Fyfe, 1993). However, the role of organizational justice (perception about the inequalities of the distribution of rewards and managerial practices) in determining corrupt behavior has been typically ignored (Wolfe & Piquero, 2011). Additionally, research into the role of alienation or self-estrangement of police officers is limited. Løvseth (2001) declared that corruption is a function of alienation; however, the association has been under-investigated. Alienated police officers are more likely to deviate, as they are detached from their jobs. Furthermore, Sunahara (2002) reported that police officers who were alienated due to perceived organizational injustice had significantly more cases of misconduct and unethical and corrupt behavior.

This study is aimed that filling the gaps in the knowledge regarding police corruption in the TTPS. Employing survey data gathered from 774 police officers from all nine policing divisions in Trinidad and Tobago, this research analyzes the influence of organizational justice on police corruption. In addition, the significance of alienation as a mediator between organizational justice and police corruption is assessed.

LITERATURE REVIEW

Organizational Justice

Overall, organizations with unjust and biased allocation of rewards have been shown to have employees whose behaviors are conducive to deviance (Aquino et al., 1999; Wolfe & Piquero, 2011). Perceptions of organizational justice have been shown to influence a plethora of work outcomes, such as job satisfaction, motivation, commitment, turnover intentions, and even theft (Greenberg, 1993). Although there are various dimensions of organizational justice, this study adopts the two-factor model of distributive and procedural justice, which surrounds equality in work outcomes and processes (Clay-Warner, Reynolds, & Roman, 2005). Distributive justice examines how social and economic commodities and services are disseminated (Longres & Scalon, 2005). This dimension measures the just distribution of rewards (Colton, 2002). Rewards described income, job security, career opportunities, training, and promotion. Ideally, workers seek a match between their input (education, experience, training, and effort) and their outputs (wages, promotions, and job security). When outcomes are believed to be unfair, employees' emotions can be negatively impacted, leading to despair, anger, and guilt and influencing their performance and withdrawal from work (Cohen-Charash & Spector, 2001). The other dimension, procedural justice, measures whether decisions made in regulating distributive rewards are fair (Thibaut & Walker, 1975). Employees measure the methods, procedures, and mechanism used to distribute rewards. The fundamental difference between distributive and procedural justice is that the distributive justice focuses on ends, while procedural justice concentrates on means (Lambert, Cluse-Tolar, & Hogan, 2005).

This review of the literature provides evidence of the significant association between distributive justice and police corruption. The lack of rewards thrust some police officers into accommodating bribes and other forms of corruption. Williams (2002) claimed that police corruption is a consequence of enrollment, promotion, income, and availability of equipment. Low earnings are the typical reasoning for corruption among police officers. Police officers often witness local criminals earning easy money and, when arrested, those criminals are also often acquitted by the court. Police officers thus reason that it may be a superior form of justice to target the pockets of the offenders and generate some money for themselves (Glazer, 1995). Offenders taken into custody typically enjoy more riches than police officers do, which creates an environment conducive to extorting bribes from criminals (Greene, 2007). According to Barker (1977), police officers do not believe they compensated adequately. They estimate that the perils they encounter are justification for them to be rewarded more and they may believe they are entitled to more money than their customary pay and benefits.

Outcomes are not only determined by disappointing wages, but also by injustice due to the lack of impartiality, consistency, accuracy of information, and ethics in the allocation of rewards. Generally, the career development model in most police organizations acts as a vehicle for corruption. White (2007) asserted that the opportunities for promotion in the police service are limited, yet it remains the single route to obtaining a significant pay. Simultaneously, this career advancement process can be source of dissatisfaction among officers. Career advancement in the TTPS has remained a sensitive issue for some officers. In 2015, 32 officers won a case against the Commissioner of Police in Trinidad and Tobago, after being overlooked for promotion whilst officers below their rank were advanced. The judge ordered that the officers be retroactively promoted and paid (La Vende, 2015). Additionally, in 2016, 35 officers sued the Commissioner of Police for excluding their names from the merit list, thereby preventing their promotions ("35 Constables Sue over Promotion.," 2016). These officers believed that they were unjustly denied of their promotions, which they had been anticipating since 2014, when Justice Charles charged that police officers were victims of prejudice. Police officers who perceived that biased procedures were employed to dispense rewards were more open to displaying unethical behavior, becoming more self-interested, and exploiting occupational resources (Sunahara, 2004). Additionally, police officers in the Philadelphia police district who believed there was equitable distribution of resources received fewer cases of misconduct based on citizen complaints (Wolf & Piquero, 2015).

Alienation

Research measuring the effects of alienation on police corruption is still in its infancy. Løvseth (2001) claimed that corruption is a result of alienation, but its association his still under investigation. The estrangement of police may lead to unethical practices, such excessive use of force, 'Dirty Harry' techniques (use of reckless practices and unquestionable behavior to achieve justice), and tolerance to their peers' unethical behavior (Shernock, 1990). The results of Shernock's study illustrated that estrangement from the public and work organization were important in influencing the tolerance of misconduct of peers, as was the perspective that the ends justify the means. "The continued police alienation from the public undermines the service ideal underlying a professional code of ethics" (Shernock, 1990, p. 39).

Sunahara (2004) reported that alienation from the community and the police service and the role of the police officer were associated with unethical behavior. However, he focused on a theoretical and descriptive analysis. The premises of the conceptual model were examined via frequencies and not through inferential statistics. Nonetheless, Sunahara's study presented the conceptual premises by analyzing the association between alienation and corruption. His research demonstrated that alienated police officers were more open to corruption. They were more likely to engage in using expedient methods that may undercut justice. These methods characteristically compose of 'Dirty Harry' tactics, such as providing incomplete evidence, inappropriately coaching witnesses, and fabricating evidence to gain a search warrant. Furthermore, alienated officers were more lenient of their coworkers' schemes to conceal crooked actions. They were more accepting of scheming and the abusive actions of their peers on the streets. These police officers were more apt to utilize their occupation to serve their personal ends, such as soliciting bribes and threatening adolescent offenders. Essentially, alienated police officers were self-indulgent or self-interested on the job.

Mediation of Alienation between Organizational Justice and Corruption

The next purpose of this study is to determine the mediation of employee alienation between organizational justice and police corruption. It is assumed that officers who are disconnected from their job due to organizational injustice are more apt to be accepting of corruption. Preceding studies with a sample frame of police officers have reported significant correlation between organizational justice and alienation (Shernock, 1990 Sunahara, 2003) and alienation and corruption (Shernock, 1990; Sunahara, 2003). This current research goes further, and assumes that alienation can act as a mediating variable between organizational justice and corruption.

Sunahara (2004) claimed that one source of employee estrangement was distributive injustice. The results of his study demonstrated that 28% of police officers felt that their wages were unjust. Additionally, publicized promotions kept officers loyal to the organization and lowered alienation. Police officers who sensed that they were unfairly denied career advancement or wage increases or who considered the distributive method to be inequitable in the provision of rewards were open to the use of unethical and corrupt practices and misconduct. Corruption was reported to be a significant by-product of alienation. Alienation occurred due to the perceived inequitable allocation of rewards and a distributive process shrouded in inaccurate information, inconsistency, bias, and favoritism. Thus, it is assumed that alienation mediates the relationship between organizational justice and corruption.

RESEARCH MODEL

In the light of the explanations provided in the literature, it is expected that the two-factor model of organizational justice and workplace alienation influences police corruption. In addition, workplace alienation is assumed to mediate perceived organizational injustice and police corruption (see Figure 1).

Figure 1: Conceptual model

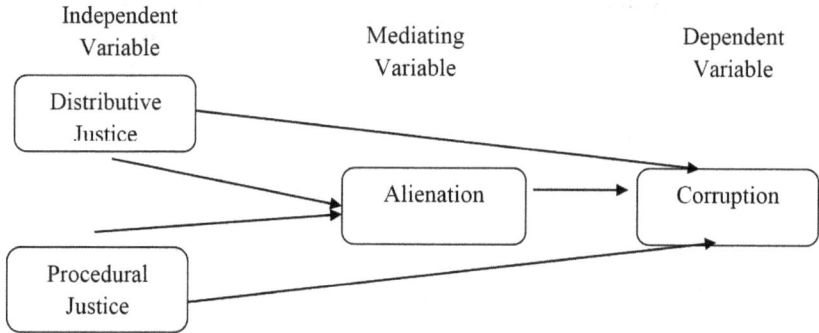

Source: Fieldwork, 2018.

The conceptual model in Figure 1 illustrates the fundamental assumptions of the theory driving the research. It applies the organizational framework to explaining both the alienation and corruption of police officers. The conceptual model assumes that distributive justice, procedural justice, and alienation influence police corruption. Additionally, it is assumed that distributive justice and procedural justice determine alienation, which directly influences corruption. Therefore, organizational justice is expected to produce an indirect effect on corruption via alienation.

METHODOLOGY

Sample

The primary data were gathered by a survey instrument distributed by the researcher. The survey was disseminated to police officers from all nine policing divisions within Trinidad and Tobago. The sample size was calculated based on Krejcie and Morgan's (1970) procedure for computing sample size. The total population of officers in TTPS stood at approximately 6,500 (TTPS figures 2018); with a .05 margin of error and 95% confidence interval, a sample size of 379 was necessary to represent the police population. To compensate for non-responses, 1,000 surveys were distributed and 774 were returned, obtaining a response rate of 77.4%.

Officers were sampled using the multistage stage cluster sample design. Police stations were randomly chosen from each of the nine police divisions. Cluster sampling is characterized by being limited by two sampling errors (Babbie, 2013). Sampling errors are produced by limited clusters integrated within the sample, which may not include a significant or diverse portion of the population. To overcome this drawback and reduce underrepresentation, police stations from each of the divisions were chosen. It is normally recommended to incorporate a larger number of clusters when employing the cluster sampling design due to intra-cluster homogeneity (Engel & Schutt, 2010). By incorporating officers from all divisions, the researcher likely lessened sampling errors.

Measures

For this study, the scale measuring distributive justice was tailored from Price and Mueller (1986). The original scale comprised of six statements, questioning participants about whether they were fairly rewarded in relation to their tasks, effort, education, experience, work stress, and accomplishments they had achieved. Procedural justice was evaluated via an adapted six-item scale developed by Niehoff & Moorman (1993). Five of the six items of the scale were re-worded to ensure that officers could clearly understand what was being asked. The scale measured consistency, accuracy of information, decisions, and the removal of bias in the process of allocating rewards.

The third scale measures alienation, which is described as the "panchreston" (Johnson, 1973). Characteristically depicted as ambiguous, alienation is conceptualized by diverse definitions. There is the one-dimensional approach, marked by powerlessness as defined by Marx, and the five-dimensional approach developed by Seeman (1959) (delineated in dimensions of powerlessness, meaninglessness, normlessness, isolation, and self-estrangement). Throughout the plethora of conceptualizations, one theme emerges: dissociation/self-estrangement (Nair & Vohra, 2009). Alienation is portrayed as a dissociative state (Schacht, 1970) or detachment from work (Hirschfield & Field, 2000). Thus, in this study, alienation is conceptualized as the separation from the self at work. The alienation scale utilized in this study was developed through a combination of alienation scales from Nair and Vohra (2009) and Maddi, Kobasa, and Hoover (1979). The scale comprised of 14 items, assessing pleasure in, disconnection from, and enthusiasm for work. The reliability of the scale has been reported to be excellent, with a Cronbach's alpha of .95 (Sookoo, 2014).

The final scale was corruption, defined as the "abuse of public office for private gain." Police corruption is difficult to gauge, and Prenzler (2009) argued that there is no certainty that all types of corrupt activities have been acknowledged, as there are no measures of the phenomenon. The measurement of corruption is an imprecise science (Klockars, Ivkovic, & Haberfeld, 2000). Nonetheless, though vague, the examination of corruption should not be abandoned, as it can still provide insights into police service. Even though police corruption is difficult to measure, Klockars et al.'s (2000) integrity scale has been universally employed. The scale is comprised of 11 scenarios, each measuring perception of integrity and the willingness to report any misconduct or corrupt and deviant behavior. The scenarios centered on questioning officers about accepting complimentary meals, accommodating discounts from businesses in their district, soliciting bribes from motorists, accepting holiday gifts, pilfering from crime scenes, abusing offenders, and approving kickbacks. One scenario questioning police officers' willingness to turn a blind eye to bars' closing times was omitted due to its cultural invalidity in Trinidad and Tobago. There are no legally specified closing times for bars in Trinidad and Tobago.

Assumptions of the Tests

Before undertaking data analysis or parametric tests, such as correlation, regression, multiple regression, and ANOVA, assumptions of normality, linearity, homoscedasticity, and independence must be met. Table 1 illustrates the statistics for each assumption. Cronbach's alpha, which tests for reliability, ranged from .763 to .933 and was categorized as good to excellent (George & Mallery, 2010). The validity of measurement scales, Kaiser-Meyer-Oklin scores, ranged from .747 to .950. Hutcheson and Sofroniou (1999) claimed that scores ranging from 0.7 and 0.8 are good, those between 0.8 and 0.9 are great and those over 0.9 are superb; therefore, the scales were observed to be valid.

The modus operandi for assessing normality is by observing skew and kurtosis. George and Mallery (2003) provided a few rules of thumb: a skew value between 1.0 and -1.0 is described as excellent for many psychometric purposes; nevertheless, a value between 2.0 and -2.0 is, in most cases, acceptable. Every one of the values fell between 1.0 and -1.0; therefore, the assumption of normality was met for each of the variables. Additionally, George and Mallery (2003) held that a kurtosis value between 1.0 and -1.0 is excellent for most psychometric purposes; a value between 2.0 and -2.0 is still considered to be satisfactory. Once more, the values were between 1.0 and -1.0, which were excellent. Finally, violations of independence were tested, using the Durbin-Watson test. Field (2009) claimed that the common rule of thumb is that values less than 1 and greater than 3 are grounds for concern and represent breaches to the assumption of independence. The Durbin-Watson scores are illustrated in Table 1; all of the scores were above 1.539 and under 2.00, portraying minor positive autocorrelations. Thus, the assumption of independence has not been violated for any of the variables.

Table 1: Test Statistics for the Assumptions of Parametric Tests

Variable	Reliability α	Validity	Normality		Independence
		KMO	Skewness	Kurtosis	
Distributive Justice	.763	.925	.028	.176	1.648
Procedural Justice	.819	.747	.088	.535	1.798
Alienation	.901	.950	.422	.817	1.539
Corruption	.933	.838	-.032	-.522	-

Source: Fieldwork, 2018.

Approximately 774 police officers participated in the randomly distributed survey across all nine policing divisions. There was a more significant male participation, with 500 male respondents compared to 263 females; 11 participants did not indicate their gender. The more distinguished male to female ratio reflected the dominance of males in the police service. Roughly 74% of the police population is male (Police Manpower Audit Committee, 2017). The subsequent results illustrate the various null hypotheses along with their findings.

Organizational Justice

Distributive justice. H_{01}: Perception of low levels of distributive justice does not influence corruption scores.

The statistical tests employed to examine the influence of distributive justice on corruption were correlation and regression. There was a significant inverse association between distributive justice and corruption ($r = -.221, p < .001$), see Table 2. Additionally, the regression coefficient reported that distributive justice significantly predicted variance in corruption ($r^2 = .049, p < .001$).

Table 2: Test Statistics for Correlation and Regression

Variable	r	r^2	Adjusted r^2	Significance
Distributive Justice	-.221	.049	.048	.001
Procedural Justice	-.226	.071	.070	.001
Alienation	.473	.223	.222	.001

Source: Fieldwork, 2018.

Procedural justice. H_{02}: Perception of a lack of procedural justice does not influence corruption among police officers.

There was an inverse correlation between procedural justice and corruption scores ($r = -.266, p < .001$). Additionally, perception of procedural injustice significantly predicted 7.1% of the variance in willingness to participate in corruption ($r^2 = .071, p < .001$).

Alienation. H_{03}: Alienation from the workplace does not determine higher corruption scores.

There was a positive correlation between alienation and corruption ($r = .473, p < .001$). Moreover, alienation significantly predicted 22.3% of the variance in corruption ($r^2 = .223, p < .001$).

Alienation as a mediator. H_{04}: Alienation does not mediate the relationship between distributive justice and alienation.

The abovementioned assumption was examined via the Sobel test of mediation. The results are presented in Table 3 below, which illustrates the β values for the influence that distributive justice had on alienation and the influence that the mediator (alienation) had on the phenomenon (corruption). Additionally, the errors for each relationship were included. Based on the results, the Sobel test was significant ($3.963, p < .001$).

Therefore, alienation significantly mediated the relationship between distributive justice and alienation.

Table 3: Sobel Test for Mediation of Alienation between Distribution Justice and Corruption

Test	Statistics
β value for path of distributive justice and alienation (A path)	.230
β value for path of alienation and corruption (B path)	.473
Error for A path	.052
Error for B path	.053
Test statistic	3.963
One tail probability	.001

Source: Fieldwork, 2018.

Figure 2: Sobel test of mediation of alienation between distributive justice and corruption

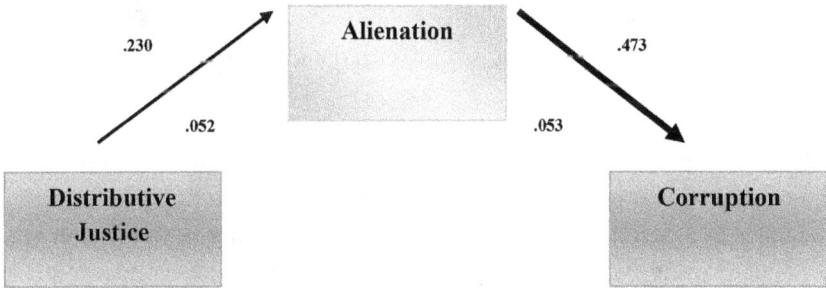

Source: Fieldwork, 2018.

H_{05}: Alienation does not mediate the relationship between procedural justice and corruption.

The mediation was examined using the Sobel test of mediation (see Table 4). Based on the calculations, the Sobel test was significant (2.878, $p < .002$). Therefore, alienation significantly mediated the relationship between procedural justice and alienation.

45

Table 4: Sobel Test for Mediation of Alienation between Procedural Justice and Corruption

Test	Statistics
β value for path of procedural justices and alienation (A path)	.301
β value for path of alienation and corruption (B path)	.473
Error for A path	.099
Error for B path	.053
Test statistic	2.878
One tail probability	.002

Source: Fieldwork, 2018.

Figure 3. Sobel test for the mediation of alienation between procedural justice and corruption

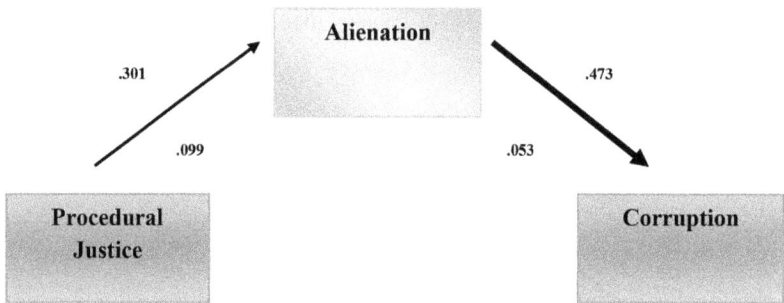

Source: Fieldwork, 2018.

H_{06}: The theoretical model does not significantly predict the influence of organizational justice on corruption and the mediation of alienation between organizational justice and alienation. The theoretical model was evaluated using path analysis, which consisted of the decomposition of two layers of multiple regression analyses.

Layer 1. Layer 1 computed the multiple regression coefficients of the effects that distributive and procedural justice had on alienation. In this layer, alienation was the criterion, while distributive and procedural justice were the predictors. The results of the first layer are provided in Table 5. Both components of organizational justice were significantly associated with alienation ($r = .325$, $p < .001$). Additionally, procedural justice exerted a stronger effect on alienation, followed by distributive justice, as seen in Table 6.

Table 5: Summary Model for Regression on Alienation

Model	r	r^2	Adjusted r^2
1	.325	.106	.103

Predictors: Distributive and procedural justice

Source: Fieldwork, 2018.

Table 6: Multiple Regression Coefficients for Alienation, as Predicted by Distributive and Procedural Justice

Model	Unstandardized Coefficients		Standardized Coefficients	Sig	Collinearity Statistics	
	B	Std. Error	Beta		Tolerance	VIF
1 (Constant)	38.198	1.339		.000		
1. Distributive Justice	-.178	.057	-.121	.002*	.792	1.263
Procedural Justice	-.718	.111	-.251	.000*	.792	1.263

*Represents significant variables.

Source: Fieldwork, 2018.

Layer 2. Layer 2 calculated the multiple regression of the effects that distributive and procedural justice and alienation had on corruption. The results of the second layer are noted in Table 7. The predictors were significantly correlated with corruption ($r = .496$, $p < .000$) and accounted for 24.6% of the variance in the outcome ($r^2 = .246$, $p < .001$). Additionally, the beta weights of the three variables were significant, as seen in Table 8. Alienation exerted the strongest effect on the variance in corruption, followed by procedural and distributive justice.

Table 7: Summary Model for Multiple-Regression for Corruption

Model	r	r^2	Adjusted r^2
1	.496	.246	.243

Predictors: Distributive justice, procedural justice, alienation

Source: Fieldwork, 2018.

Table 8: Multiple Regression Coefficients for Corruption and Multicollinearity Statistics

Model	Unstandardized Coefficients		Standardized Coefficients		Collinearity Statistics	
	B	Std. Error	Beta	Sig	Tolerance	VIF
1 (Constant)	39.696	2.935		.000		
1. Distributive Justice	-.179	.087	-.074	.040*	.744	1.291
Procedural Justice	-.484	.172	-.104	.005*	.747	1.339
Alienation	.696	.055	.425	.000*	.895	.117

*Represents significant variables.

Source: Fieldwork, 2018.

Figure 4: Model illustrating path analysis.

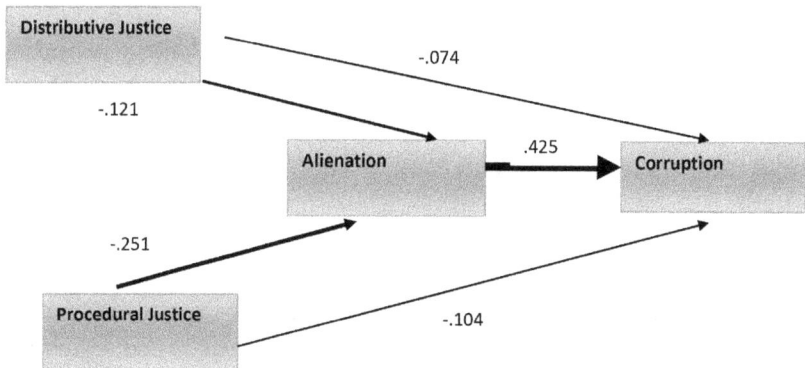

Source: Fieldwork, 2018.

On examining the path diagram (Figure 4 above), the following were revealed:

1. Alienation had the strongest direct effect on corruption (β = .425).

2. Distributive justice and procedural justice both had significant direct effects on alienation, with procedural justice having the stronger effect (β -.251).

3. Via its direct effect on alienation, distributive justice had an indirect effect on corruption. Distributive justice had an indirect ef-

fect of .134 (distributive justice → alienation → corruption = .121 x .425 = .051). Following the calculation of the indirect effect of distributive justice, the total effect was calculated by adding the direct effect of the independent variable on corruption (β – standardized beta weights) and the indirect effect. Distributive justice had a total effect of .125 (.074 + .051).

4. Via its direct effect on alienation, procedural justice had an indirect effect on corruption. Procedural justice had an indirect effect of .134 (procedural justice → alienation → corruption = .251 x .425 = .107). Additionally, procedural justice had a total effect of .211 (.104 + .107).

5. Both distributive (β = -.74) and procedural justice (β -.104) had significant effects on corruption.

DISCUSSION

Organizational Justice

This study followed the two-factor model of organizational justice, and it was assumed that perceptions of skewed distribution of rewards significantly lowers employees' integrity or increases values associated with corruption. The results from the survey distributed to randomly distributed police officers throughout the nine policing divisions revealed that distributive justice was significantly inversely associated with police corruption ($r = -.221, p < .001$). Moreover, distributive justice influenced 4.9% of the variance in corruption and, at the multivariate level of analysis, it had a β of .085 ($p < .022$). Officers who believed that they were treated unjustly based on their income, promotion, and other occupational compensation were more likely to hold unfavorable outlooks supporting and sustaining corrupt behavior. Low earnings frequently present a predictable validation for corruption within the police service Glazer 1995; Greene, 2007). Police officers who sensed that their establishment employed unequal management measures and an inequitable distribution of assets may be more inclined to defy standards and values of the organization and display deviant behavior (Wolfe & Piquero, 2011).

Additionally, low salaries provide the grounds for making ends difficult to meet. Mauro (1997, p. 5) reasoned that when wages are small, civil servants are often bound to exploit their profession to canvass bribes as a *modus operandi* to subsist. Additionally, Palmier (1985, p. 5) recognized low incomes as a significant influence of corruption: "If the official is not to be tempted into corruption and disaffection, clearly there is an obligation on the government to provide or at least allow such benefits that will ensure his loyalty; one might call it an implicit contract." Adequate pay is typically recommended as a fundamental component in reform. If "workers are paid a high enough salary, it shall discourage them from being corrupt" (Banerjee, 1996, p. 10). However, if salaries diminish severely, "even the most honest workers will be tempted into corruption in the effort to safeguard their standard of living" (Banerjee, 1996, p. 10). Thus, low salaries act as a stimulus to corruption; once salaries meet a reputable stand of living, it is argued that police officers will be discouraged from corruption (Klockars, Kutnjak, & Haberfeld, 2004).

The second component of organizational justice was equally significant in explaining police officers' integrity values. Procedural justice was significantly inversely associated with police corruption $(r = -.266, p < .001)$ and influenced 7.1% of the variance in the phenomenon $(r^2 = .071, p < .001)$. Workplaces committed to organizational justice have highly motivated employees who are committed to conforming to ethical standards (Quinton, Bradford, Fildes, Fildes, & Porte, 2015). Police officers who perceive that the process of distributing rewards was unjust were likely to embrace attitudes that favor corruption. Biased career advancement can also act as a vehicle for unethical and corrupt behavior. White (2007) argued that opportunities for promotion in the police service are restrictive, yet it is the sole means to achieve a considerable pay increase. Officers who believed that they are hindered by a biased promotion system are more likely to hold lower integrity values.

Unjust practices in allocating rewards, such as promotions and assigning officers, have been sore issues for several officers in Trinidad and Tobago. As previously mentioned, 32 police officers registered their complaints of discriminatory promotional practices in court and were retroactively promoted in 2015 (LaVende, 2015). The Police Manpower Audit Committee (2017) also demonstrated perception of favoritism in assigning police officers to divisions, units, and sections. Approximately 68% of officers felt there was favoritism in the assignment of officers very often or often. Such instances and perceptions of biased practices can influence

unethical behavior (White, 2007). Sunahara (2004) contended that police officers who maintain a cynical perspective of their conditions of employment are more open to unethical behavior, such as the self-interested
utilization of professional resources.

Alienation

Alienation of police officers from their workplace was also assumed to
increase values associated with corruption. At the bivariate level of analysis, alienation was significantly associated with corruption ($r = .473, p <$
.001) and predicted 22.3% of the variance in the phenomena ($r^2 = .223$,
$p < .001$). At the multivariate level of analysis, alienation had a β of .425
($p < .001$). The results of this survey reflected previous research, in which
the significance of police alienation was reported to have a positive effect
on unethical and corrupt practices (Sunahara, 2004; Shernock, 1990).

Locally, alienated police officers had a negative outlook supporting corrupt values. They viewed running a personal business, receiving free
meals, soliciting bribes, and displaying abusive behavior as not serious
and they were less likely to report unethical behavior. These results mirrored Sunahara's (2004) research claims. Sunahara (2004) claimed that
estranged officers are expected to implement their occupation for their
private means, agree to gratuities, and threaten juvenile offenders. Additionally, he argued that alienated police officers were more self-interested in their profession. These officers were more likely to minimize the
gravity of using police assets, such as vehicles for personal responsibilities
and office space for private advantage. Therefore, alienation validates corruption. Furthermore, alienation can oppose the values of civic culture
and promulgate self-interest (Løvseth, 2001). When officers become estranged from their jobs, values supporting citizenry and moral behavior
are undermined while values sustaining corruption germinate.

Additionally, alienation represented a significant mediating variable.
The mediation of alienation between distributive justice and police
corruption was tested via the Sobel test of mediation. The results indicated that alienation was a significant mediator (3.963, $p < .001$).
Police officers who were alienated due to inequity in the distribution
of work-related rewards had values that predisposed them to favor corrupt behavior. Police officers who felt that they were victims of missed
opportunities and who had become estranged from their workplace

had values and attitudes that supported unethical behavior, corruption, and misconduct.

The mediation of alienation between procedural justice and police corruption was tested via the Sobel test of mediation, and the results indicated that it was a significant mediator (2.878, $p < .02$). Officers who were alienated due to the belief that the distributive process was unsystematic and rigged were more likely to have attitudes and behavior that supported corruption. The arbitrary nature of organizational justice, as evidenced by the litigations of inequity of promotions against the TTPS, resulted in police officers' frustrations. Such inequities have been shown in past empirical research to influence alienation or estrangement of police officers (Shernock, 1990; Sunahara, 2004).

Theoretical Model

The assumptions of the theoretical model were that both factors of organizational justice influence the corruption scores of police officers. Additionally, it was assumed that alienation mediates the relationship between organizational justice and corruption scores. This model was examined via path analysis, which significantly predicted 24.6% of the variance in police corruption. The results also indicated that both distributive and procedural justice, along with alienation, significantly determined police corruption. Finally, alienation significantly mediated the relationship between organizational justice and corruption. Thus, police officers who were estranged from their job due to perceived injustices of work-related rewards and the process of distribution of rewards had lower integrity scores and higher values supporting corruption.

CONCLUSION

Corruption presents a problem plaguing police officers in the TTPS. This study was aimed at measuring the effects of organizational justice and police officer alienation on corruption/integrity. The results demonstrated that police officers who believed that they were denied just rewards and deemed the distributive process as unfair had lower integrity scores. Additionally, police officers who were estranged from their work organization held attitudes skewed towards corruption. Furthermore, police officers who were alienated from their job due to distributive and procedural injustice had lower integrity scores. As shown, alienation was a significant mediator variable in clarifying the relationship between organizational justice and police corruption. This research not only added to the local understanding of police integrity and corruption, but also examined the assumption that alienated police officers are ripe for corruption. Officers who find themselves disconnected from their jobs are more predisposed to using their jobs for personal advantage. Deviant and corrupt behavior becomes more acceptable to police officers who are more and more separated from their job due to unjust rewards and unsystematic processes in allocating rewards. Therefore, management should attempt to reduce alienation among police officers by promoting a fair social exchange process in a bid to reduce corruption and increase integrity.

REFERENCES

Aquino, K., Lewis, M.U., & Bradfield, M. (1999). Justice constructs, negative affectivity, and employee deviance: A proposed model and empirical test. Journal of Organizational Behavior, 20(7), 1073-1091.

Babbie, E. (2013). Practices of social research. Belmont, CA: Wadsworth Thomson Learning.

Banerjee, A. (1996). Can anything be done about corruption? In M. G. Quibria & J. Malcolm Dowling (Eds.), Current issues in economic development: An Asian perspective (pp. 107-131). Hong Kong, China: Oxford University Press for the Asian Development Bank.

Barker, T. (1977). Peer group support for police occupational deviance. Criminology, 15(3), 353-366.

Bayley, D. H., & Robert P. (2011). Police corruption: What past scandals teach about current challenges. Washington, DC: U.S. Institute of Peace.

Clay-Warner, J., Reynolds, J., & Roman, P. (2005). Organizational justice and job satisfaction: A test of three competing models. Social Justice Research, 18(4), 391-409.

Cohen-Charash, Y., & Spector, P. E. (2001), The role of justice in organizations: A meta-analysis. Organizational Behavior and Human Decision Processes, 86(2), 278-321.

Colton, M. (2002). Special Issue Editorial. *British Journal of Social Work,* 32(6), 659–667.

Engel, R. J., & Schutt, R. K. (2010). *The fundamentals of social work research.* Thousand Oaks, CA: SAGE Publications.

Ezeanya, C. (2012, September 12). Colonialism, corruption and the future. *Pambuzuka News.* Retrieved from https://www.pambazuka.org/global-south/colonialism-corruption-and-future.

Field, A. (2009). *Discovering statistics using SPSS: (And sex, drugs and rock'n'roll).* London, England: SAGE Publications.

George, D., & Mallery, P. (2003). *SPSS for windows step by step: A simple guide and reference. 11.0 Update.* Boston, MA: Allyn & Bacon.

Glazer, S. (1995). *Police corruption: Can brutality and misconduct be rooted out?* Washington, D.C: Congressional Quarterly Inc.

Gomes, C. (2007). "Police accountability In The Caribbean: Where are the people." *Proceedings From Workshop On Police Accountability At The Civicus World Assembly. Glasgow.* Retrieved from https://www.humanrightsinitiative.org/programs/aj/police/intl/docs/police_accountability_paper_gomes.pdf.

Greenberg, J. (1993). The social side of fairness: Interpersonal classes of organizational justice. In R. Cropanzano (Ed), *Justice in the workplace: Approaching fairness in human resource management* (pp .79-103). Hillsdale, NJ: Erlbaum.Greene, J. (2007). *The encyclopedia of police science.* New York, NY/London, England: Routledge.

Griffith, I. L. (2015). *The quest for security in the Caribbean: Problems and promises in subordinates state.* Oxon: Routledge Press.

Griffith, I.L. (1995). Drugs in the Caribbean: An economic balance sheet. *Caribbean Studies,* 28(2), 285-303.

Hirschfeld, R. R and Feild, H. S. (2000). "Work centrality and work alienation: Distinct aspects of a general commitment to work." *Journal of Organizational Behavior,* 21(7), 789-800.

Hutcheson, G., & Sofroniou, N. (1999). *The multivariate social scientist: Introductory statistics using generalized linear models.* Thousand Oaks, CA: SAGE Publications.

Ivkovic, S. K. (2003). "To serve And collect: Measuring police corruption." *Journal of Criminal Law and Criminology, 93*(2-3), 593-649.

Johnson, F. (1973). *Alienation: concept, term, and meanings.* New York, NY: Seminar Press.

Kleinig, J. (1996). *The ethics of policing.* Cambridge, England: Cambridge University Press.

Kirton, R., Anatol M., & Braithwaite, N. (2010). *The political culture of democracy Trinidad and Tobago 2010: Democracy in action.* St Augustine, Trinidad: The University of the West Indies.

Klockars, C. B., Ivkovic, S. K., & Haberfeld, M. R. (2000). *Measurement of police integrity* Retrieved from https://www.ncjrs.gov/pdffiles1/nij/181465.pdf

Klockars, C. B., Ivkovic, S. K., & Haberfeld, M. R. (2004). *Contours of police integrity.* Thousand Oaks, CA: SAGE Publications.

Krejcie, R. V., & Morgan, D. W. (1970.) Determining sample size for research activities. *Educational and Psychological Measurement, 30,* 607-610.

Lambert, E. G., Cluse-Tolar, T., & Hogan, N. L. (2007). This job is killing me: The impact of job characteristics of correctional staff job stress. *Applied Psychology in Criminal Justice, 3*(2), 117-142.

LaVende, J. (2015, October 01). Back pay for 32 bypassed cops. *Trinidad and Tobago Guardian Newspapers.* Retrieved from http://www.guardian.co.tt/news/2015-10-01/back-pay-32-bypassed-cops

Longres, J., & Scalon, E. (2001). Social justice and the research curriculum. *Journal of Social Work Education, 37*(3), 447-463.

Loree, D. (2006). Corruption in policing: Causes and consequences —A review of the literature. Retrieved from http://dspace.africaportal.org/jspui/bitstream/123456789/22286/1/Corruption%20in%20Policing%20Causes%20and%20Consequences%20A%20Review%20of%20the%20Literature.pdf?1.

Løvseth, T. (2001). *Corruption and alienation.* Retrieved from https://ecpr.eu/Filestore/PaperProposal/777893a9-cf86-44d0-9ca2-99f1c04c7344.pdf

Maddi, S. R., Kobasa, S. C., & Hoover, M. (1979). An alienation test. *Journal of Humanistic Psychology, 19*(4), 73-76.

Mars, J. (2002). *Deadly force, colonialism, and the rule of law—Police violence in Guyana.* Westport, CT: Greenwood Press.

Mauro, P. (1997). *Why worry about corruption?* Washington, DC: International Monetary Fund.

Nair, N., & Vohra, N. (2009). Developing a new measure of work alienation. *Journal of Workplace Rights, 14*(3), 293-309.

Nazario, O. (2007). A strategy against corruption. CARICOM Conference On the Caribbean: A 20/20 Vision. Retrieved from https://www. cpahq.org/CPAHQ/CMDownload.aspx?ContentKey=efd36893-8265-4a69-9370-350130278795&ContentItemKey=08be8177-d8d4-454c-a4db-916395dc3078.

Newburn, T. (2015). Literature review: Police integrity and corruption: Inspecting police in the public interest. Retrieved from https://www.justiceinspectorates.gov.uk/hmicfrs/wp-content/uploads/pic-literature-review.pdf

Niehoff, B. P., & Moorman, R. H. (1993). Justice as a mediator of the relationship between methods of monitoring and organizational citizenship behavior. *Academy of Management Journal, 36*(3), 527-556.

Palmier, L. (1985). *The control of bureaucratic corruption: Case studies in Asia.* New Delhi, India: Allied Publishers.

Pfaff, D. J. (2010). *Investigating the Determinants of Police Corruption in Three Caribbean Nations.* PhD dissertation, American University.

Police Complaint Authority. (2017). *Police Complaint Authority 2016/2017 annual report.* Retrieved from http://www.pca.org.tt/wp-content/uploads/2018/05/PCA-2016-Annual-Report.pdf

Police Manpower Audit Committee. (2017). *Final report of the police manpower audit committee—Now is the time, no sacred cows.* Retrieved from http://parlcloud.ttparliament.org:8081/PapersLaidViewer/TempFiles/Final%20Report%20of%20the%20Police%20Manpower%20Audit%20Committee.pdf

Prasanna, S. B. M. (2013). The role of police in the protection of human rights: A review. *Indian Social Science Journal, 2*(2), PAGES. https://www.questia.com/library/journal/1P3-3358585851/role-of-police-in-protection-of-human-rights-a-review

Prenzler, T. (2009). *Police corruption: Preventing corruption and maintaining integrity.* Boca Raton, LA/London, England/New York, NY: CRC Press.

Price, J., & Mueller, C. (1986). *Handbook of organizational measurement.* Marshfield, MA: Pittman.

Quinton, P., Bradford A., Fildes, B., Fildes, A., & Porte, G. (2012). *Fair cop 2: Organisational justice, behaviour and ethical policing.* Retrieved from https://whatworks.college.police.uk/Research/Documents/150317_Fair_cop%202_FINAL_REPORT.pdf

Ryan, S., Rampersad, I., Bernard, L., Mohammed, P., & Thorpe, M. (2013). *No time to quit: Engaging youths at risk. Executive report of the committee on young males and crime in Trinidad and Tobago.* Retrieved from http://www.ttparliament.org/documents/2197.pdf

Scotland Yard Drug Report. (1986). *Trinidad and Tobago.* London: Metropolitan Police Office.

Seaby, G. (1993). *Final report for the government of Trinidad and Tobago on investigations carried out by the officers from the New Scotland Yard in respect of allegations made by Rodwell Murray and others about corruption in the Trinidad and Tobago Police Service.* Great Britain: Metropolitan Police Service.

Seeman, M. (1959). On the meaning of alienation. *American Sociological Review, 24*(6), 783-791.

Shernock, S. K. (1990). The effects of patrol officers' defensiveness towards the outside world on their ethical orientation. *Criminal Justice Ethics, 9*(2), 24-42.

Sookoo, N. (2014). Perception of injustice and alienation: Dynamics within the workplace. *Journal of Behavioural Sciences, 3*(1), 81-99.

Sunahara, D. F. (2002). *A social-psychological model of unethical and unprofessional police behaviour. police ethics and performance.* http://

cacole.ca/Resource%20Library/Conferences/2004%20Conference/
2004%20Conference%20Presentations/Sunahara,%20D.%202004.
pdf.

Sunahara, D. F. (2004). *Searching for causes: entitlement and alienation as precursors of unethical police behaviour.* Ottawa, Canada: Canadian Police College.

Thibaut, J., & Walker, L. (1975). *Procedural justice: A psychological analysis.* New York, NY: Erlbaum.

Trinidad and Tobago Newsday. (2016, February 1). 35 constables sue over promotion. Retrieved from http://www.newsday.co.tt/news/0,223431.html

Trotman, D. (1986). *Crime in Trinidad: Conflict and control in a plantation society, 1838–1900.* Knoxville, TN: University of Tennessee Press.

Williams, H. (2002). Core factors of police corruption around the world. *Forum on Crime and Society, 2*(1), 85-99.

White, M. D. (2007). *Current issues and controversies in policing.* New York, NY: Pearson-Allyn and Bacon.

Wolfe, S. E., & Piquero, A. R. (2011). Organizational justice and police misconduct. *Criminal Justice and Behavior, 38*(4), 332-353

CHAPTER III

GANGS, STRUCTURAL DISADVANTAGE, AND HOMICIDE IN A CARIBBEAN NATION

Charles M. Katz[1], Andrew M. Fox[2] and Lexi Gill[3]

[1]*Arizona State University, Phoenix, AZ, USA*
[2]*Department of Children, Youth, and Families, State of Washington, Olympia, WA, USA*
[3]*University of Missouri-Kansas City, Kansas City, MO, USA*

ABSTRACT

The relationship between community, gangs, and homicides has been well established in the United States. We are still learning how these factors are related in other countries, specifically in Caribbean nations. The current study combines three sources of data (gang expert survey, census data, and official homicide data) to better understand how gangs and community social structure are related to homicide in Trinidad and Tobago. Overall, the findings indicated that after controlling for community social structure, communities with higher numbers of gangs and gang members experienced significantly higher rates of homicide. Implications and direction for future research are discussed.

Keywords: Gangs, structural disadvantage, homicide, Caribbean, Trinidad and Tobago

INTRODUCTION

Homicide rates in the Caribbean are among the highest in the world. Countries in the Caribbean with the highest homicide rates include Jamaica, Saint Kitts and Nevis, and Trinidad and Tobago (UNODC, 2015). High homicide rates within these countries negatively affect their resident's human growth and development, quality of life, mortality rates, decreases their mobility, and results in psychological harm and family disruption (UNODC, 2007). Additionally, violence can impact local economies in numerous ways, such as increased costs for health and security services; inhibits the success of businesses; reduces property values; undermines governments; and disrupts human services (Krug, Mercy, Dahlberg, & Zwi, 2002; UNODC, 2007).

Gangs are believed to be one of the primary contributors to the region's high homicide rates. For example, in Trinidad and Tobago, gang members are involved in 35%–60% of its homicides (Hill, 2012; Katz, Maguire, & Choate, 2011). About three-quarters (74%) of homicides in St. Kitts and Nevis and almost half (52%) of homicides in Jamaica are recorded as gang-related (Hill, 2012). Some researchers have attributed the disproportionate involvement of gang members in homicide to their heavy reliance on firearms and disproportionate involvement in violence, especially when compared with gang members in the United States (Katz et al., 2011).

While a small body of literature has provided evidence that Caribbean gang members self-report more delinquency (Katz & Fox, 2010) and are arrested more often than nongang members (Katz et al., 2011), there is no research that has examined whether increased numbers of gangs and gang members are related to increased aggregate levels of crime and violence. Nevertheless, policymakers, researchers, and practitioners have assumed that because gang members exhibit higher individual levels of crime and violence, that the communities where gangs and gang members are present will also exhibit higher levels of crime and violence.

The purpose of the present study is to address this gap in the literature and examine whether the prevalence of gangs and gang members at the community level is related to community levels of homicide in the Republic of Trinidad and Tobago. We do this by drawing on theoretical measures and statistical controls evident in the larger body of literature on community correlates of homicide, and simultaneously examine how varying levels of gangs and gang members are related to homicide. More simply stated, the number of gangs and gang members in a community serves as our intervening variable, which should remain significantly related to homicide after accounting for community structural factors. In the next section, we briefly review the prior literature. Next, we describe our methods, data, and measures, and present our findings and their implications.

LITERATURE REVIEW IN BRIEF

The staggering homicide rates in the Caribbean have sparked interest in determining its causes and correlates for the purpose of better understanding the phenomenon and to inform responses to it. Previous research examining the predictors of homicide in the Caribbean, including the role of gangs, is significantly underdeveloped, especially considering the magnitude of its homicide problem. Below we briefly review the body of literature on gang presence, concentrated disadvantage, and community levels of violence; and then discuss related research in the Caribbean to provide context to the present study.

It is well established that structural covariates are related to homicides in a community, however, we are still learning about the role gangs play in this process at the macro-level. Research has shown that gang members are more likely to engage in crime and violence at the individual level, but the relationship becomes more complex at higher levels of aggregation as we have to control for the social and structural factors related to violence at the macro-level. One of the first macro-level studies to examine this issue was Pyrooz (2011) in his study of the structural covariates of gang homicide in 88 large cities in the United States. He used survey data from the police to obtain data on the number of gang members and gang homicides and census data to provide data on community size and the social structural characteristics of each city.

While Pyrooz (2011) reported that U.S. cities with more gang members have more gang homicides, the number of gang members in a community was unrelated to the total number of homicides in a community. He further reported that social–economic deprivation and population density were significantly related to both gang and nongang homicide, nongang homicides were more strongly related to social–economic deprivation and gang homicides were more strongly related to population density. These findings suggest that gangs are an important factor for understanding the variation in homicides in a community, and that social structural factors are related to both gang and nongang homicides, albeit the relatively influence of social structural factors varies by type of homicide (Pyrooz, Fox, Katz, & Decker, 2012).

Tita and Ridgeway (2007) reported that gang presence was related to trends in some forms of community levels of violence in neighborhoods across Pittsburgh. The authors examined emergency calls for service to measure crime, maps of gang territories to measure gang presence, and U.S. Census data to measure the social structure of neighborhoods. Tita and Ridgeway's (2007) analysis indicated that gang presence facilitated overall levels of drug and shots-fired activity at the neighborhood level. They concluded that the presence of gangs and gang members "clearly serves as a crime attractor or generator" (p. 232). Conversely, Katz and Schnebly (2011) reported that gang presence in a community was unrelated to community levels of violence, net controls. The authors used police intelligence data to map the number of gang members in 93 neighborhoods in Mesa, Arizona. They also used U.S. Census data from 1990 to 2000 to examine neighborhood levels of social and economic change and police incident data to measure neighborhood levels of violent crime. Katz and Schnebly (2011) reported that even after controlling for neighborhood social structural characteristics, neighborhood levels of violence were unrelated to the number of gang members in a community.

Prior macro-level research on social structural factors, gang presence, and community levels of violence in American cities suggests that it is important to model and control for structural correlates in order to isolate the impact that gangs might have on community levels of violence. These findings should not be surprising. Over the past 30 years, researchers have observed that homicide rates at the community level are consistently and highly related to social structural characteristics such as economic deprivation and population structure in the United States, Canada, and across Europe (Cotte Poveda, 2012; Kennedy, Silverman, & Forde, 1991; Land, McCall, & Cohen, 1990; McCall, Land, & Parker, 2010; McCall & Nieuwbeerta, 2007). However, researchers should not assume that community structural correlates related to violence are the same in the Caribbean, and if they are related, researchers should not assume that the magnitude of the relationship is as robust.

A recent study suggests that the Caribbean might be at least somewhat unique with respect to the structural factors associated with neighborhood levels of homicide. In Jamaica, Morris and Maguire (2015) examined the social structural factors associated with homicide to better understand the role of political solidarity in violence. The authors reported that traditional measures of concentrated disadvantage such as population, economic disadvantage, and residential instability were positively associated with homicide. But they also reported that homicide in Jamaica can be understood through the defended neighborhood thesis. In the case of Jamaica, Morris and Maguire (2015) argued that high levels of homicide in some neighborhoods (particularly garrison communities) were a result of high levels of informal social control where increased levels of violence were facilitated by local gang leaders (dons) and elected officials to protect territories in response to external threats. In support of their hypothesis, the authors found that after controlling for community structural factors, higher levels of voter participation, which served as a proxy for the defended neighborhood thesis, were associated with increased community levels of homicide. A limitation to the study was the absence of data on gang presence. Regardless, the author's findings suggest that gangs might have a significant effect on overall levels of homicide in the region.

While we are unaware of other research on community correlates of homicide in the Caribbean, it should be noted that Maguire, Willis, Snipes, and Gantley (2008) examined spatial concentrations of homicide within a few high-crime police station districts in Trinidad and Tobago. They reported that even in the highest crime communities, homicides were clustered within a few hot spots, or micro-places. While the authors did not examine the structural correlates of homicide, qualitative interviews suggested that a commonality among all of the hot spots was the presence of gangs and their use of violence to defend turf and resolve disputes. Wallace (2018) reported similar results in his study of the evolution of street gangs in Laventille, Trinidad. Through the analysis of interview data, he suggested that gangs contribute to violence through the protection and control of turf. Wallace (2018) concluded that since the late 1980s, social structural changes in the nation—tied to the oil and gas industry—led to gang joining in "economically depressed communities"; to control territory for the purpose of increasing profits from drug sales. He stated, "gangs began targeting their communities and surrounding neighborhoods for drive-by shootings, assaults, murders, and other heinous crimes and violence became a way of life as they sought to keep out perceived outsiders from their drug enclaves" (pp. 12–13). It is with these studies in mind that we seek to quantitatively determine whether the presence of gangs and gang members significantly increase community levels of homicide in Trinidad and Tobago.

METHODOLOGY

Setting

The present study reports on findings from the Republic of Trinidad and Tobago. The Republic of Trinidad and Tobago is a twin-island nation located about seven miles off the northeastern coast of Venezuela, between the Caribbean Sea and the North Atlantic Ocean. Trinidad and Tobago obtained independence from Great Britain in 1962; however, it remains a member of the Commonwealth of Nations, and it continues to be highly influenced by British culture and law. Although Trinidad and Tobago was once an agrarian society, over the past 30 years, it has transformed into one of the wealthiest and most industrialized Caribbean countries, largely through petroleum production and the provision of regional finance. During the study period, it possessed one of the highest gross national incomes (per capita) and the second-fastest-growing economy among all Caribbean, Central American, and South American countries (Dubinsky & Derrick, 2007). In 2000, the nation was comprised of about 1.26 million people, of whom 40% are East Indian, 37.5% are African, and 20.5% are Afro-Indian (Mixed).

During the study period, as seen in Table 1, Trinidad and Tobago experienced a 313% increase in homicides, from 151 incidents in 2001 to 473 incidents in 2010. Its homicide rate (36 per 100,000 population) was substantially higher than other nations in the region. For example, it was about two times higher than Guyana (19 per 100,000), about three times higher than St. Lucia (11 per 100,000), about four times higher than Antigua and Barbuda (8 per 100,000), and five times higher than Barbados (7 per 100,000). Most of the increase was attributed to firearms-related violence (Wells, Katz, & Kim, 2010) and gang warfare (Katz & Fox, 2010). The increase in violence led to a significant increase in fear among residents in high-crime neighborhoods. For example, a study of one high-crime community found that "56% of residents [believed that] the risk of being injured or killed because of crime [was] high, and many [felt] unsafe in their own neighborhood" (Johnson, 2006).

Study Design

Three sources of data were used to conduct the analysis for the present study. First, data from the 2006 Trinidad and Tobago Gang Expert Survey provide measures of the number of gangs and gang members by community. Second, the 2000 Trinidad and Tobago population and housing census provide measures of population, ethnicity, education, employment, income, and mobility. These data were obtained directly from the Trinidad and Tobago Central Statistics Office along with GIS base maps to geo-code the data by community. Third, 2006 homicide data obtained from the Trinidad and Tobago Police Services (TTPS) provide a measure of the number of homicides by community. The three data sources provide a unique opportunity to understand the relationship between community structure, gang presence, and homicide in a Caribbean nation. We discuss each of these three data sources in detail below.

Table 1: Number of Homicides Per Year in Trinidad and Tobago

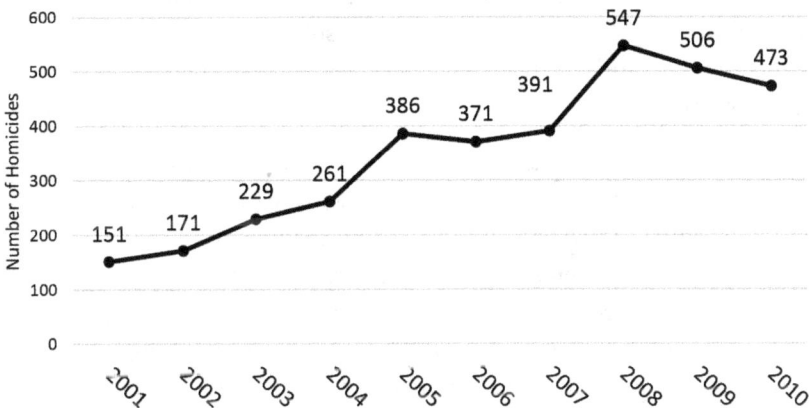

Source: Fieldwork (2006).

Trinidad and Tobago Police Gang Expert Survey

The Trinidad and Tobago Police Gang Expert Survey was modeled after the Eurogang Expert Survey. The Eurogang Expert Survey was created by a group of prominent European and American scholars, later known as the Eurogang Working Group, which has met annually since the late 1990s (Decker & Weerman, 2005, p. viii). The instrument was created to collect data on the scope and nature of gang problems from individuals who have a strong understanding of gangs and gang problems such as police officers, street workers, and teachers (Van Gemert, 2005). The instrument was specifically developed with the goal that it be used to "build a foundation of international comparative research" (Van Gemert, 2005, p. 148).

A copy of the preliminary instrument was provided to a group of executives and line level officers within the TTPS for their review. Their input and suggestions lead to the text of the survey instrument being altered to reflect local culture and language. Additionally, changes were made so that it captured unique issues related to Trinidad and Tobago gangs. The instrument was then pre-tested in three station districts; after which slight modifications were made to increase the readability of the survey instrument.

The instrument collects information related to the scope and nature of the gang problem in their station district (analogous to a relatively small police precinct in the United States) based on a formal definition of a street gang so that police experts could distinguish between youth groups and gangs. The definition of a gang used for the present study was that created by the Eurogang Working Group, and was subsequently adopted for use by the Trinidad and Tobago Police Services' Repeat Offender Program/ Gang Unit which is:

> A street gang is any durable street-oriented youth group whose involvement in illegal activity is part of their group identity. "Durability" means several months or more and refers to the group, which continues despite turnover of participants. "Street-oriented" means spending a lot of group time outside home, work and school—often on streets, in shopping areas, in parks, in cars, and so on. "Youth" refers to average ages in the teens or early twenties or so. "Illegal activity" generally means delinquent or criminal behavior, not just bothersome activity. "Identity" refers to the group, not individual self-image (Van Gemert, 2005, p. 148).

The survey instrument was designed by the Eurogang Working Group to estimate the number of street gangs and gang members' in specific geographic areas and to gather data on their general characteristics and behavior. For example, the instrument included questions related to the age, ethnicity, and gender composition of each gang in a specific area, and included questions related to each street gang's size, organizational structure, and involvement in delinquency and criminality. For organizational purposes, TTPS is divided into 9 divisions and 66 police station districts. Each police station district represents a community. Within each station district, police officers are assigned a position within Uniform Services or to the Criminal Investigation Division (CID). Uniform officers are primarily responsible for taking crime reports and conducting random preventative patrol within the boundaries of the station district. CID officers are responsible for gathering intelligence and investigating all criminal activity within the station district. CID officers are typically more experienced and are expected to have stronger relationships with those their district including citizens, informants, known criminals, and key community stakeholders. CID officers frequently provide intelligence to other specialized units within the TTPS. For this reason, CID officers from each station district were selected to complete the Trinidad and Tobago Expert Survey.

A list of all 66 police station districts was provided to the researchers to facilitate and track the completion of each survey instrument. In January 2006, survey instruments were sent through inter-departmental mail to each district commander who was asked to forward a copy of the instrument to the most senior CID officer in each district, or the officer who they believed had the most knowledge about gangs and gang problems in their district. Five rounds of data collection in May 2006 yielded 66 returned instruments. This strategy resulted in a response rate of 100% (n=66). These data were then geocoded by station district boundaries. A total of 93 gangs and 1,310 gang members were identified through the survey.

Census Data

Trinidad and Tobago conducts a population and housing census every 10 years, and has done so since 1851. Similar to other countries, the census collects information through personal interviews from every person in the nation. Through the census, data is collected on a variety of issues related to population size and characteristics, as well as the spatial distribution of the population (see www.cso.gov.tt, 2011). While described in the Measures section, in the present study, we use data related to population size, age, gender, education, employment, household composition, ethnicity, income, and mobility. The data were collected in 2000 at the address level and GIS layer maps obtained from the Trinidad and Tobago Central Statistics Office were used to aggregate data at the station district level.

Homicide Data

Police homicide data from the year 2006 were used to construct the study's measure of community-level homicide. These homicide data were provided by the crime analysis unit within the TTPS in electronic form. All duplicate records were eliminated from the dataset. These homicide data were aggregated at the station district level. The final dataset included 371 homicides in the Republic of Trinidad and Tobago in 2006. Prior research examining police homicide data in Trinidad and Tobago has shown these data to be valid and reliable (Seepersad, 2016).

Measures

The dependent variable for the present study is the number of homicides in each police district. As discussed above, the homicide data were obtained from the crime analysis unit of the TTPS. The variable represents the homicide rate for each community in Trinidad and Tobago. Our measure of the number of gangs and gang members in each community was obtained through the gang expert survey. These two measures represent the number of gangs and gang members known by the police at the level of the station district. Our measures of community structure were obtained from the 2000 Trinidad and Tobago Census. The measures used in our analysis include: percent residents aged 12–24, percent of residents foreign born, percent of residents without a secondary education, percent of residents unemployed, percent of female-headed households with kids, median household income, percent of residents who have a 5-year address, and percent African. These measures are consistent with those used in prior research examining the relationship between neighborhood structure and gangs (Katz & Scnebly, 2011) and are grounded in theoretical models of social disorganization and concentrated disadvantage in the United States (Shaw & McKay, 1942; Wilson, 1987).[1]

We used principal components analysis (PCA) to reduce the number of covariates included in our models, instead of using the individual measures, for two reasons. The first reason was to reduce the total number of covariates included in our regression analyses. The sample size used in the present study is relatively small and the inclusion of too many variables can result in low statistical power. The second reason was that variance inflation factor scores and condition indices indicated multicollinearity between many of our measures. Therefore, we addressed these issues us-

---

1　We are unaware of prior research examining the dimensionality of structural covariates (e.g., social, economic, and physical factors) within the context of the Caribbean. We recommend that future researchers examine the theoretical and quantitative dimensionality of structural covariates in the region.

ing PCA (Land et al., 1990), which resulted in two components based on our eight measures of community structure. The component loadings are shown in Table 2. We designated one component *cultural/traditional disadvantage*, which displayed high loadings for percent male residents aged 12–24, foreign-born residents, percentage of residents without a secondary education, median household income, and percentage of residence who lived at the same address for 5 years or longer. We designated the second component *social/family disadvantage*, which displayed high loadings for percentage of residents unemployed, percentage female-headed households with children, and percent Afro-Caribbean. The correlation between the two components was low (r=0.135). In addition to our two measures of disadvantage, we include a measure of population density. Population density was measured as the population per square kilometer.

Table 2: Component Loadings

	Component 1	Component 2
	Cultural/ traditional disadvantage	Social/familial disadvantage
% male residents aged 12–24	0.702	—
% of residents foreign born	−0.749	0.311
% of residents without a secondary education	0.899	−0.006
% of residents unemployed	0.230	0.731
% female-headed households with kids	−0.504	0.686
Median household income	−0.752	−0.269
% of residents who have a 5-year address	0.825	−0.108
% African	−0.065	0.853

Note: Principal components analysis with varimax rotation

Source: Fieldwork (2006).

Analytic Strategy

First, as noted above, PCA with varimax rotation was used to address multicollinearity and identify community-level structural factors. Second, these components were then included in negative binomial regression models predicting homicide counts (using population as an exposure variable). Negative binomial regression was selected because the outcome variable is a count of the number of homicides. A control for population density was included across models. Given the strong correlation between the number of gangs and gang members in a community, both variables could not be included in the same models. As such, one set of models included the number of gang members and one set of models included the number of gangs. Third, final model estimates were used to predict the expected number of homicides, given the number of gang and gang members in a police district, after controlling for community-level correlates. We tested the model residuals for spatial clustering using the Moran test. To test the error structure, a contiguity weights matrix was created to identify police districts that shared a border. The Moran test of the residuals indicated non-significant results for both the intercept only and the full regression models. With residuals that were i.i.d., we did not include a spatial autoregressive term (Kelejian & Prucha, 2001; Moran, 1950; StataCorp, 2017).

Results

Descriptive information on each of the variables can be found in Table 3. The dependent variable is the number of homicides in each police district. The average district had 5.18 homicides, ranging from 0 to 67. The two components, social/familial disadvantage and cultural/traditional disadvantage were both normally distributed variables with a mean of zero and standard deviation of one. The average number of gangs per district was 1.36 and ranged from 0 to 19. The average number of gang members was 20.02 and ranged from 0 to 385. The descriptive information about the variables that were included in the components are also provided in Table 3.

Tables 4 and 5 show the negative binomial models predicting homicides at the police district level. Table 4 has three models. The first model indicates that social/familial disadvantage is significantly and positively associated with homicides. A one-unit increase in social/familial disadvantage

Table 3: Descriptive Statistics (n=61)

	Mean	SD	Min	Max
Dependent variable				
# of reported homicides	5.18	11.04	0.00	67.00
Independent variables				
Social/familial disadvantage	0.00	1.00	−1.73	3.87
Cultural/traditional disadvantage	0.00	1.00	2.56	2.53
Number of gangs	1.36	3.00	0.00	19.00
Number of gang members	20.02	56.73	0.00	385.00
Variables included in components				
% male residents aged 12–24	13.28	1.19	8.70	15.80
% of residents foreign born	3.66	2.74	0.50	14.40
% of residents without a secondary education	49.75	9.18	2,739	74.9
% of residents unemployed	6.07	2.08	1.97	13.13
% female-headed households with kids	19.83	4.94	5.30	32.30
Median household income	1,976.97	470.36	1,000.00	3,400.00
% of residents who have a 5-year address	16.92	4.36	8.42	26.37
% African	36.84	19.97	3.20	80.50

Source: Fieldwork (2006).

(or a one standard deviation increase since the variable is standardized) results in an increase in the homicide rate by a factor of 1.68. Model 2 includes the number of gang members in each police district. With the inclusion of gang members, the magnitude of social/familial disadvantage is reduced. The addition of one gang member in a community results in an increase in the homicide rate by a factor of 1.005. The final model adds squared terms of the two disadvantage components. Interestingly, the final model shows that social/familial disadvantage becomes marginally significant, but cultural/traditional disadvantage becomes significant along with the squared term. Analysis showed that both are negatively associated with homicides. This indicates that there is an overall negative relationship between cultural/traditional disadvantage and homicide; and that the relationship is even stronger where cultural/traditional disadvantage is the most pronounced. Put another way, there are fewer homicides in those Trinidad and Tobago communities that experience the most extreme levels of cultural/traditional disadvantage. The effect from gang members remains, with each additional gang member in a police district, there is an increase in homicides by a rate of 1.004. The pseudo-r^2 for the final model in Table 4 is 0.121.

Table 4: Results from Negative Binomial Regression Models Predicting Homicide Counts, Controlling for Gang Members

Independent variables	Model 1			Model 2			Model 3		
	Coeff.	Rob.SE	IRR	Coeff.	Rob.SE	IRR	Coeff.	Rob.SE	IRR
Cultural/ traditional disadvantage	−0.174	(0.331)	0.838	−0.219	(0.189)	0.803	−0.559	(0.211)	0.572*
Squared							−0.345	(0.144)	0.708*
Social/familial disadvantage	0.522	(0.201)	1.686*	0.427	(0.148)	1.532*	0.263	(0.161)	1.301ᵃ
Squared							0.151	(0.093)	1.162
Population density * 10⁴	0.017	(0.832)	1.000	0.807	(0.796)	1.000	1.066	(0.751)	0.999
Number of gang Members				0.005	(0.001)	1.005*	0.004	(0.002)	1.004*
Log likelihood	−131.38			−128.68			−125.12		
Wald chi-square (df)	27.85* (3)			81.06* (4)			54.53* (6)		
Pseudo R-square	0.077			0.096			0.121		
n	60			60			60		

*p<0.05; ᵃ p<0.10

Note: Police district population is used as the exposure variable in all models.

Source: Fieldwork (2006).

Table 5 replicates the same models as presented in Table 4, but includes the number of gangs, not gang members, in a police district. The findings are substantively identical except for the marginal significance of the squared social/familial disadvantage. This indicates that there were a greater number of homicides in communities with higher levels social/familial disadvantage. Also in the final model, each additional gang in the community was associated with an increase in the homicide rate by a factor of 1.091. The models with gangs (instead of gang members) are slightly better models as is evidence by the lower log likelihood and slightly higher pseudo-r^2.

Table 5: Results from Negative Binomial Regression Models Predicting Homicide Counts, Controlling for Gangs

Independent variables	Model 1			Model 2			Model 3		
	Coeff.	Rob.SE	IRR	Coeff.	Rob.SE	IRR	Coeff.	Rob.SE	IRR
Cultural/ traditional	−0.174	(0.331)	0.838	0.204	(0.185)	0.815	−0.539	(0.214)	0.583*
Squared							−0.326	(0.138)	0.515*
Social/familial disadvantage	0.522	(0.201)	1.686*	0.424	(0.141)	1.528*	0.262	(0.157)	1.299[a]
Squared							0.157	(0.093)	1.169[a]
Population density * 10^4	0.017	(0.832)	1.000	0.979	(0.820)	0.999	1.210	(0.769)	0.999
Number of gangs				0.106	(0.174)	1.112*	0.087	(0.036)	1.091*
Log likelihood		−131.38			−128.09			−124.682	
Wald chi-square (df)		27.85* (3)			49.34* (4)			59.23* (6)	
Pseudo R-square		0.077			0.100			0.124	
n		60			60			60	

*p<0.05; [a] p<0.10

Note: Police district population is used as the exposure variable in all models.

Source: Fieldwork (2006).

The final step in the analysis was to illustrate the relationship between the number of gang members and gangs in a community and the number of homicides in the community. The predictions are based on the final models from Tables 4 and 5. Table 6 shows how incremental increases in both gang members and gangs correspond with increases in homicides. Specifically, one additional gang member in a police district results in an increase in homicides by 0.4%, extrapolated further, 50 additional gang members would result in 22.1% increase in homicides, and 200 additional gang members in a police district would result in a 122.22% increase in homicides. In terms of gangs, one additional gang in a police district would result in a 9.1% increase in homicides, and 10 additional gangs would result in a 138.9% increase in homicides.

Table 6: Interpreting the Estimated Incidence Rate Ratios:
Based on Final Models

Increase in # of gang members	Percent increase in homicides	Increase in # of gangs	Percent increase in homicides
1	0.4%	1	9.1%
5	2.0%	2	19.0%
10	4.1%	3	29.9%
50	22.1%	4	41.7%
100	49.1%	5	54.6%
150	82.0%	10	138.9%
200	122.2%	20	470.8%
400	393.7%		

Source: Fieldwork (2006).

CONCLUSION

Over the past 20 years, Trinidad and Tobago has experienced a substantial increase in homicides. While there has been a burgeoning body of literature on crime and violence in the nation, as well as the Caribbean, there is still much research to be done to understand the causes and correlates of violence in the nation and region. The current study examined the relationship between gang presence, community social structural factors, and homicide in Trinidad and Tobago. To our knowledge, this is the first study to examine the role of gangs and their relative influence on neighborhood levels of homicide in the Caribbean. We relied on three sources of data: homicide data obtained by the police, census data, and police expert survey data that contained information on the number of gangs and gang members in each community.

Our analyses examined the role of community social structural factors through the inclusion of several structural variables. We were unable to find any prior Trinidadian research that identified the neighborhood social structural factors that might be related to violence so we relied on a statistical approach known as PCA. PCA allowed us to simultaneously reduce multicollinearity between our covariates (Land et al., 1990) and identify the common social structural dimensions across communities. Our analyses identified two types of community-level disadvantage in Trinidad and Tobago. We labeled the first type of disadvantage as cultural/traditional disadvantage. It was related to communities with high rates of young males, low rates of foreign born, low educational attainment, low household income, but high levels of residential stability. We labeled the second type of disadvantage as social/familial disadvantage. It was related to neighborhoods that exhibited high rates of unemployment, female-headed households with children, and high rates of African residents.

We found that neighborhoods with greater levels of social/familial disadvantage exhibited higher rates of homicide, and that neighborhoods with extreme levels of cultural/traditional disadvantage exhibited lower rates of homicide. Our findings related to the relationship between neighborhood disadvantage and homicide are at least somewhat supported in prior research. Researchers have long found that neighborhoods with higher levels of concentrated disadvantage have high levels of violent crime (Sampson, Raudenbush, & Earls, 1997). Therefore, our findings that higher rates of homicide were found in those neighborhoods with higher levels of unemployment, female-headed households with children, and Africans is not surprising. However, our finding that homicide rates were lower in neighborhoods with extremely low levels of cultural/traditional disadvantage (e.g., high levels of poverty, more young males, and fewer foreign-born residents, residents who are less educated and less likely to have moved in the past 5 years) was somewhat surprising.

We are unsure how to fully interpret this finding in the context of Trinidad but Wallace's (2018) qualitative assessment of gang formation in Laventille offers some insight. He noted that gangs in Laventille, which is a community located in the urban hills of the capital of the nation (Port of Spain), started as "loose-knit groups" of migrant youth who came together "for unity, socialization and for the protection/preservation of claimed territories for incoming migrants into these created enclaves where the same culture, customs, and language prevailed" (p. 12). Our findings provide at least some support for his conclusions. We encourage Caribbean scholars to further examine the issue. To be sure, there is little research that has examined the social structure of homicide in the Caribbean in general, and Trinidad and Tobago specifically. Given the high rates of homicide in the Caribbean, and the lack of prior research on the social structural factors related to homicide in the Caribbean, we believe that future research in this area of study would make an important contribution to the body of literature on violence in the Caribbean.

The primary focus of the study was on the relationship between gang presence and homicide in Trinidad and Tobago. Our results indicated that after controlling for community levels of social/familial disadvantage, cultural/traditional disadvantage, and population density, community's with higher numbers of gangs and gang members experienced significantly higher rates of homicide. In particular, we found that for every five gang members in a police district, the number of homicides increased by 2%, and 100 additional gang members in a police district resulted in homicides increasing by 49.1%. Likewise, one additional gang in a police district result in homicides increasing by a 9.1% and five additional gangs result in homicides increasing by 54.6%. While we can only speculate as to why the number of gangs and gang members in a community are positively related homicide, our findings support that of past research (Tita & Ridgeway, 2007; Wallace, 2018) that increased numbers of gangs and gang members in a community result in increased opportunities for status violations, disputes over turf, and competition for illicit income. Gangs and gang members, in other words, might serve to generate and enhance community levels of violence by increasing community opportunities for violence to take place (e.g., drug market activity, location-specific fraud schemes). Future research should further examine these and other possible causal mechanisms.

Addressing the formation of gangs and gang joining in Trinidad and Tobago is vital to the health and wellbeing of the nation and multiple strategies should be applied that strategically and comprehensively address the problem. For example, evidence-based gang prevention programs such as G.R.E.A.T. should be widely adopted by the Ministry of Education to reduce the prevalence of gang joining. With that said, G.R.E.A.T. has not been rigorously evaluated outside the United States and should be concomitantly evaluated within the Caribbean context with its implementation. Systematic reviews should also be undertaken to identify barriers to youth leaving gangs. These can include such obstacles as poor education and economic opportunities, threats of violence from the gang, threats to self-image and identity, and labeling by school, police, and employers (Arciaga Young & Gonzalez, 2013). Policies and programs that remove barriers to gang desistence have the potential to reduce community levels of gang prevalence. Enhancing the effectiveness of formal mechanisms of social control is also vital. Prior research in Trinidad and Tobago found that of the 53 gang homicides in the Besson police station district from January 2005 through January 2006, only 3 (5.6%) resulted in an arrest, and none (0.0%) of the homicides resulted in a conviction (Katz & Maguire, 2015). Without adequate levels apprehension and imprisonment, active violent offenders, as well as others, will not be effectively deterred. A contemporary and comprehensive gang assessment is an important next step by researchers to determine the most appropriate responses to gangs, gang members, and gang violence in the nation (Katz & Nuno, 2015).

It is important that further research be conducted on this issue in the Caribbean and determine whether these results can be replicated. As noted above, Pyrooz et al. (2012) reported that the prevalence of gang members in a community was not significantly related to the total number of homicides after controlling for factors such as socio-economic deprivation, population heterogeneity, residential stability, population density, and youth population. In other words, Pyrooz did not find that the number of gang members played an independent and significant role in the number of homicides in a community. Future research should further examine the unique role of gang presence on homicide in the Caribbean and its relatively powerful contribution to violence when compared with developed nations. Data that allows for comparisons between nations would be especially valuable. Future research should also take the next step of disaggregating homicide by type. Several studies (Kubrin & Weitzer, 2003; Mares, 2010; Papachristos & Kirk, 2006; Pyrooz et al., 2012; Rosenfeld, Bray, & Egley, 1999) have reported that community structural factors underlying gang and nongang homicides differ; although the specific community structural factors believed to be associated with gang homicides is still being debated. This research might further refine our understanding of the role of gangs and gang members on homicide, and the unique social structural conditions that might be associated with gang-related homicides.

ACKNOWLEDGMENTS

Funding for this research was provided by the Ministry of National Security of Trinidad and Tobago. The points of view expressed in this paper are those of the authors alone and do not represent the official policies or positions of the Ministry of National Security, Trinidad and Tobago Police Service, or Arizona State University. This research was approved by the Institutional Review Board at Arizona State University.

REFERENCES

Arciaga Young, M., & Gonzalez, V. (2013). *Getting out of gangs, staying out of gangs: Gang intervention and desistence strategies.* US: National Gang Center.

Colin, D., Dubinsky, W., & Derrick, C. (2007). *Latin America and the Caribbean selected economic and social data.* Washington, DC: United States Agency for International Development.

Cotte Poveda, A. (2012). Violence and economic development in Colombian cities: A dynamic panel data analysis. *Journal of International Development, 24*(7), 809–827.

Decker, S. H., & Weerman, F. M. (Eds.). (2005). *European street gangs and troublesome youth groups* (Vol. 3). Lanham, MD: Rowman Altamira.

Dubinsky, C., & Derrick, C. (2007). *Latin America and the Caribbean: Selected economic and social data.* Washington, DC: United States Agency for International Development.

Hill, S. (2012). Gang homicide in the Caribbean. Symposium on gangs and gang violence in the Caribbean. American University, Washington, DC. February 17, 2012. https://cvpcs.asu.edu/sites/default/files/content/events/Hill%20presentation.pdf

Johnson, D. (2006). *Results from the gonzales IMPACT study.* Manassas: George Mason University.

Katz, C. M., & Fox, A. (2010). Risk and protective factors associated with gang involved youth in a Caribbean Nation: Analysis of the Trinidad and Tobago Youth Survey. *Pan-American Journal of Public Health/Revista Panamericana de Salud Pública, 27*(3), 187–202.

Katz, C. M., & Maguire, E. (2005). *Improving homicide detection rates in Trinidad and Tobago*. Phoenix, Arizona: Arizona State University.

Katz, C. M. & Maguire, E. (2006). *Reducing gang homicides in the Besson Street Station District*. Phoenix, Arizona: Arizona State University.

Katz, C. M., Maguire, E. R., & Choate, D. (2011). A cross-national comparison of gangs in the United States and Trinidad and Tobago. *International Criminal Justice Review, 21*(3), 243–262.

Katz, C. M., & Maguire, E. R. (2015). Diagnosing gang violence in the Caribbean. Gangs in the Caribbean: Responses of state and society, 118-175.

Katz, C. M., & Nuno, L. (2015). Diagnosing your community's gang problem: Avoid the kitchen sink approach. National Gang Center Fall 2015 Newsletter. Retrieved from https://www.nationalgangcenter.gov/Content/Newsletters/NGC-Newsletter-2015-Fall.pdf

Katz, C. M., & Schnebly, S. M. (2011). Neighborhood variation in gang member concentrations. *Crime & Delinquency, 57*(3), 377–407.

Kelejian, H. H., & Prucha, I. R. (2001). On the asymptotic distribution of the Moran I test statistic with applications. *Journal of Econometrics, 104*, 219–257.

Kennedy, L. W., Silverman, R. A., & Forde, D. R. (1991). Homicide in urban Canada: Testing the impact of economic inequality and social disorganization. *Canadian Journal of Sociology/Cahiers canadiens de sociologie*, 397–410.

Krug, E. G., Mercy, J. A., Dahlberg, L. L., & Zwi, A. B. (2002). The world report on violence and health. *The Lancet, 360*(9339), 1083–1088.

Kubrin, C., & Weitzer, R. (2003). Retaliatory homicide: Concentrated disadvantage and neighborhood culture. *Social Problems, 50*(2), 157–180.

Land, K., McCall, P., & Cohen, L. (1990). Structural covariates of homicide rates: Are there any invariances across time and social space? *American Journal of Sociology, 95*(4), 922–963.

Maguire, E. R., Willis, J. A., Snipes, J., & Gantley, M. (2008). Spatial concentrations of violence in Trinidad and Tobago. *Caribbean Journal of Criminology and Public Safety, 13*(1–2), 48–92.

Mares, D. (2010). Social disorganization and gang homicides in Chicago: A neighborhood level comparison of disaggregated homicides. *Youth Violence and Juvenile Justice, 8*(1), 38–57.

McCall, P. L., Land, K. C., & Parker, K. F. (2010). An empirical assessment of what we know about structural covariates of homicide rates: A return to a classic 20 years later. *Homicide Studies, 14*(3), 219–243.

McCall, P. L., & Nieuwbeerta, P. (2007). Structural covariates of homicide rates: A European city cross-national comparative analysis. *Homicide Studies, 11*(3), 167–188.

Moran, P. A. P. (1950). Notes on continuous stochastic phenomena. *Biometrika, 37*, 17–23.

Morris, P. K., & Maguire, E. R. (2015). Political culture, neighbourhood structure and homicide in urban Jamaica. *British Journal of Criminology, 56*(5), 919–936.

Papachristos, A. V., & Kirk, D. S. (2006). Neighborhood effects on street gang behavior. *Studying Youth Gangs, 12*, 63–84.

Pyrooz, D. (2011). Structural covariates of gang homicide in large U.S. cities. *Journal of Research in Crime and Delinquency, 49*(4), 489–518.

Pyrooz, D. C., Fox, A. M., Katz, C. M., & Decker, S. H. (2012). Gang organization, offending, and victimization: A cross-national analysis. In Finn Esbensen and Cheryl Maxson (Eds.), *Youth gangs in international perspective* (pp. 85–105). New York: Springer.

Rosenfeld, R., Bray, T. M., & Egley, A. (1999). Facilitating violence: A comparison of gang-motivated, gang-affiliated, and nongang youth homicides. *Journal of Quantitative Criminology, 15*(4), 495-516.

Sampson, R. J., Raudenbush, S. W., & Earls, F. (1997). Neighborhoods and violent crime: A multilevel study of collective efficacy. *Science, 277*(5328), 918–924.

Seepersad, R. (2016). *Crime and violence in Trinidad and Tobago: IDB series on crime and violence in the Caribbean.* Washington, D. C.: Inter-American Development Bank.

Shaw, C. R., & McKay, H. D. (1942). *Juvenile delinquency and urban areas.* Chicago: University of Chicago Press.

StataCorp. (2017). Stata: Release 15. Statistical Software. College Station, TX: StataCorp LLC.

Tita, G., & Ridgeway, G. (2007). The impact of gang formation on local patterns of crime. *Journal of Research in Crime and Delinquency, 44*(2), 208–237.

United Nations Office on Drugs and Crime. (2015). Intentional homicide, counts and rates per 100,000 population. [Data file]. Retrieved from https://data.unodc.org/#state:1.

United Nations Office on Drugs and Crime and the Latin America and the Caribbean Region of the World Bank (2007). Crime, Violence, and Development: Trends, Costs, and Policy Options in the Caribbean. United Nations: Washington, DC. Retrieved from https://www.unodc.org/pdf/research/Cr_and_Vio_Car_E.pdf

Van Gemert, F. (2005). Youth groups and gangs in Amsterdam: A pretest of the Eurogang expert survey. In S. Decker & F. Weerman (Eds.), *European Street Gangs and Troublesome Youth Groups (pp. 147-157).* Lanham, MD: Altamira Press.

Wallace, W. C. (2018). Understanding the evolution of localized community based street gangs in Laventille, Trinidad. *Journal of Gang Research, 26*(1), 1–16.

Wells, W., Katz, C. M. & Kim, J. (2010). Firearm possession among arrestees in Trinidad and Tobago. *Injury Prevention, 16*(5), 337–342.

Whyte, W. F. (1943). Social organization in the slums. *American Sociological Review, 8,* 34–39.

Wilson, W. J. (1987). *The truly disadvantaged: The inner city,* The Underclass, and Public Policy. Chicago: University of Chicago Press.

CHAPTER IV

Jamaica's Transnational Crime Problems of Drug Trafficking and Money Laundering

Suzette A. Haughton and Trevor Smith

The University of the West Indies, Mona, Kingston, Jamaica

Abstract

Drug trafficking and money laundering are two intricately connected transnational organized crimes affecting Jamaica. The main connection between these problems is well established. Drug traffickers smuggle illegal drugs to foreign destinations and receive substantial illicit profits. From the huge illicit funds, drug traffickers launder these monies into legitimate businesses to hide its tainted origins from law enforcers. Given this reality, the chapter argues that crime control remains a major challenge and a fundamental responsibility of the Jamaican state. Utilizing secondary source information and desk-based review of governmental documents and laws, the study explores this problem from a criminology perspective. The chapter is organized as follows: first, transnational organized crime is explored within the context of Jamaica's drug trafficking and money laundering problems. Second, Rational Choice theory is explored for explicating these crimes. Third, existing institutions and legislation for addressing these problems are discussed. Fourth, the study concludes with the rationale and recommendations on the strategic alliances that are required to mitigate these problems.

Keywords: Transnational organized crime, drug trafficking, money laundering, Jamaica

INTRODUCTION

Jamaica has a population of 2.9 million people and is the largest English-speaking and the fourth largest among Caribbean countries (CIA Factbook, 2019). The country is prone to natural disasters and is considered to be an upper-middle-income country that continues to experience low growth and high public debt. Jamaica is also the fourth most murderous country in the world (Jamaica Observer, 2017). The inner cities in Jamaica are among the most violent in the world due to criminals and drug lords who reside within these communities.[1] Poverty in Jamaica remains high and was recorded at 17.1% in 2016. Jamaica's unemployment rate in 2017 was 12.2% with youth unemployment at 28.3% (CIA Factbook, 2019). Poverty along with high unemployment among the youth, particularly within inner city communities, are associated with the high levels of crime and violence in the country (Amnesty International, 2011; UK Home Office, 2015).

Jamaica is geographically located in the Caribbean region and situated on the direct air and sea routes to North and South America (Haughton, 2008; Vasciannie, 1997). Jamaica's location therefore lies in the middle of air and sea routes linking the consumers of drugs in the North to the producers of drugs in the South. Jamaica's geo-strategic position is also suited for geo-narcotics and supports Jamaican criminals in the trafficking of cocaine and marijuana from production and transshipment countries in the region to markets in North America and Europe. Further, Jamaica has established a reputation of marijuana cultivation. This started with the eighteenth-century indentured laborers who brought the plant to the island and used it as a herb (Rubin & Comitas, 1976). As such, marijuana is not considered as a plant new to Jamaica or to the Jamaican transnational criminals. Instructively, in explaining the connection between the drug problem, power, politics, and the strategic geographic location of Caribbean states, Griffith (1994) coined the notion of "geo-narcotics."

Despite the early uses of the drug in Jamaica, the trafficking of marijuana to overseas destination markets by Jamaican criminals began only in the early 1980s (Haughton, 2011). The diversification of marijuana trafficking with the transshipment and trafficking of cocaine is utilized by Jamaican transnational criminals to maximize profits while serving a larger

---

1   https://devtracker.dfid.gov.uk/countries/JM, retrieved April 6, 2019.

drug consumption market in their targeted areas. For this reason, Jamaica attained the U.S. Department of State categorization of being a major marijuana trafficking and cocaine transshipment country. As such, the transnational criminals violate the border security of various territorial jurisdictions to traffic drugs and launder monies into and out of Jamaica.

Drug addiction, illnesses, and hospitalization that result from drug consumption have proven challenging for countries that provide a market for these drugs. It also creates challenges for the transshipment and production countries. For many years, drug trafficking has been a prime source of violence and corruption in Jamaica. In this context, drug dons (drug dons are similar to crime bosses in North America and Europe) exert their economic power, use violence to settle scores among rivals and challenge the Jamaican state to keep pace with criminal activities (Warnecke-Berger, 2018). The intricate connection between drug trafficking and money laundering also create problems for the state's criminal justice apparatus amidst the scarce resources allotted to Jamaica's Ministry of Justice. Drug trafficking proceeds laundered into legitimate businesses are difficult to trace as such laundered monies make it extremely hard for law enforcers to differentiate good money from bad money (Reuter & Truman, 2004).

This perennial problem is exacerbated by huge levels of profits that drive the transnational criminal acts of drug trafficking and money laundering (Van Duyne & Levi, 2005). With this profit motive, Jamaican criminals have smuggled illicit drugs to profitable destination markets in the United States and the UK. Haughton (2016) noted the primacy of foreign markets, such as the United States, for Jamaican traffickers. This was highlighted as destination markets in the United States and Britain provide foreign exchange which yield high rates of return when the dollar is converted. Drug trafficking and money laundering are lucrative for drug traffickers but create problems for the state and law-abiding citizens.

The current study seeks to address the twin evil of drug trafficking and money laundering in Jamaica. Strategies for addressing this problem along with inhibiting factors are also explored. Recommendations are also presented for addressing this situation at the level of policy. The chapter is arranged as follows. First, the criminological theory of Rational Choice is used for explaining the twin problem of drug trafficking and money laundering. Second, transnational organized crimes across Jamaica's borders are explored. Third, the laws to address these problems and the collaborative efforts are discussed. Fourth, the chapter is concluded with recommendations on the strategic alliances that are required to mitigate these problems. Given the complexity of Jamaica's transnational crime situation, the Rational Choice Theory is proffered as the framework for explaining these problems.

Rational Choice Theory

The Rational Choice Theory was developed by the Italian criminologist Cesare Beccaria (Siegel, 2009). There are many studies on criminal decision making (Cornish & Clarke, 1987) and the Rational Choice Theory is one of the popular theories that is utilized in this area (Piquero & Tibbets, 2002). In 1764, Beccaria's work entitled *Crime and Punishments* made the case that criminal reforms should be based on rational principles and noted that criminals willfully and rationally opt to engage in crime (Siegel, 2009). Rational Choice Theory argues that self-interest plays a significant role in decision making. To this end, before an act is committed, an individual calculates the cost and benefits of carrying out this act. Beccaria argues that Rational Choice Theory is premised on four (4) main principles. First, criminal behavior is based on individual choice. Second, individuals decide to engage in criminal behaviors based on the perceived pleasure to be received while at the same time, aiming to reduce pain or displeasure. Third, the fear of punishment is central in controlling criminal choices. Fourth, to curtail criminal behavior, punishment must be severe, certain, and swift.

The Rational Choice Theory contends that since criminals are rational individuals who act based on calculations, then the use of punishment can control or determine their actions. As such, the fear of punishments can deter individuals from engaging in criminal acts, while the deterrent effect would be lost if punishments are not feared. Despite the existence of punishment, Beccaria believed that the egoistic and self-centered nature of individuals will propel them into criminal activities to satisfy their nature. For this reason, he argues that punishment must instill fear in criminals in order for it to obtain compliance with the law.

Beccaria argued that the crime committed and the punishment imposed must be proportional. This is important because in the absence of exercising the principle of proportionality, criminals will be motivated to commit more serious crimes when they expect that they will be given harsher punishments than is deserving of the crime if they are caught. As such, the punishment for offenses, such as drug trafficking, should be less than the punishment for murder. Hence, the punishment must fit the crime. For Beccaria, petty offenses cannot be subjected to the same penalty as serious offenses because if this happens offenders are likely to engage in more serious offenses since the punishment would be the same. Given Beccaria's reasoning, marginal deterrence becomes critical. Marginal deterrence refers to a situation in which the punishment level for criminal acts are ranked based on the types of acts committed.

Modern Rational Choice Theorists argue that offenders who break the law do so after pondering both personal and situational factors (Siegel, 2009). Personal factors are anything which benefits the individual such as money and other tangibles. On the other hand, situation factors are those that are external to the individual and are based on the situational context. These may involve situations such as a vulnerable target or a state of efficiency in law enforcement activities. Criminals are considered to be rational because they reason and evaluate the likelihood of being caught, the severity of the attached punishment, the potential value of the criminal enterprise and the extent of the criminal gain. Based on their calculations, criminals have opted to use the easy route by cutting corners in utilizing illegal means to achieve their desired goals. As such, they will use unlawful means to obtain their desired goals which might have normally been out of their reach.

For Rational Choice Theorists, crime is offense-specific as well as offender-specific. Offense-specific means that criminals will selectively respond to a particular crime. Hence, for traffickers to decide to engage in drug trafficking, the traffickers would assess the potential financial yield, the security devices installed at the ports of entries and exits, effectiveness of maritime patrols availability, and ease of corrupting port workers with bribes, ease of delivering the drugs to targeted destination, the ease of moving large amounts of cash across state borders, and the ease of transferring drug proceeds into lawful businesses.

Offender-specific, on the other hand, means that criminals do not routinely enter into random criminal acts. They assess their own characteristics to determine if they have the skills needed, the attributes and patterns of behavior to execute the chosen criminal activity. These assessments may include their ability to carry out the criminal act successfully, their need for the money to be derived from concluding the act successfully, their possession of the resources required to carry out the criminal act, the options of poly-criminal acts and their health, and physical strength to execute the act along with the fear of the possible punishment if caught. Therefore, the Rational Choice Theory suggests that criminal acts may be minimized if prospective offenders believe that they can reach their desired goals through lawful means and if they are hugely afraid of been caught and punished for conducting crimes.

The Rational Choice Theory supports the view that personal factors are a significant part of the criminal's calculation to commit crimes. Prominent personal factors in this regard include financial prospects, knowledge, and familiarity as well as awareness of criminal techniques. In terms of financial prospects, the existence of multiple economic opportunities may influence one's decision to commit criminal acts. For instance, criminals who are involved in marijuana trafficking may increase their involvement in criminal activities by engaging in poly-drug trafficking, that is, to increase their profitability, they may smuggle cocaine or heroin along with marijuana shipments. The attractiveness of poly-drug trafficking may be sufficient to convince individuals to smuggle drugs due to its combined profitability.

Rational Choice Theory also evaluates the individual's views of normal law-abiding alternatives and compare them with alternatives derived from criminality. In this regard, it purports that prospective criminals may refuse to enter into criminal activities if they anticipate that returns from crime is minimal and that attractive legal alternatives exist. However, if individuals perceive that criminal activities, such as drug trafficking, will yield excessive profits with minimal risk then they will be motivated to undertake such activities. Hence, knowledge of the illegal drug industry and an understanding of the clandestine techniques involved in smuggling drugs without detection are critical to successful engagement in drug trafficking and money laundering. The section below discusses the nature of Jamaica's drug trafficking and money laundering problems.

UNDERSTANDING JAMAICA'S DRUG TRAFFICKING AND MONEY LAUNDERING

Drug trafficking is a transnational criminal activity and ranks as one of the largest crime problems affecting peoples and states globally. International estimates of drug trafficking is worth USD400 billion yearly (Emmers, 2007). Jamaica is a major marijuana planting and cocaine transshipment state. It is also listed among the countries described as major money laundering jurisdictions by the U.S. State Department (INCSR, 2018).

Jamaican waters are used as shipment routes to transport Colombian cocaine (Griffith, 2010; Haughton, 2016; Vasciannie, 1997). In fact, the coves and inlets of the rugged Jamaican 550 miles long coastline are used by criminals to hide Colombian cocaine before it departs for American and British markets (Griffith, 2010; Haughton, 2011). Bolivia, Colombia, and Peru are major coca cultivation hubs and cocaine is produced from the coca bush (INCSR, 2018; World Drug Report, 2018). Jamaican criminals have formed alliances with Colombian cocaine traffickers and most of the cocaine entering Jamaica comes from Colombia (Haughton, 2011; INCSR, 2018). Colombia accounts for 68.5% of the global coca cultivation and there were 146,000 hectares of coca bush under cultivation in Colombia in 2016 (World Drug Report, 2018, p. 29).

Marijuana, on the other hand, is planted in Jamaica and there is a paucity of data on marijuana cultivation (World Drug Report, 2018). The World Drug Report has also highlighted the reduction in marijuana seizures in countries, especially in the Americas where there is a shift in law enforcement priorities due to decriminalization of marijuana for personal or medicinal purposes. This exemplifies the case in Jamaica where the decriminalization of marijuana in 2015 resulted in reduced penalties in the form of a *ticketable* offense for individuals found in possession of 2 ounces or less (The Dangerous Drugs (Amendment) Act, 2015). This has freed up the over-burdened Jamaican court system from marijuana cases involving small quantities. However, an issue raised with decriminalization of marijuana concerns its impact on young people and its possibility in fueling crime (Abel, Sewell, & Eldemire-Shearer, 2011). Studies have shown the negative effects of marijuana use, including motor vehicle accidents, anxiety, dysphoria, and panic attacks (Abel et al., 2011; Elvik, 2013; Morgan et al., 2013). However, whereas an association exists between marijuana usage and crime, there is no indication of a causation between these two constructs, that is, the evidence does not reveal that marijuana usage is a cause of criminal behaviors (Caulkins et al, 2015). Moreover, of all the substances banned as illegal through the 1961, 1971, and 1988 United

Nations Conventions, marijuana is the one that is least likely to result in individuals committing violent crimes.

Jamaican traffickers have used maritime and aerial transportation to traffic their drugs to foreign markets (Griffith, 2010). Assessment of drug trafficking across the Caribbean's maritime zone revealed that criminals have utilized fast speed boats to transport cocaine from Colombia into Jamaica's waters. Speeding go-fast vessels are determined by law enforcement agents to transport up to 100 metric tonnes of cocaine from Colombia through Jamaica's waters each year (Haughton, 2011). Criminals have also used semi-submersibles that are difficult to detect from land. Further, the moving of drugs with the assistance of corrupt agents and through the cover of dark have been strategies planned and executed by drug cartels and their organized team of criminal operatives to traffic drugs (Haughton, 2011).

Drug cartels are drug traffickers who own and operate drug empires but do so by employing front runners who act in executing aspects of the drug business. These cartels are not usually the ones who deal with the day-to-day activities required to traffic drugs. They are the ones who engage in the business not because they are poverty-stricken and in need but because they are greedy (Haughton, 2011). Further, the drug cartels benefit the most from the huge profits generated through the drug industry. As the Rational Choice Theory suggests, these cartels are driven by self-interest and their drug trafficking decisions are based on how to maximize profits for themselves (Siegel, 2009). In Jamaica's case, this holds true, although there have been instances in which drug cartels were known to have spent their monies in assisting children in some vulnerable communities to attend school. They are also known to sponsor football matches and help with school feeding programs.

Monies from illicit drug trafficking forms the main source of money laundering in Jamaica. However, to a lesser extent, money laundering is also executed through funds derived from illicit gun trafficking, financial fraud schemes, corruption, and extortion (Ali, 1998; INCSR, 2018). Despite the high levels of crime, however, conviction rates for drug cartels and for money launderers remain low in Jamaica. For instance, in 2016, of the 18 money laundering prosecution, only 6 culminated in a conviction. Further, from January to August 2017, Jamaica's Financial Investigative Division only forfeited USD 220,000 in cash and assets associated with money laundering activities (INCSR, 2018). The UNODC in 2009 estimated that criminal proceeds totaled 3.6% of global Gross Domestic Product (GDP), with 2.7 percent or USD 2 trillion being laundered. Money laundering therefore constitutes a significant portion of world GDP with anecdotal evidence, suggesting that Jamaica's estimate in this area could be far ahead of the world averages.

Law enforcement estimates have indicated that as much as 100 metric tonnes of cocaine traverse the Caribbean Sea and are transshipped through Jamaica each year (Haughton, 2011). The multiple players involved in the drug trade and the intricate coordination required to circumvent law enforcement support the notion that the movement of drugs from production or transshipment states to consumption states necessitates strategic and operational planning by drug cartels and their employees (Haughton, 2011). Activities such as the cultivation or processing of drugs, the internal transportation within a country, the trans-border transportation to destination countries in foreign markets all require detailed planning and precise execution. Therefore, drug trafficking activities are not coincidental nor do they occur in a haphazard manner. Drug traffickers carefully plan their drug trafficking illicit activities. These activities are coordinated and often involve many persons but led by a drug cartel. The drug cartel is usually the mastermind behind the drug trade and often command and control the sequenced processes of the drug trafficking activities.

Other planned activities include the planting of marijuana and the transportation of cocaine through Jamaica's waters. Successful execution of these activities requires skillful maneuvering in order to avoid law enforcement detection. Hence, the implementation of a systematic supply chain moves drugs from Jamaica to destination locations in the United States and the UK. However, the safe delivery and sale of the drugs to retailers in the United States or the UK does not terminate the process. The intermediary traffickers must be able to safely transport the large sums of cash obtained from this illicit activity to Jamaica or into the hands of the drug cartels.

A significant part of the drug trafficking process involves the safe return of drug monies to the cartels. This is particularly crucial as these monies crosses states' territorial borders and must be delivered without the attention of law enforcers. They must also be dispatched outside the formal banking system where "dirty money" or money obtained through criminal activities is likely to be traced. As a calculated mechanism to prevent detection and to reduce traceability, drug trafficking sales are either conducted using cash or done through a system of barter. The barter system may involve cash but traffickers, at times, exchange their drugs for small arms and light weapons. Law enforcement sources have indicated that Jamaican drug traffickers utilized this system to exchange marijuana and cocaine for guns from Haitian criminals.

The illicit profits from drug trafficking are mixed into lawfully obtained funds through the money laundering process. To make the origins of drug money appear to be emerging from lawful sales and trade, it is often transferred into legitimate businesses. When this happens, it is difficult to determine the drug proceeds as distinct from proceeds obtained through normal legal business operations (Van Duyne & Levi, 2005). Another way in which drug traffickers undertake a reasoned calculation to support their drug trafficking efforts is through innovative schemes to circumvent law enforcers when they are using maritime means to trafficking drugs to their desired locations. For instance, in the Caribbean Sea, fast speed boats called Go-fast Vessels were utilized by drug traffickers to outrun Jamaican law enforcers' slower 40-foot patrol vessels. These Go-fast Vessels also have refueling capacity which means that they can make the trip between Colombia to Jamaica without having to stop to add fuel. However, increased presence in the Caribbean waters and the collaboration emerging from the U.S.–Jamaica Shiprider Agreement has since strengthened Jamaica's capacity to police its territorial waters.

Like any good business operator who stays ahead of his competitors, drug traffickers respond to law enforcement activities by changing their strategies in order to maximize profits. Hence, when there are greater law enforcement efforts to curtail maritime drug trafficking, drug cartels respond with alternative strategies by utilizing drug couriers or target cargo consignments to traffic drugs via airplanes (Griffith, 2010). Traffickers have calculated that by dispatching human couriers, a flow of cocaine can be sent to their targeted markets. More importantly, couriers serve as a deliberate way to test the vulnerability of air transportation system from which a pattern can be crafted by cartels to establish low check points on vulnerable routes. For the drug cartels, vulnerable routes are those with the lowest risk for the drug couriers and for confiscation of their drugs. The calculated actions of drug traffickers are in sync with the Rational

Choice Theory as these actions involve the decision to embark on drug trafficking and money laundering activities through detailed conceptualization, planning and decision making aimed at maximizing profits and minimizing capture and punishment.

Further, Jamaica's drug traffickers' decision to sell drugs is based on rational decision making fueled by personal reasons, inclusive of greed and need. Drug traffickers make calculations in the determination of the societal image they portray to others. Indeed, Jamaican drug cartels portray the trappings of success and affluence. As such, they have very expensive clothing, jewelries, homes, and cars. On the face of it, some have legitimate businesses that are spill over business from their drug runnings. They also tend to attract the most beautiful and high maintenance women. The wealthy lifestyle is part of what they use in their recruitment drive to attract drug couriers and other workers in the illicit drug industry. The outward attributes of the drug cartels are sometimes enough to appeal to the interest of some individuals who surmise that this is the way to obtain the affluent dream. Further, compared to this lifestyle, acquiring education as a means of social mobility is not likely to attract many Jamaican youth as they believe they can make faster and more profits from drug trafficking activities, obtain greater admiration and economic status, and achieve instant gratification.

In this regard, Jamaica's drug problem is organized and traffickers are motivated by the huge profits that a consignment of marijuana and cocaine yield. This supernormal profit from the illicit drug trafficking far outweighs the possible risk of apprehension. Indeed, from the Rational Choice Theory, it is conceived that the decision to commit a crime is made only after the drug trafficker and money launderer carefully weighs the potential benefits and consequences of their planned action. Thereafter, they decide that the benefits of this crime far surpass its consequences. In this calculation, the penalties for money laundering and drug trafficking are paltry compared to the returns that can be made for engaging in these crimes.

Jamaica's drug trafficking and money laundering problems are further compounded by gangs and dons who operate in garrison communities. Jamaica, like many other Caribbean countries, such as Trinidad and Tobago, Guyana, and St. Lucia, has a huge gang problem (Harriott & Katz, 2015; Wallace, 2013). The estimated number of criminal gangs operating in the country ranged between 120 and 266 (IACHR, 2012; UK Home Office, 2017) and comprised a large number of juvenile delinquents, thus creating a next generational problem for Caribbean societies (Wallace, 2013). Added to the aforementioned problems is the prevalence of garrison communities.

A garrison community is an informal enclave, which is maintained by dons, supported by political interests and operates within a framework of violence (Henry-Lee, 2005; Stone, 1986). In essence, a don is an informal community leader who controls the community with the use of violence (Henry-Lee, 2005). *Donmanship* evolves through social and economic conditions of urban poverty and limited access to employment opportunities. The strategy of the don is to use fear and material resources afforded through ill-gotten gains to create an unofficial power base for operating within these communities. These dons provide financial assistance to community citizens and in many cases fill an economic void created by the absence of state actors (Johnson & Soeters, 2008).

Christopher "Dudus" Coke, along with his deceased father, Lester Lloyd Coke, before him, are perhaps the two most reputed dons that Jamaica has seen. Christopher Coke was extradited to the United States in 2010 for drug trafficking and gun-running and was the don of the garrison community of Tivoli Gardens, which is located in Western Kingston where the former Prime Minister Bruce Golding was the Member of Parliament (Lewis, 2012).

The Rational Choice Theory is also applicable to the criminal justice system in the curtailment of drug trafficking and money laundering. It appears that the Jamaican authorities have calculated the benefits of implemented strategies and laws aimed at apprehending and punishing drug traffickers and money launderers, for example, they have engaged the United States in the Shiprider Agreement to combat drug trafficking. They have also evaluated the impact on societal core values and the heavy burden of corruption and violence which are associated with these illicit activities. This is being undertaken through social intervention in vulnerable communities. In addition, calculations are made on the best ways by which such punishments may be imposed to curb the criminal activities. The laws and strategies devised by governmental agents and institutions are designed to apprehend criminals and to impose the punishment on them. The section below presents the core institutions and their efforts to reduce drug trafficking and money laundering. It also discusses the laws implemented to arrest these transnational criminals and to deprive them of the gains derived from illicit activities.

CURBING THE PROBLEM: INTER-AGENCY COLLABORATION AND LAWS

Inter-Agency Collaboration

The United States continues to play a geo-strategic role through the Shiprider Agreement for mitigating Jamaica's drug trafficking problem. The Shiprider Agreement is a maritime counter-drug agreement aimed at curtailing Jamaica's drug trafficking by air and sea. It gives the U.S. permission on a case-by-case basis to board, search and seize suspected drug trafficking vessels that are operating in Jamaican waters. Jamaican suspected vessels operating in international waters can also be seized through this agreement (Vasciannie, 1997). This Shiprider Agreement has now been broadened to include third-party states such as Britain, France, and Holland since 2004 (Haughton, 2008).

The Foreign Account Tax Compliance Act (FATCA) was enacted in 2014 by the United States for strengthening the legislative framework around these illicit activities. The Jamaica–U.S. FATCA Intergovernmental Framework supports information sharing regarding the requirements of FATCA. As a requirement of the bilateral agreement, Jamaica's tax authority must facilitate compliance with the Government of the USA. Further, Jamaica's financial institutions must review their customers to determine if they are citizens of the United States. For U.S. citizens, the Jamaican financial institution must report their financial standing to the U.S. Internal Revenue Service. This increased monitoring of accounts and information sharing with the U.S. Government has made it difficult for drug traffickers to launder their illicit gain through the formal financial system without detection.

International and local institutional collaboration as well as the imposition of legal penalties are used to deter drug trafficking and money laundering activities in Jamaica. International collaboration has often taken the form of the Jamaican authorities partnering with other countries in order to obtain the expertise and training required to curb the dynamic problems of drug trafficking and money laundering. Hence, in 2017, the

U.S. Federal Reserve Board of Governors provided training seminars and technical assistance to banking supervisors on detecting and addressing money laundering activities. Further, the International Unit of the USA's Money Laundering and Assets Recovery Section also provided varying Jamaican stakeholders with training on techniques in recovering assets from many types of criminal money laundering activities (INCSR, 2018).

The USA's Narcotic Kingpin Act was established in the post-September 11th era by the United States. To reduce the connection between terrorism and drug trafficking acts, the U.S. President Bush in 2004 cooperated with Jamaica and other drug production countries globally to apprehend drug cartels and to provide stiff penalties for those drug cartels who transport illicit drugs into the United States. Since this Act, at least 10 Jamaican drug cartels were listed as drug kingpins and were arrested and charged in the United States.

In addition, local collaboration that involves the sharing of information among different security agencies in Jamaica are also instituted in order to prosecute drug traffickers and money launderers. For instance, the Major Organised Crime and Anti-Corruption Unit cooperates with the Financial Investigative Unit in the apprehension of drug traffickers and in confiscating their assets once a court seizure order is issued following a guilty conviction. Further, the establishment of the 2016 Financial Investigations Division Anti-money Laundering software has resulted in the identification of increased suspicious transaction filings from a number of regulated entities, including financial institutions, cambios, and real estate agents. This is the case as the software facilitates online filings while providing law enforcers with an updated report of filed transactions to support their money laundering and drug trafficking investigations.

The Laws

The 1996 Dangerous Drugs Act covers the penalty involved for the possession, use, cultivation, manufacture, storage, and transportation of illicit drugs, such as opium, marijuana, cocaine, and morphine. However, Jamaican Government amended this Act in 2015 to decriminalize marijuana for medical and personal uses. Individuals in possession of two (2) ounces or less are ticketed and fined for possession of marijuana, but no criminal record is attached to this possession. Decriminalization must not be confused with legalization and despite this change to the law, the large-scale trafficking of marijuana is still illegal under Jamaican law and hence attracts the fines and penalties stipulated under the Dangerous Drugs Act.

The Dangerous Drugs Act stipulates harsh fines for those individuals who violate the law. Section 8A, paragraph 2 (a) stipulates that individuals who are convicted before a circuit court on cocaine charges are to be fined or imprisoned for a period not surpassing thirty-five (35) years or to be given both a fine and imprisonment. Part III A, Section 1 (a) stipulates that persons who are involved in the importation or exportation of marijuana are guilty of an offense. Upon conviction in a Circuit Court, these persons must be fined no less than JMD500 per ounce of marijuana found or be imprisoned for a term not exceeding thirty-five (35) years or to both a fine and imprisonment.

Jamaica's passage of the 2007 Proceeds of Crime Act is aimed at depriving criminals of their illicit gains derived from transnational crime. Once an individual is criminally convicted, the Proceeds of Crime Act allows for the seizure of cash and the civil forfeiture of assets obtained from criminal activity. Regulation 7 of the Act authorizes an Interim Receiver to seize property to which a seizure order has been issued.

Paragraph 3 (2) of Jamaica's Proceeds of Crime Act mandates financial institutions to report certain transactions from persons or entities other than Ministries of Government, Statutory Bodies, Registered Companies, Embassies, and High Commissions. Further, Paragraph 4 prohibits reporting financial institutions from disclosing the contents of their reports to any person or entity other than the competent authority. Jamaica's 1996 Money Laundering Act outlines money laundering offenses, stipulates penalties for such offenses, and mandates businesses to implement measures to facilitate the detection and prevention of money laundering. Section 2 of the Act outlines the specified offenses as the violation of the Dangerous Drugs Act, the contravention of the provisions of the Firearms Act, the acquisition, use, and possession of criminal property and aiding, abetting or procuring criminal property through fraud, dishonesty, or corruption. Further, to stem the flow of money laundering through greater information sharing across financial institutions, in 2014, the Banking Services Act was passed. This Act mandated the Bank of Jamaica and Jamaica's Financial Services Commission to share information with each other and the other international financial counterparts.

Like the Proceed of Crime Act, the 1996 Drug Offences (Forfeiture of Proceeds) Act was passed to curtail drug trafficking activities and to deprive drug traffickers of their monies derived from trafficking. Among the acts listed as prescribed offenses under the Drug Offences (Forfeiture of Proceeds) Act are money laundering activities in contravention of the Money Laundering Act as well as the production, manufacture, supply, storage, and transportation of drugs in contravention of the Dangerous Drugs Act. Part II, paragraph 3 (2) of the Drug Offences (Forfeiture of Proceeds) Act allows the Director of Prosecutions to apply to the Supreme Court for a forfeiture order against any property in relation to drug trafficking and money laundering offenses.

Taken as a whole, these laws have made it difficult for drug trafficking and money laundering activities. Despite the strategies implemented for containing drug trafficking and money laundering, it appears that the levels of criminal convictions are not commensurate with the high levels of crime in these areas (Levi & Reuter, 2006). For money laundering, in 2017, the Jamaican authorities had 27 prosecutions that resulted in only one conviction. Similarly, for the first nine months of 2018, there were 13 prosecutions and only three convictions (INCSR, 2019b). Similar to money laundering, Jamaica continues to underperform in the seizure of drugs. For example, while Jamaican farmers cultivate approximately 15,000 hectares of marijuana per year, in 2018, only 186 hectares were eradicated and 20.2 metric tonnes of cured marijuana were seized. This underperformance is also reflected in cocaine seizure with a mere 658 kilogram of cocaine confiscated in 2017 (INCSR, 2019a). It should be highlighted that the estimate of the underground market in drug trafficking and money laundering are at best sparse. This twin problem continues to be a pervasive challenge for the Jamaican authorities.

In the absence of such laws, drug trafficking would occur unfettered and the laundering of drug money into legitimate businesses would possibly be the norm for many traffickers. However, with these laws in place, the stakes are higher for traffickers as they must find ways to operate without detection and prosecution. Jamaica's transnational crime problem is no doubt mitigated by these legislation and regulations. However, enforcement of laws in the area of money laundering remains problematic as it is difficult to trace these nefarious activities for successful prosecution.

Recommendations

As the trafficking of drugs and the laundering of these illicit proceeds continue to be a problem in Jamaica, this study makes the following recommendations:

- The Jamaica state must continue to collaborate with external partners to provide training to multiple stakeholders who are central to curbing drug trafficking and money laundering activities.

- There is need to strengthen Jamaica's criminal justice system by building capacity of the state's law enforcement, prosecutors, and court system to effectively and efficient prosecute financial crimes.

- Drug trafficking and money laundering are high-profit-driven activities; hence, the Jamaican government must aim to remove the profit from these transnational criminal activities by apprehending the cartels. This will make these activities less financially attractive for transnational criminals.

- The government must focus intervention efforts on at-risk-youths and vulnerable communities to prevent individuals from pursuing a life of crime and to protect communities from degenerating to crime and violence.

CONCLUSION

Drug trafficking will continue as long as there is a lucrative market for drugs and as long as existing and potential drug traffickers visualize no other normal legitimate ways of earning a livelihood. As the Rational Choice Theory suggests, drug traffickers make calculated decisions to embark on a lucrative life of crime. In the case of Jamaica, calculated decisions to traffic drugs and to launder proceeds are based on the supernormal profits that drug trafficking generates. Indeed, the decision to invest "dirty" money into legitimate businesses is a drug trafficker's calculated strategy to surpass the laws of the state and to circumvent arrest, fines, and prison time.

Given this reality, the best way to deter traffickers and launderers is to take the profitability out of these illicit activities. Without the huge profits, traffickers will calculate that it makes no financial sense to pursue these activities. Additionally, penalties for these illicit acts must be immediate and harsh to deter drug trafficking and money laundering activities in Jamaica. However, as is well established in the drug trafficking literature, most incarceration happen among the lower-level drug traffickers. Major drug cartels are infrequently caught and it is difficult to obtain money laundering convictions in Jamaica.

REFERENCES

Abel, W. D., Sewell, C., & Eldemire-Shearer, D. (2011). Decriminalization of marijuana: Is this a realistic public mental health policy for Jamaica?. *West Indian Medical Journal, 60*(3), 367–370.

Ali, S. A. (1998). Jamaica: Combating money laundering—A review of the Money Laundering Act 1996. *Journal of Money Laundering Control, 1*(3), 261–267.

Amnesty International. (2011). Annual Report: Jamaica. Retrieved from https://www.amnestyusa.org/reports/annual-report-jamaica-2011/.

Caulkins, J. P., Kilmer, B., Kleiman, M. A. R., MacCoun, R. J., Midgette, G., Oglesby, P., & Reuter, P. H. (2015). Options and issues regarding marijuana legalization. Santa Monica, CA, RAND Corporation, coll. *Perspectives.*

Central Intelligence Agency (CIA) Factbook. (2019). Jamaica. Retrieved from https://www.cia.gov/library/publications/the-world-factbook/geos/print_jm.html.

Cornish, D. B., & Clarke, R. V. (1987). Understanding crime displacement: An application of rational choice theory. *Criminology, 25*(4), 933-948.

Elvik, R. (2013). Risk of road accident associated with the use of drugs: A systematic review and meta-analysis of evidence from epidemiological studies. *Accident Analysis & Prevention, 60*, 254–267.

Emmers, R. (2007). Securitization. In A. Collins (Ed.), *Contemporary security studies* (pp. 109–125). Oxford: Oxford University Press.

Griffith, I. L. (1994). From cold war geopolitics to post-cold war geo-narcotics. *International Journal, 49*(Winter 1993–1994), 1–36.

Griffith, I. L. (2010). *Drugs and security in the Caribbean: Sovereignty under siege.* Pennsylvania State University Press, University Park, PA, USA.

Harriott, A., & Katz, C. M. (Eds.). (2015). *Gangs in the Caribbean: Responses of state and society.* University of the West Indies Press.

Haughton, S. (2008). Bilateral diplomacy: Re-thinking the Jamaica-USA Shiprider Agreement. *The Hague Journal of Diplomacy, 3*(3), 253–276.

Haughton, S. (2011). *Drugged out: Globalisation and Jamaica's Resilience to Drug Trafficking.* Lanham, MD: University Press of America.

Haughton, S. (2016). Border security and cooperative initiatives to counter illicit drug trafficking: The case of Jamaica and the USA. In M. Dawson, D. R. Kisku, P. Gupta, J. K. Sing & W. Li (Eds.), *Developing next generation countermeasures for homeland security threat prevention* (pp. 104–120). Hershey, United States: IGI Global.

Henry-Lee, A. (2005). The nature of poverty in the garrison constituencies in Jamaica. *Environment and Urbanisation, 17*(2), 83–99.

Inter-American Commission on Human Rights (IACHR), Annual Report. (2012). Retrieved from http://www.oas.org/en/iachr/docs/annual/2012/toc.asp.

International Narcotics Control Strategy Report (INCSR). (2018). Money laundering, 2, The Bureau of International Narcotics and Law Enforcement Affairs, The United States Department of State.

International Narcotics Control Strategy Report (INCSR). (2019a). Drug and chemical control, United States Department of State Bureau for International Narcotics and Law Enforcement Affairs, 1. Retrieved from https://www.state.gov/documents/organization/290501.pdf.

International Narcotics Control Strategy Report (INCSR). (2019b). Money laundering, United States Department of State Bureau of International Narcotics and Law Enforcement, II. Retrieved from https://www.state.gov/documents/organization/290502.pdf.

Jamaica Observer (November 06, 2017). Richard Hugh Blackford. JA's murder figures tell of a state of emergency. Retrieved from http://

www.jamaicaobserver.com/opinion/ja-8217-s-murder-figures-tell-of-a-state-of-emergency_115377?profile=1096.

Johnson, H. N., & Soeters, J. L. (2008). Jamaican dons, Italian godfathers and the chances of a "reversible destiny." *Political Studies*, 56(1), 166–191.

Levi, M., & Reuter, P. (2006). Money laundering. *Crime and Justice*, 34(1), 289–375.

Lewis, R. (2012). Party politics in Jamaica and the extradition of Christopher "Dudus" Coke. *The Global South*, 6(1), 38–54.

Morgan, C. J., Page, E., Schaefer, C., Chatten, K., Manocha, A., Gulati, S., & Leweke, F. M. (2013). Cerebrospinal fluid anandamide levels, cannabis use and psychotic-like symptoms. *The British Journal of Psychiatry*, 202(5), 381–382.

Reuter, P., & Truman, E. M. (2004). Chasing dirty money: Progress on anti-money laundering. *Institute for International Economics, United States: Washington*.

Rubin, V. D., & Comitas, L. (1976). *Ganja in Jamaica: The effects of marijuana use.* Garden City, N.Y.: Anchor Books.

Siegel, L. (2009). *Criminology* (10th ed.). Canada: Thomson, Wadsworth.

Stone, C. (1986). *Class, state and democracy in Jamaica.* New York: Praeger.

United Kingdom (UK) Home Office. (2015). Country information and guidance Jamaica: Fear of organised criminal gangs. Retrieved from https://www.refworld.org/pdfid/55a3bb434.pdf.

United Kingdom (UK) Home Office. (2017). Country information and guidance Jamaica: Fear of organised criminal gangs. Retrieved from https://assets.publishing.service.gov.uk/government/uploads/system/uploads/attachment_data/file/598136/Jamaica_-_Org_Crim_Gangs_-_CPIN_-_Feb_2017_-_v.2.pdf.

United Nations Office on Drugs and Crime (UNODC). (2009). Money laundering and globalisation. Retrieved from https://www.unodc.org/unodc/en/money-laundering/globalization.html.

Van Duyne, P. C., &. Levi, M. (2005). *Drugs and money: Managing the drug trade and crime money in Europe.* London: Routledge.

Vasciannie, S. (1997). Political and policy aspects of the Jamaica-United States Shiprider Negotiations. *Caribbean Quarterly, 43*(3), 38–60.

Wallace, W. (2013). *Better to be alone than in bad company: A handbook about gangs for Caribbean parents and children.* Kingston, Jamaica: Arawak Publications.

Warnecke-Berger, H. (2018). Jamaica: Transationalization by force and the transformation of violence. In H. Warnecke-Berger (Eds.), *Politics and Violence in Central America and the Caribbean* (pp. 163–195). Cham: Palgrave Macmillan.

World Drug Report. (2018). Analysis of drug markets: Opiates, cocaine, cannabis and synthetic drugs, United Nations Office of Drugs and Crime (UNODC), United Nations, June.

LAWS

The Dangerous Drugs Act, 1996, Ministry of Justice, Kingston, Jamaica.

The Dangerous Drugs (Amendment) Act, 2015, Ministry of Justice, Kingston, Jamaica.

The Drug Offences (Forfeiture of Proceeds) Act, 1996, Ministry of Justice, Kingston, Jamaica

The Money Laundering Act, 1996, Ministry of Justice, Kingston, Jamaica.

The Proceeds of Crime Act, 2007, Ministry of Justice, Kingston, Jamaica.

CHAPTER V

CRIMINOLOGICAL DIMENSIONS OF AGRICULTURE IN THE CARIBBEAN

Wendy-Ann P. Isaac, Wayne G. Ganpat, Marlene Attzs, and Thomas E. Isaac

The University of the West Indies, St. Augustine, Trinidad and Tobago

ABSTRACT

Criminological research globally has focused on the more conventional or salacious higher profile type crimes in society and trivialized agricultural/farm crimes as inconsequential. Agricultural/farm crime or praedial larceny refers to the theft of agricultural produce, namely crops, livestock, and fisheries. This chapter discusses the development of agricultural crimes from socially accepted cultural activities to highly complex and organized criminal activities. It provides an overview of these crimes from a Caribbean historical perspective, with a specific focus on the characterization of crime. The chapter also highlights the degree of agricultural crimes commonly facing the Caribbean region and reviews the various strategies employed throughout the Caribbean to address these types of criminal activity. The authors examine this now organized criminal activity and focuses on the opportunistic and professional nature of praedial larceny on the one hand and the dependency and abuse issues embroiled in pesticide overuse, air and water pollution, and illegal hunting. The chapter then provides an ethnographic explication by analyzing the narratives of the victims of praedial larceny, and then examines the anthropological, cultural, and historical roots of the problem. Finally, the mechanisms which can be introduced to reduce this social problem are explored.

Keywords: Agriculture crime, praedial larceny, Routine Activity Theory, food security, Caribbean

INTRODUCTION

The Agricultural sector in Trinidad and Tobago contributes less than 0.5% of the GDP. The sector has historically been overlooked in favor of the petroleum industry and has been confined mainly to rural areas across both islands, although pockets of farming activities can be seen throughout many urban areas. Due to Trinidad and Tobago's colonial history, cocoa, coffee, and sugar were the main agricultural exports to Europe, but the Government has over the past decades been prioritizing agriculture in an effort to increase the country's food and nutrition security, diversify the economy, reduce the growing food import bill, conserve foreign exchange, and provide sustainable employment opportunities. One of the most serious constraints to agriculture has been farm theft or praedial larceny, an intractable problem that has catapulted losses to considerable proportions, making it a risky investment. This crime has been recognized throughout the Caribbean as one of the most significant constraints to food security in the region (Isaac, Ganpat, & Joseph, 2017; Little, 2011) and its proliferation is primarily driven by the increased demand for fresh food.

Agricultural crime/farm theft or praedial larceny includes any statutory or common law offense which may be committed against people in agricultural communities or against their businesses and property (Isaac et al., 2017). While including a wide spectrum of offenses, some of more prevalent acts include theft, vandalism, illegal hunting, illegal dumping of rubbish, and trespassing. These offenses are often overlooked or underestimated, but they can have a significant impact on the economic stability of agricultural operations and negatively impact on the development of the agriculture sector. Most of the agricultural production in food crops in the Caribbean constitutes the livelihood of small farmers utilizing plots of 2–5 acres, planting green produce, ground provisions, fruit crops, vegetables, much of which ends up in the groceries or weekend markets and road-side stalls. The wealthier farmers, with expensive trucks, tractors, and shiny farm technology, own plots of 5, 10, or more acres. For the latter group, losses resulting from larceny may not be as disastrous as it may be for small farmers, many of whom may be squatters occupying state land or rented acreages. For those who farm livestock, the losses can be equally disastrous. Few farms are equipped with effective surveillance technology to detect the night-raider possessing fast-moving transport vehicles and deadly ammunition. Farmers are really at the mercy of the criminal element, and the losses suffered can hardly be offset by a higher price for produce at market. Farm incomes among small and middle-size farmers are used as family finances, funding home-maintenance, food bills, education, transport, and the electronic and digital equipment for a decent middle-class lifestyle. Praedial larceny threatens simultaneously the quality of life of a productive social class of citizens and the entire economic fabric of a society working toward food security and import substitution.

A regional survey conducted in 2010 among stakeholders revealed that more than 90% of the respondents regarded praedial larceny as the single most discouraging aspect of agriculture (CARICOM, 2011; Isaac et al., 2017) and the study further revealed that 18% of the value of farm output regionally is taken by thieves, accounting for losses in excess of USD $321 million annually (CARICOM, 2011). Worldwide losses are estimated as high as USD $5 billion on an annual basis (Isaac et al., 2017; Swanson, Chamelin, & Territo, 2000) with some countries in Europe, reporting losses between 6% and 18% of agricultural output (Isaac et al., 2017). In addition to the expected risks of frequent flooding during the rainy season or the occasional wild-fire during the dry season, coupled with volatile price fluctuations in the market, much of which may be predictable, larceny of one's produce after months of tedious labor and postponed gratification, has disastrous effects on one's economic and psychological well-being.

Often overnight, several acres of high-priced commodities can be trucked away to be sold to middlemen, or directly to salesmen engaged in the retail business with no traceability (Ganpat & Isaac, 2019; Isaac et al., 2017). Often because of some farm's remoteness and absentee farmers, valuable, accessible, and portable farm equipment and supplies have disappeared when left unguarded. In some cases, thieves have been reported to pose a serious threat to farmers, their workers, and even their families. This has resulted in farmers abandoning their entire enterprise due to heavy losses and the high cost paid for security. Such unscrupulous practices bring enormous profit to those engaged in this sordid underworld of agricultural criminality, even as it spells economic ruin to the practicing farmer and his inability to repay banks or credit unions.

The experience of massive financial losses to families in this manner constitutes an enormous disincentive to farmers and has partly been responsible for some degree of estate abandonment and low production levels on manageable land holdings, less vulnerable to petty theft. There is hardly a day that goes by in Trinidad where the media does not report an incident involving praedial larceny. For example, farmers of the Edinburgh Food Crop Farmers Association report several incidents of praedial larceny, with calls to the praedial larceny squad being unanswered.

Most praedial larceny incidents reported by the media include thefts to farm tools and equipment, food crops, and illegal planting of marijuana. The theft of livestock is increasingly a major threat to small holder producers. Larcenists steal livestock during the night, slaughter them, and either leave the carcass on the farms or secretly sell meat to unsuspecting citizens. Unfortunately, most of these crimes are not correctly recorded by police and usually ignored. In some areas, as in the Wallerfield district in Trinidad, farmers have retained their holdings and diversified the farm economy to include taxi-driving, small-engine repairs, the trucking business, or auto-mechanics which are regarded as more reliable and lucrative areas of employment. Most farmers have over the last few generations guided their progeny away from agriculture to more reliable and lucrative careers. This has been so among both the Afro- and Indo-Trinidadian populace. Initially, law and medicine, there-after a range of recently attractive professions as engineering or business have offered escape routes for farm children distressed over the experience of repeated family losses. Instructively, students from Trinidad and Tobago who study agriculture at university level seldom return to family farms or venture into their own agricultural enterprises. Employment is sought in the public service or the education system.

The national government's paltry budgetary allocation to agriculture not only betrays a developmental policy framework that points in other directions to significant growth sectors of the economy such as tourism, national celebrations, banking, infrastructural development, shipping, and the upgrading of port facilities. This reflects a middle-class privileging of urban over rural development as well as a widespread Afro-Trinidadian contempt for agriculture out of a collective reminiscence of the woes of plantation slavery. Successive governments over the last few decades which have largely represented the interests of this group have therefore paid little attention to farming and the anxieties of the rural communities. Lip service is paid to agriculture in the school curricula which have traditionally been skewed toward the humanities for middle-class, and technical–vocational subjects for working-class children. The resulting de-valorization of agriculture in the national consciousness relegates farm-related crimes to virtual insignificance within the spectrum of transgressive activities that bedevil the population. The fact of praedial larceny reinforces the pervasive negativism toward agriculture as a viable career, offering an attractive lifestyle.

There is a growing body of academic studies in rural criminology from Africa, America, Australia, Britain, and Scotland, examining the changing ecology of agricultural crime, criminality, and policing (Agozino, 2017; Barclay, 2001; Donnermeyer & Barclay, 2005; Donnermeyer, Scott, & Barclay, 2013; Isaac et al., 2017; Jones, 2008; Little, 2011; Smith, 2010; Smith, Laing, & Mcelwee, 2013; Smith & McElwee, 2013; Spore, 2009; Sugden, 1999; Yarwood & Gardener, 2005). These studies all show that farm theft is regarded as one of the major deterrents to agricultural production. Smith (2010) explains that rural crime is now organized, semi-organized, or committed by outsiders or sometimes committed by "rogue farmers" or "exploitative farmers" themselves (Wilkinson, Craig, & Gaus, 2010). In Africa, Agozino (2017) describes modern thieves of farm produce as being better armed with machine guns and using lorries to cart away their loot.

The impact of this crime worsens when other issues such as the hidden cost to agriculture production, productivity, and food security are factored in. The FAO (2013) study posits these hidden costs to include the decision by farmers to leave the sector or even when high-quality genetic breeds of livestock and crop varieties are stolen from breeding stations and agriculture research facilities and sold as food sometimes threatening public health issues from tainted and uncertified produce food entering into the domestic food chain. Table 1 presents a typology of most farm-related crimes throughout the Caribbean (adapted from Smith, 2010, and modified by Isaac et al., 2017). Smith (2010) categorizes farm crimes as situation-specific and context-bound, wildlife crime as predatory (carried out by organized gangs of urban criminals), illegal rural enterprise (symbiotic/entrepreneurial), and village crime (opportunistic or context-bound), a further contamination crime (situational-based) was added, which has similarities to conservation crimes.

Table 1: A Typology of Rural-Related Farm Crimes in the Caribbean

Farm crime (predatory/ organized/ context-bound)	Wildlife crime (predatory)	Illegal rural enterprise (symbiotic/ entrepreneurial)	Village crime (opportunistic/ context-bound)	Contamination crime (situational-based)
Theft—farm equipment (irrigation lines, tractors, diesel, water pumps, weed whackers, fertilizer, and pesticides, etc.)	Hunting out of season for wildlife—agouti, manicou, lappe, deer	Theft of livestock/ sheep, goat, cattle, poultry, and small stock stealing	Petty theft (pipers)— generally opportunistic	Overuse of agricultural inputs (fertilizers and pesticides)
	Illegal fishing for tilapia etc.	Theft of seedlings, fruits, and vegetables	Illegal trespassers and shooters	Water pollution due to improper storage and disposal of pesticides
Vandalism— to farm and buildings and fences, damage to crops	Trapping	Squatting on private lands	Breaking and entering	
	Theft of turtle eggs, etc.	Drug cultivation— cannabis farming	Dumping of rubbish on farmland	Air pollution from drift of pesticides
Fire-raising— buildings and farms				
Cruelty to livestock				

Source: Adapted from Smith (2010) and modified by Isaac et al. (2017).

HISTORICAL TRENDS OF AGRICULTURAL AND ENVIRONMENTAL CRIMES IN THE CARIBBEAN

Praedial larceny has powerful anthropological roots in the collective historical experience of Caribbean peoples. But it is easy to read the history of the Caribbean, written from a Eurocentric perspective by the conquerors celebrating the glory and wealth of empire, and not detect the collective horrors experienced by natives, bond-servants and slaves from elsewhere. Looked at from the standpoint of the conquered and the subjugated, centuries of empire-building marked the historical origins of West Indian colonies in an imperial enterprise of global theft of the land and resources of others and the brutal exploitation of the vanquished in the Prospero-Caliban encounter that defined European colonialism. The institution of slavery itself disenfranchised millions of human beings, who were denied the right to property itself and therefore survived only as they rejected the ethics of the conqueror. Survival on slave plantations spawned a range of resistance mechanisms to the ambient oppression and the brutalization of body and spirit. Malingering, vandalism, brutality to animals, violence, vituperation, lying, physical and verbal abuse, and stealing whatever was available, typified plantation culture among the Africans during slavery. Many of these learned transgressive behaviors survived emancipation and have become ingrained in the lifestyle practices of many Caribbean people. Under conditions of oppression and abuse, blacks experienced considerable self-contempt and came to introject the negative stereotypes of the ruling classes. The act of stealing, without shame or remorse, has become a functional behavior and lifestyle option for many, psychologically and ethically unprepared to cope with the demands of contemporary living.

The origins of praedial larceny itself have its roots that can be traced to the small agricultural plots that were given to blacks during the later period of plantation slavery. To supplement the food supply, slaves were allowed to plant food crops on small acreages of estate land and even sell at the newly developing Sunday markets (an institution that still survives in many islands). Profits made in these enterprises were even used by the thrifty to purchase their freedom through manumission, and as well purchase land holdings for agricultural production. Slaves developed quite ingenious strategies to market produce for sale, often stealing from neighbors' plots to increase earnings. This practice did not diminish after emancipation, surviving with the Sunday markets up to the present. In Trinidad, slaves abandoned the plantations and bought or squatted on available land to continue small-scale farming of ground provisions and green vegetables. This development constituted a veritable underground economy, outside of and very much opposed to the economics of sugar production and export to the metropolitan markets and serving the interests of empire. Vigilant supervision of a bastard economy by colonial governments could not be expected. Indeed, it was precisely this development that directly increased labor costs on the sugar estates and led to the advent of Asiatic indentureship as a source of labor. Colonial governments could not be expected to address the trivial issue of praedial larceny or minor infringements of petty theft among the plebeian populace. Blacks as second-class citizens had to find native strategies to solve such illegal practices, such as covert retaliations or occasional visits to the "obeah-man." Even up to today gardens can still be seen with upturned green or blue bottles to ward off thieves through necromancy. Some even resort to using salt and garlic as deterrents to thieves.

Stealing is perceived as a desperate act perpetrated by people in dire need of sustenance and deprived of the resources to meet basic physiological demands. In Trinidad and Tobago, stealing is often simply a pastime when a group of deviants may well avail themselves of a fowl-cock from a nearby farm to arrange a cook-out by the river. Such incidents serve almost as a confirmation of St. Augustine's lament in The Confessions over the problem of original sin and his own admission of a compulsion to steal as a boy merely for the fun of it. Few of our social analysts have been willing to probe the moral fabric of our society. Those who have paid attention to the persistent culture of poverty generated and sustained by conditions of political hegemony and colonial exploitation have focused almost exclusively on the objective conditions of economic deprivation of the masses and the lack of opportunities for institution-building.

Clearly, in historical hind-sight, such a record of centuries of managed dehumanization of the masses that attended the colonial order could only have resulted in an existential and moral deficit that has persisted in our cultural practices and modalities of being and consciousness. It has taken the acute, though morbid sensitivity of a Vidia Naipaul to describe our society here in Trinidad as a "picaroon society" (King, 2003) where ethical standards are ignored or unknown and where we live in a truly Hobbesian universe of a war of all against all. The Marxian hypothesis which extends the existential problem of alienation emerging out of the conditions of British industrial exploitation to the entire imperial project serves as an impressive launching-pad for theorizing the experience of existential alienation underlying many of the moral negativities perceptible in the social and cultural conditions within the Caribbean space.

Despite the pervasive Carnivalesque laughter and *joie de vivre* that characterize so many of the cultural practices and traditions in the Caribbean, the ambient cultural and economic poverty of the masses has bred an unmistakable banality and perverseness perceptible in attitudes to women, authority, language-use, property, squatting, celebration, children, race, and ethnicity, among other things. Praedial larceny is not a social aberration *sui generis*; it can be located on a continuum of moral transgressions together with car theft, extortion, kidnaping, drug trafficking, house burglary, murder, violence against women, vandalism, and general lawlessness that continue to plague the society.

The fact that poverty reduction and rising personal incomes (Trinidad and Tobago is among the high-income countries of the world) have not occasioned a significant reduction in these illicit activities is a clear indication that there is a moral and psychological dimension to the phenomenon and that it is a distinguishable cultural feature of the folk. The alleged corruption that is rampant in those occupying high political office provides a kind of spurious legitimation and a sop to conscience to many and discloses the depth and pervasiveness of the problem. It is amazing that most Trinidadians identify with some of the major religions of the world, regard themselves as "God-fearing," and hardly perceive any moral conflict between alleged belief based on religious affiliation and moral behavior in their everyday practices.

The Trinidad and Tobagonian society as with many of the other Caribbean islands such as Jamaica and Guyana has been a relatively unique demographic space that has, more than any other small-island population, sustained a rich cultural and ethnic diversity, fueled on the one hand by immigration from the neighboring islands after emancipation, together with the advent of Indian, Chinese, and Portuguese indentureship during the nineteenth century. With political independence, this amazing diversity described by ethnographers and historians as a proto-globalization, only now witnessed in the metropolitan centers of the North, has been perceived as a threat to creation of the nation-state.

The early nationalist ideology of the 1960s–1980s obliquely attempted to unify this bewildering plurality of truly organic regional communities through strategic dislocation of major population centers. Houses for the burgeoning populations in depressed suburbia around the Port of Spain in the West were built in the East along what is referred to as the "corridor." In addition to such demographic dislocations through planned housing policies, the patterns of allocating secondary students to schools, based not on geographic location but school choice and examination performance, have contributed significantly to the virtual dismantlement of organic community throughout most of the country. This has brought strangers into close proximity with indigenous inhabitants and created conditions of anonymity and hostility between neighbors.

Such radical demographic dislocations have generated environments where customary neighborly civilities have vanished (The singing group

Three Canal's popular song Good Morning Neighbour registers the stark anonymity and hostility that define neighborhood transactions today), and the individual conscience finds it easier to prey remorselessly on the stranger next door. Large residential communities surfaced during the oil-boom years throughout north, central, and south Trinidad as demographic oddities among rural or semi-rural communities, threatening traditional folk-ways and communal practices that had developed over decades of social integration and acculturation. The pathological rise in criminality throughout the country that continues to plague and frustrate governments since the 1990s is clearly symptomatic of the catastrophic demographic disorientations of a failed ideology. Trinidad has now become one of the most homicidal societies in the world with astounding levels of serious crime.

Nevertheless, these negative cultural retentions may well have been overcome if the pilfering of crops and livestock together with the fear for personal safety did not constitute the dreaded disincentive that it does. National institutions set up to provide safety and security to farmers as to the rest of the population have been woefully ineffective in delivery and mismanaged. Successive governments have failed to provide effective institutions at the level of national security through efficient policing and crime detection, as well as a proficient judicial process aimed both at retribution and deterrence, to deter the potential thief from intruding into someone else's farm or homestead. The abnormally high levels of both petty and serious crimes in the country are tied both to the failure of the political directorate to create effective security mechanisms for the population and the inner moral and psychological flaws in a population coming out of a tragic moral past. Where habits become engrained in the collective psyche of a people, it requires committed political action and stern government legislation, effectively implemented, to alter cultural and social mores that have solidified over centuries.

STRATEGIES TO MITIGATE AGRICULTURAL CRIMES

Crime prevention strategies to mitigate agricultural crimes can be adopted proactively before crimes occur, or as a reaction to the experience of crime. Many governments in the region have been strengthening policies in an attempt to build strategies which will secure the economic gains from public investment in the sector. The United Nations Food and Agriculture Organization Praedial Larceny Prevention Act of 1983 granted agricultural wardens the power to detect offenses and arrest suspects in the Caribbean.

Isaac et al. (2017) reported that early strategies of dealing with praedial larceny in many Caribbean islands included a traditional folk belief that if the maljo bean (*Canavalia ensiformis*) is planted around crops, it prevents petty theft (Winer, 2009). This bean is also reportedly planted in West African gardens in order to protect (them) from praedial larceny. Mitigation strategies are aimed at reducing opportunities for this activity to occur by increasing the risk to someone who intends to commit the crime (Isaac et al., 2017). The situational crime prevention theory focuses on the fact that offenders calculate the risk, which, in turn, influences their decision to target (or not) either the property or person for crime. Felson (2002) describes this as improving guardianship, where visibility, accessibility, and attraction of crime targets are reduced.

Craig (2011) described the 3Ds; deterrence, detection, and delay, as considerations when attempting to mitigate the impacts of crime. According to Craig (2011), deterrence involves the use of lighting, gates, fencing, no trespass signs, security systems, and dogs. Detection includes systems to alert you when someone enters your property, which may include the use of motion lights, cameras, sensors and detectors, visual surveillance by your employees or neighbors. Delay is part of the strategy to slow access to your property or equipment and may include fencing, locking doors on equipment storage facilities, parking equipment away from public viewing when left in fields overnight (Craig, 2011) to reduce the incidence of visibility.

Instructively, at a Public Consultation on Food Prices held in 2007, the Association of Professional Agricultural Scientists of Trinidad and Tobago (APASTT) presented a proposal designed primarily to secure food production and mitigate praedial larceny (Isaac et al., 2017). The proposal included the establishment of Designated Agricultural Zones which with controlled access to necessary physical infrastructure: roads, electricity, and water and inputs from the Police service to ensure security concerns. In a regional context, the Jamaican Government has sought to address the problem of praedial larceny by implementing a receipt book system whereby farmers and agricultural traders can establish legal proof of sale or purchase of agricultural products. They also initiated a Praedial Larceny Public Education Programme and Praedial Larceny Prevention Unit (PLPU) which aimed at increasing awareness about praedial larceny and more recently the National Animal Identification and Traceability System (NAITS) (Isaac et al., 2017). What is significant is that all persons involved in agricultural transactions in Jamaica have to register with the Rural Agricultural Development Authority (RADA). Further, Island Special Constabulary Force (ISCF) officers are assigned to various parishes to preside over the implementation of the Praedial Larceny Programme. The Jamaican Government has plans to tag animals using biometric tags and RFID biometric markers and intent to even issue passports to them. Drone technology is already in use to track down perpetrators and this is backed up by the police prevention support.

In St. Lucia, the Ministry of Agriculture attempted to address the praedial larceny problem by implementing a "four-pronged strategy." The first arm of this strategy involved the enactment of stronger legislation to deal with praedial larceny to regulate the sale of agricultural produce. The second arm aimed at a national identification program and licensing of registered farmers and traders. Third, the government began working with Local Government and with funding from the European Union Social Recovery Programme, they re-introduced the Rural Constabulary. They then embarked on an intensive public sensitization program aimed at educating the public on the importance of praedial larceny. In Antigua/Barbuda where "the agriculture sector continues to lose millions of dollars through the effects of praedial larceny" (Hilson Baptiste, Minister of Agriculture, Lands, Housing and the Environment, Antigua/Barbuda, 2009), the government also introduced an agricultural receipt book system and farmers were encouraged to register their business or form cooperatives (Isaac et al., 2017). A public education program was also established to increase awareness of praedial larceny and to educate farmers to use prompt action in detecting and reporting praedial larceny.

The FAO (2013) recommends a multi-sectoral and multifaceted approach to ensure the appropriate integration of policy issues when addressing the mitigation of praedial larceny. Their approach, in addition to those identified by Isaac et al. (2017) and CARICOM (2011), considers the following crucial elements:

1. Regularization of land tenure and proof of ownership of land and produce under the law.

2. Employment programs for improved livelihoods through projects in rural communities targeting the youth in vulnerable and poor households with the aim of building skills for employment.

3. Public education and communication strategies that empower and build resilience in farmers and fisher folks and their organizations at all levels—regional, national, and community—in praedial larceny prevention and reduction.

4. Promotion of investment and incentives in information technology systems that provide clarity in the relationships in the legitimate businesses in the trafficker (higgler/huckster) trade between islands.

5. Introduction and awareness of new technologies to foster traceability, surveillance, and deterrence, such as use of electronic fences using solar power, mobile apps, DNA paints, and more.

6. Promotion of sharing of best prevention programs among countries.

Some specific actions should revolve around:

1. Policy and legislative frameworks to support the work of the police and the judiciary through the criminal justice system and the Agriculture Ministry.

2. Mainstreaming of praedial larceny into the work of Agriculture Ministries and technical partners for implementation of a Plan of Action for praedial larceny prevention.

3. Integration of praedial larceny prevention into the planning and monitoring systems of the National Agriculture Strategy and the national strategies for crime prevention.

4. Information generation and knowledge management at the Ministries of Agriculture and partners including baseline data and mechanisms for knowledge-based planning and evaluation such as mapping praedial larceny hotspots.

5. Capacity building for praedial larceny prevention among all stakeholders, Ministries of Agriculture in collaboration with re-

gional and national farmers and fisher folks and their organizations.

6. Strategic partnerships for development and implementation of the Plan of Action for praedial larceny prevention.

7. Use of the Comprehensive Disaster Management Strategy framework to provide additional coordination for praedial larceny at the regional level. The processes of CDM already provide a mechanism for management and sharing.

8. Research to identify solutions to praedial larceny—The University of the West Indies to lead.

CONCLUSION

Praedial larceny is indeed a very complex and serious social problem affecting the agricultural sector globally and impacting food security of many vulnerable developing countries. Historically, the problem of praedial larceny was not given the attention it deserved, but as the global problem of food availability and food security comes to the fore, attention is inevitable. The plight of farmers throughout the region are increasingly gaining traction and concerted efforts are being made to mitigate the prevalence of this serious crime through the implementation of various programs.

In developing countries, food producers are generally embattled with the impact of the changing climatic conditions such as intense rainfall and drought, frequent pests, and disease outbreaks, little or no support from the government, trade barriers, and unfair regulations. Many farmers encounter great difficulties in making ends meet and rarely even generate enough profits to reinvest into their agricultural enterprise. Praedial larceny further compounds existing production constraints farmers may face causing them to become further impoverished and unable to feed their families. Managing this menace is paramount to advancing a productive and vibrant agricultural sector. Farmers can reduce the impact of praedial larceny by reducing opportunities for the crime, but actions at the higher level can be more effective. This chapter reviewed this now organized criminal activity from an anthropological, cultural, and historical perspective, with a specific focus on the characterization of this opportunistic crime. Finally, mechanisms and suggestions are presented to reduce this social problem are explored.

REFERENCES

Agozino, B. (2017). Critical perspectives on deviance and social control in rural Africa. *African Journal of Criminology and Justice Studies, 10*(1), 1-21.

Brereton, B. (2010). The historical background to the culture of violence in Trinidad and Tobago. *Caribbean Review of Gender Studies: A Journal of Caribbean Perspectives on Gender and Feminism, 4*, 1–16.

Bryan, P. E. (2000). *The Jamaican People 1880–1902, race, class and social control*. Kingston 7, Jamaica: The University of the West Indies Press.

CARICOM. (2011). Food security in Caricom. Caricom view. Retrieved from http://www.caricom.org/jsp/communications/caricom_online_pubs/caricom_view_jul_2011.pdf

Craig, P. H. (2011). Protecting you farm from theft. Penn State Extension, Cumberland County. Retrieved from http://extension.psu.edu/cumberland/news/2011/protecting-your-farm-from-theft.

Donnermeyer, J., Scott, J., & Barclay, E. (2013). How rural criminology informs critical thinking. *International Journal for Crime, Justice and Social Democracy, 2*(3), 69–91.

Donnermeyer, J. F., & Barclay E. M. (2005). The policing of farm crime. *Police Practice and Justice Research, 6*, 3–17.

Felson, M. (2002). *Crime and everyday life* (3rd ed.). London: Sage.

Food and Agriculture Organization. (2013). Praedial larceny in the Caribbean. Issue Brief #3, July 2013.

Ganpat, G., & Isaac, W. (2019). Facing boldly the scourge of praedial larceny on food production in the Caribbean. *Journal of International Agricultural and Extension Education, 24*(4), 52–62.

Isaac, W. P., Joseph, M., Ganpat, W., Wilson, M., & Brathwaite, R. (2012). The Caribbean's Windward Islands banana industry: A heritage of dependency. *The Journal of Rural and Community Development*, 7(2), 98-117.

Isaac, W. P., Ganpat, W., & Joseph, M. (2017). Farm security for food security: Dealing with farm theft in the Caribbean Region. In W. Ganpat, R. Dyer & W.-A. P. Isaac (Eds.), *Agricultural development and food security in developing nations* (pp. 300–319). Pennsylvania, USA: IGI Publications.

Jones, J. (2008). Farm crime on Anglesey: Local partner's and organisations. Views on the Issue, second report, January 2008. http://www.aber.ac.uk/en/media/jane-jones---second-report.pdf

King, B. (2003). In B. King & V. S. Naipaul (Eds.), *Miguel street, the mystic masseur* and *the suffrage of Elvira* (pp. 23–40). London: Palgrave Macmillan.

Little, D. (2011). Praedial larceny: Its consequences for Caribbean agriculture. Caricom View. http://www.caricom.org/jsp/communications/caricom_online_pubs/caricom_view_jul_2011.pdf.

Smith, R. (2010). Policing the changing landscape of rural crime: A case study from Scotland. *International Journal of Police Science & Management*, 12(3), 18–30.

Smith, R., Laing, A., & Mcelwee, G. (2013). The rise of illicit rural enterprise within the farming industry. *International Journal of Agricultural Management*, 2(4), 185–188.

Smith, R., & McElwee, G. (2013). Confronting social constructions of rural criminality: A case story on "Illegal Pluriactivity" in the farming community. *Sociologia Ruralis*, 53(1), 112–134.

Spore Magazine. (2009). Theft: Tactics for battling crime. Publication of the Technical Centre for Agricultural Land Rural Cooperation (CTA), 129, 10–11. http://spore.cta.int/images/stories/pdf/SE139-web.pdf.

Sugden, G. (1999). Farm crime: Out of sight, out of mind: a study of crime on farms in the county of Rutland, England. *Crime Prevention and Community Safety: An International Journal*, 1, 29–36.

Swanson, C. R., Chamelin, N. C., & Territo, L. (2000). *Criminal investigation*. Boston: McGraw Hill.

Wilkinson, M., Craig, G., & Gaus, A. (2010). *Forced labour in the UK and Gangmaster licensing authority, Report for the Contemporary Research Centre.* University of Hull.

Wilson, W. J. (1987). *The truly disadvantaged: The inner city,* The Under-class, and Public Policy. Chicago: University of Chicago Press.

Winer, L. (2009). *Dictionary of the English/Creole of Trinidad and Tobago.* Montreal: McGill Queen's University Press.

Yarwood, R., & Gardener, G. (2005). Fear of crime, cultural threat and the countryside. *Area,* 32(4), 403–411.

CHAPTER VI

EXAMINING MIGRATORY SEX WORKERS IN BELIZE: CHALLENGING STIGMAS AND STEREOTYPES

Avekadavie Parasramsingh Mano

The University of the West Indies, St. Augustine, Trinidad & Tobago

ABSTRACT

Globally, though the sex trade has been one of the most discussed topics in academia, it remains one of the most enigmatic. This chapter examines the impact of stereotypes and stigmas on sex workers (SW) in Belize and the need for changes in societal perceptions. The current research effort adopts a micro-level approach based on field research and the use of relevant examples to analyze and understand the lived experiences of migratory SW in Belize. Results from detailed, semi-structured interviews with several key informants (N=34) indicate that the coercive and forceful practices associated with the sex trade in other parts of the world are absent within the Belizean context. The structured interviews revealed that sex work in Belize is highly profitable and its continuance assured; however, it was emphasized that sex worker discrimination is prevalent and exacerbated since those who migrate illegally to Belize for sex work have very little access to social, economic, and legal protections. The study also found that the Belizean sex trade is widely characterized by migratory SW and is markedly different from the dominant trafficking discourse. Other key findings are that: (1) SW voluntarily migrate into Belize's sex industry primarily from other parts of Central America, (2) stigmatization affects legal, social, and cultural attitudes toward SW and encourages a reality where they are perceived as victims, in need of rescuing or as having the "pretty woman" syndrome, and (3) stereotypes surrounding sex work heighten the difficulties faced by

SW and include notions of labor, pursuing alternatives to sex work and the debate between victimization and the "happy hooker." This chapter demonstrates support for the decriminalization of sex work and implementation of rights and labor protections for SW in Belize.

Keywords: Migratory sex workers, stigmatization, stereotypes, decriminalization, Belize

INTRODUCTION

Belize's sex industry, despite being an integral component of the country's social, cultural, and economic environment, remains widely misunderstood. This chapter focuses on an issue that has unfortunately received insufficient attention among researchers, namely: migratory sex workers (SW) in Belize. It looks at the stigmas and stereotypes associated with the sex trade focusing on SW and contradictions within the research literature. Discussions are based on findings from independent research conducted in Belize over a ten-month period. The overall aim was to examine participants' perceptions of migratory sex work and to present criminal justice policy recommendations to address the emergent issues (Mano, 2018). Interviews were held with those directly involved in the sex trade as well as those locally identified as knowledgeable or experienced with the Belizean sex industry. These persons included SW, bar owners (BO) (often locally referred to as traffickers), clients, and both governmental and nongovernmental officials.

According to Goffman (1963), a stigma is an attribute, behavior, or reputation that is socially discrediting in a particular way. It causes an individual to be mentally classified by others in an undesirable, rejected stereotype rather than in an accepted, normal one. The literature identifies several components of stigma such as labeling, discrimination, separation, status loss, and stereotyping (see Link & Phelan, 2001; Green, Davis, Karshmer, Marsh, & Straight, 2005; Murray, Crowe, & Overstreet, 2018).

Stereotypes are pre-conceived, oversimplified ideas of a particular type of person. Unlike stigmas, which are entirely negative, stereotypes can be negative, positive, or even neutral. According to Green et al. (2005,

p. 198), this involves the "assignment of negative attributes to socially salient differences. Stereotypical differences are differences that matter and are also deemed by others to be undesirable." The insights provided by the study's participants allow for a discussion on the impact of stigmas and stereotypes such as the "pretty woman syndrome," "the happy hooker," and "the powerless victim." It also discusses how such discrimination needs to be challenged, because it negatively affects the rights and well-being of the women involved within the Belizean sex industry.

Historically, within the Caribbean region, there exists a culture of migration whereby people have been prepared to migrate whenever and wherever better economic opportunities arose. Within this general context, and especially in those countries experiencing high poverty rates, many persons have actively sought out migratory opportunities. These migratory patterns are heavily influenced by socioeconomic inequalities, tourism, and human trafficking (Kempadoo & Doezema, 1998). In particular, Caribbean women face a growing familial responsibility because of their increasing economic role. This has been referred to as the feminization of migration (Guinn & Steglich, 2003). In Belize, among the many women and girls who voluntarily migrate to work in the nation's sex industry, most often originate from other parts of Central America, notably Guatemala, El Salvador, and Honduras.

An understanding of the evolution of the Caribbean sex trade is important since there exists a strong adherence to policies and practices that are both outdated and impractical. The sex trade, like many other societal issues, has evolved creating a need for research that explores this evolution. Changes ought to reflect policies and initiatives that will be both pertinent and effective in addressing the Caribbean region's current reality. Another emergent concern is the decriminalization of sex work. Research has shown that SW are discriminated against access to goods and services, accommodation, employment, and legal protections (see Banach & Metzenrath, 1999; Overs & Loff, 2013). This chapter argues for the decriminalization of sex work in Belize and the provision of legal rights and protections for SW akin to those legislated in New Zealand.

REVIEW OF THE LITERATURE

According to Abel (2014), much of the current discourse on the sex industry uses the terms "trafficking" and "prostitution" interchangeably leading to the perception of SW as being powerless victims who lack rational decision-making autonomy. In Belize, as in many other countries, there have been policies implemented in support of global governance, state policing, exclusionary immigration policies, and border control. The result is that the legislation intended to address issues stemming from the sex trade only served to target migrants and positioned them in situations that were even more precarious (Kempadoo, 2005). Such policies do not address the root causes of the problem, but offer temporary, ineffective alternatives. Such an account adequately reflects Belize's current system.

As noted earlier, the Caribbean region has a culture of migration. Rates of migration increased after emancipation with people migrating in search of an improved quality of life and this trend has continued. In actuality, migratory SW comprise a minority of trafficking cases (Mai, 2013) and are an integral component of the commercial sex industry worldwide. Migrants enter the sex trade for varying reasons; some intend to work as commercial SW while others may turn to sex work as a response to their perceived lack of alternative opportunities coupled with their familial and financial responsibilities. There are also some migratory SW who engage in sex work because of debt bondage. Unfortunate socioeconomic conditions increase migrants' vulnerability to exploitation and coercion mechanisms that can closely resemble, or become human trafficking (Mano, 2018).

Raymond et al. (2002) identified several push and pull factors that promote female migration. They claimed that it is therefore not only poverty that forces women to migrate in search of better opportunities but a "whole complex of natural, economic, social and political circumstances" (Raymond et al., 2002, p. 12). Demir and Finckenauer (2010, p. 60) added that poverty and unemployment compel women to leave their countries in search of a better life, since "when push factors are very strong, young women are ready to accept any job irrespective of the risks involved" (Demir & Finckenauer, 2010, p. 80). Many migrants "described problems in their homelands, such as economic hardships, unemployment, domestic problems in their families and terrible marriages" (Demir & Finckenauer, 2010. p. 69).

The majority of female SW, whether forced or through their own volition, often found it difficult to reintegrate into society (Brunovskis & Tyldum, 2004). A woman who left in an attempt to improve the quality of life for herself and family may find that the economic realities she had attempted to escape from did not change. According to Sanders (2007), "sex workers suffer terribly from the sexual stigma wrongly attributed to their behaviour, leaving them open to a multitude of deviant labels relating to their sexuality, morality, femininity, and criminality" (p. 91). For many involved in the sex trade, stigmas effectively depersonalize them, "labelling, violence and discrimination were, to them, normal and expected conditions. Therefore, the women were living with stigma as part of their day-to-day lives" (Sallmann, 2010, p. 150).

Miller and Schwartz (1995) explored various rape myths that contribute toward the violence experienced by many SW, including "social beliefs that prostitutes are unrapeable, no harm is done when raping a prostitute, prostitutes deserve the violence and prostitutes are all the same" (p. 1). Despite the apparent illogical nature of these statements, Sallmann (2010) stated that the life stories she collected revealed there was indeed a social acceptance of these myths. This acceptance effectively served in "perpetuating the invisibility and normalization of harm against participants" (Sallmann, 2010, p. 151) whose "experiences of violence were minimized, dismissed, and/or normalized by both informal and institutional support systems" (Sallmann, 2010, p. 152).

Karandikar and Gezinski (2012) explored the issues of stigmas and stereotypes through the theme of male validation and rationalization of sex work as a profession. Some clients respected SW rights to control their own bodies; while other clients' were prejudiced against them. Some men perpetrated violence against SW and tended to blame the women by claiming they (the women) deserved it (Karandikar & Gezinski, 2012). They added that clients generally believed that SW remained in their positions because of poverty, and emphasized the importance of legalizing sex work, not to protect SW, but instead to protect the virtue of women from "good" families and to satiate male sexual desires (p. 364). According to Karandikar and Gezinski (2012), SW are considered to be tainted and immoral, "they don't have a good family, their mothers sell them ... they are soiled. They can't go back. This is their life. Men use women like machines. They use the women to make money ... women are objects of desire and pleasure" (p. 364).

Among those SW who sought assistance from the criminal justice system, many were not supported but were "revictimized through discriminatory and victim-blaming responses" (Sallmann, 2010, p. 152). Such institutionalized discrimination involves victim-blaming responses based on stigmas and negative stereotypes (Blume, 1991) such as the "whore stigma" (Pheterson, 1996, p. 39). According to Sallmann (2010), the implicit acceptance of violence and discrimination by several participants revealed a "consciousness of their social rejection and disempowerment" (p. 153). She concluded that these women "are targets of a societal belief that women who engage in prostitution and substance use deserved to be raped or otherwise harmed because they have placed themselves at risk for such abuses by the very nature of their behaviour" (Sallmann, 2010, p. 153).

Sallmann (2010) added that the stigma associated with SW impact their "self-perceptions, the ways in which they saw others as viewing them, and how they interacted in the world" (p. 154). For some women, being a prostitute was a permanent status and continuously affected their lives even after they stopped. Karandikar and Gezinski (2012) also looked at how clients perceive their role within the sex trade, "[I]f there is no rain in the village we can't till the land. For these girls we are like rain. Without us sex workers will die like weeds ... It is a job for them and we are paying" (p. 364). In exploring sex work in Kamathipura, Mumbai, Karandikar and Gezinski (2012) described a reality where, "if you are soiled once then you are soiled forever" (p. 361), effectively describing the sex trade as a cycle that is near impossible to break free.

While there are SW who have negative self-perceptions, there are those who do not self-depreciate. Sallmann (2010) stated that the latter "took full responsibility for their actions; however, they also recognized the social double standards against which they were judged and ultimately found deficient," such a "resistance involves rejection of the dichotomies that are considered between 'prostitute' and 'others' in the dominant culture" (p. 155). There is the belief that "other" women also trade sex for material items, the housewife for instance, trades sexual favors but her conventional role as "wife" makes it socially acceptable. There is the recognition that although men purchase sex, their behavior is socially acceptable. These women resist "their differential status as stigmatized women.

Furthermore, they ... assert their own human rights and refuse to believe that they are 'less than' others" (Sallmann, 2010, p. 155). Despite this recognition, stigmas and negative stereotypes regarding sex work continue to significantly affect the overall well-being of the women involved.

METHODOLOGY

This study's methodology was developed within a constructivist framework. This framework encompasses the belief that in order to attain knowledge; it is imperative to examine the ways knowledgeable participants describe their own realities. Gubrium and Holstein (2008) significantly contributed to the constructivist literature describing knowledge as "plural and fallible, and conversations and social interactions are the ultimate contexts in which knowledge is produced and understood" (p. 432). This study employed an emic-oriented, qualitative approach, which employed detailed semi-structured interviews with participants. This allowed for "focused, conversational, two-way communication" (Fontana & Frey, 1994, p. 14). Hannabuss (1996, p. 14) added that such an approach is "preferable when complex, personal or sensitive issues are being probed." The predominantly clandestine nature of the sex industry and the general lack of secondary data in Belize contributed toward the utilization of such an approach.

In attempting to achieve a holistic understanding into the Belizean sex industry, four distinct yet inter-related groups were examined. Participants included 4 BO (also identified as traffickers), 16 SW, 4 clients, and 10 relevant governmental and nongovernmental officials. Some participants, notably BO and SW, refused to be recorded, given the illicit nature of their activities, this was expected. Instead, detailed notes were taken during the interviews with their consent. In all instances, the interviews were transcribed shortly after they were concluded. A major challenge to researching hard-to-access groups such as SW and BO is that it is nearly impossible to acquire an optimum sample of participants (Wahab & Sloan, 2004). The illegal nature of the activities involved as well as the social stigmas attached to sex work has resulted in the effective use of two nonrandom sampling methods, snowball sampling, and through the use of gatekeepers.

Analysis in qualitative research is the "process a researcher uses to reduce data to a story and its interpretation" (LeCompte & Schensul, 1999).

With this in mind, Attride-Stirling's (2001) Thematic Network Analysis (TNA) was successfully applied to allow the effective organization and analysis of both content and discourse as they emerged from the interview transcripts. This method is also more rigorous than basic thematic analysis since it allows for the emergence of significant themes throughout varying levels within a text while simultaneously providing structure and allowing for interpretation of the data.

THE EXPANSION AND REFINEMENT OF TNA TECHNIQUE

Four global themes were derived, each reflective of one of the four groups examined. This has been the commonly accepted route adapted by researchers employing TNA, since it has until now, been applied to single group, single-site research from which emerged multiple global themes (see Braun & Clarke, 2006; Fereday & Muir-Cochrane, 2006; Goldbart & Marshall, 2014). In looking at previous studies employing TNA, it was found that in 64 studies, 22 used a single group, single-site study, 15 used multiple groups in a single site, 19 had a single group in multiple sites, and only 8 had multiple groups in multiple sites. In all 64 studies, only seven produced multiple global themes. These researchers nonetheless stopped their analysis at this level and discussed their findings for each emergent global theme.

In an attempt to develop a more holistic understanding that would incorporate the perceptions of all the groups interviewed, the original TNA was modified to create a new level of analysis, what is termed here a "supra-global theme" (Mano, 2017). Basically, the four global themes were treated as if they were a second group of organizing themes. The emergence of a new supra-global theme meant that sex trafficking and sex work in Belize could now be understood from the combined points of views of officials, SW, BO, and clients. This constructs a pertinent understanding into the Belizean sex trade and is a useful methodology when devising strategies and policies to address studies involving multiple sites and multiple groups (Mano, 2017).

ROUTINE ACTIVITIES THEORY

Routine activities theory or RAT (Cohen & Felson, 1979) is a subsidiary of rational choice theory. RAT explains that crime is more likely to occur when three essential components of crime converge in space and time, for a crime to occur, there must be a motivated offender, a suitable target, and the absence of capable guardians. The main assumption of RAT is that crime can be committed by anyone who has the opportunity (Figure 1).

Figure 1: Routine Activities Theory and the Sex Trade

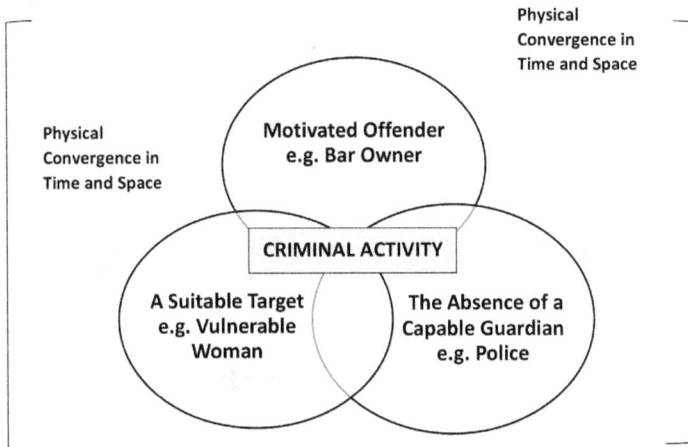

Figure 1: Routine Activities Theory and the Sex Trade

Component of RAT	Description	Example
Motivated Offenders	The motivated offender must have the willingness and ability to commit predatory crime	Bar owners, pimps
Suitable Targets	A suitable target has good value, and are both easily visible and accessible	Vulnerable targets come from situations of poverty, lack of viable economic alternatives, financial dependents, lack of education, physical and/or sexual abuse, drug abuse, homelessness
Absence of Capable Guardians	Guardians could either prevent the occurrence of the crime or serve as potential witnesses to the crime	Police officers, Immigration officials, parents and other family members

Source: Adapted from Cohen and Felson (1979); Williams and McShane (2010).

Figure 2 reveals a level of complexity within the Belizean sex trade. There are no clearly delineated boundaries among the groups, for example, SW are recognized as both motivated offenders (e.g. public nuisance, spreaders of diseases, immoral) and suitable targets (e.g. vulnerable, exploited, in need of rescuing).

Figure 2: Validation of Routine Activities Theory to Belizean Context

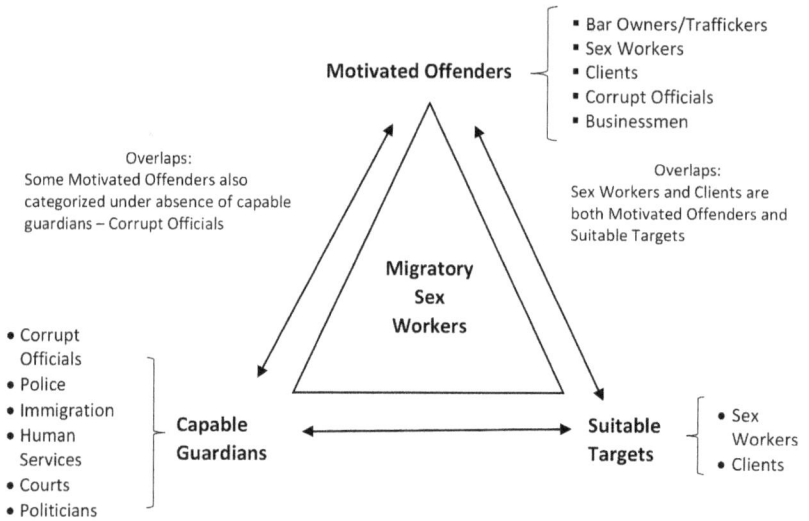

Source: Fieldwork (2014–2015).

RESULTS

Bar Owners (Traffickers)

Although often brought into Belize legally and willingly, many SW live and work under restrictive conditions. BO stereotyped SW as "happy hookers," claiming that many actively pursued sex work since they were primarily concerned with earning fast, easy money because of their familial responsibilities. Described as migratory SW, they were fully aware of the nature of the sex trade. RAT when applied recognizes BO as motivated offenders, they operate with impunity and expressed no guilt or remorse for exploiting SW since they rationalized that their actions were beneficial to those women.

> In Central American countries like in Guatemala, some of the young girls look forward to being prostitutes because they feel that this is one of the business that pays very well. It is about making money real fast (BO2).

> Some just come and pass by and stopping and checking these places, if there is vacancies here, I'm looking for a job and I

*say yes there's a job ... others are brought here and they know
exactly what they are getting into (BO4).*

Additionally, they were not seen as victims since they had been involved
in sex work in their own countries prior to their arrival in Belize, with one
bar owner describing sex workers as being "old beef" in their countries of
origin.

*What we always say when they reach here, you call them
fresh meat but over there they are old beef because the same
thing they do over there. They know exactly what they come
here to do, that's not a maybe, that's definitely (BO1).*

Sex Workers

Interviews with SW provided valuable insight into the Belizean sex trade.
The issue of sex work being immoral often arose, with many women ad-
mitting that their families were unaware of the nature of their employment, while others said that their work was both known and accepted.
One sex worker opined:

*He doesn't mind because it is a job and he knows that I love
him, I have many friends, but I have sex with my boyfriend,
he works in construction. The other people, that is work
(SW5).*

Another sex worker proffered the following view:

*My husband doesn't know I am here, he would kill me. It is
a good thing he is back in Guatemala. He is happy for the
money, be he cannot know ... I tell them I work in a resort
with a lot of Americans ... I earn good money, my children
can live good with the money I send for them because my
husband, he does not earn much (SW1).*

Importantly, although these SW saw themselves as gainfully employed,
and often the sole financial providers for their families, they expressed a
desire for change. For another interviewed sex worker, her narrative was:

*I am working here for now but if something else, something
better comes up I will take it up ... I stay because I want to
earn money. Other girls will tell you that they don't go with*

men .... the men pay more money for sex so it is easier to just have sex with them, it does not mean anything, it's work (SW3).

SW face economic hardships, a lack of viable alternatives and familial responsibilities, which makes them suitable targets (RAT) with the "whore" stigma being a significant factor in their continuance of sex work.

Clients

Despite an apparent recognition of the vulnerability of SW, clients rationalized that it was acceptable to procure sexual services. Client (C) motivation increased through an accepted rationalization that SW were in need of financial relief. Considering RAT, such motivated offenders fuel the demand for paid sex. The following narratives emanated from interviews with two clients:

They want the money and the guys want a good time, it's a win-win (C2).

They have a tough life and they come here because they want a better life, sometimes you have to do what you have to do ... they need the work ... in Guatemala or Honduras, how much can a man really pay? They earn little here but it is much more than over there (C3).

Officials (Governmental and Nongovernmental)

Officials (O) presented a dichotomy where, on the one hand, SW were rational decision makers while on the other hand, they were trafficking victims. In the middle of this dichotomy are the women who voluntarily enter the sex trade but are exploited. Officials stated that these women come mainly from other parts of Central America seeking to escape situations of extreme poverty, lack of opportunities, and abusive homes. SW, described as vulnerable, easily manipulated, and exploited, become "suitable targets" for motivated offenders. According to one official:

I remember one person told me ... regardless of the situation that I am having here, it is much better than where I came from (O2).

Another official cogitated:

> *Clearly, people are being trafficked because of the issues of eco-*
> *nomics that they are often recruited. Its classic what we find*
> *with our victims. When we do interview the story, is the classic*
> *story of the human trafficking victim where they're recruited,*
> *they're promised certain things that do not turn out to be true*
> *... coming from mostly Central American countries (O3).*

DISCUSSION

This study has shown that the coercive and forceful practices associated
with sex trafficking in other parts of the world are nearly absent in the Belizean context as most SW voluntarily migrate to Belize from other parts
of Central America. The issue of stigma was an emergent issue throughout this research. Existing policies focus on SW as being victims of sex
trafficking. Issues surrounding their agency and willingness to engage in
the sex trade due to familial responsibilities and lack of viable alternatives
continue to be inadequately addressed by policymakers. Additionally, the
many stereotypes which exist hinders SW who want to leave the industry,
being labeled as "immoral" and "loose," they are left with relatively little
alternative but to continue in the sex trade.

The stigmatization, discrimination, and criminalization that are often
faced by migrant SW in Belize (see Figure 3) leads to substantial hin-
drances in accessing basic prevention, treatment, and care services. They
are often faced with judgmental treatment and breaches of confidentiality.
Within the sex trade, SW are often stigmatized and labeled as a public nuisance, spreaders of disease, indecent, victims, and home wreckers. This
makes it very difficult for these women to develop healthy relationships
and makes leaving sex work more challenging. The thematic network in
Figure 4 illustrates the societal perceptions of the Belizean sex trade that
significantly affect SW' lives. Sex worker stigmatization and stereotypes
have significant impact and should be given adequate attention in the development of pertinent responses.

The "Whore" Stigma

The majority of SW claimed that their families and friends in their home
countries unaware regarding the kind of work they did in Belize because

Figure 3: The Impact of Stigmas and Stereotypes on the Sex Work Cycle

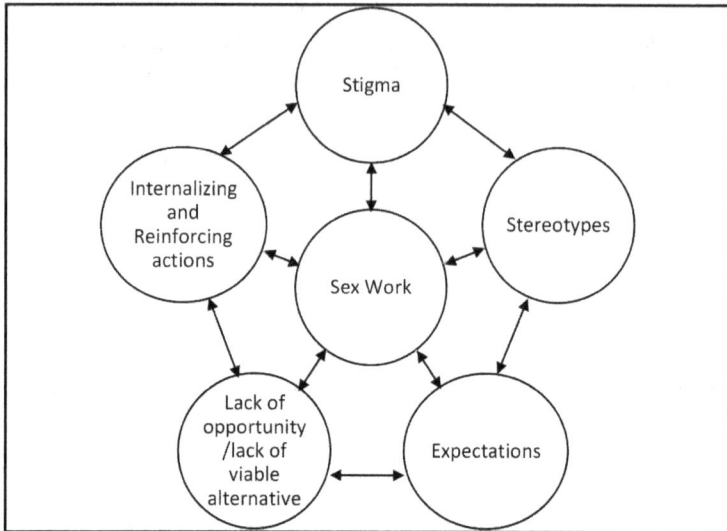

Source: Fieldwork (2014–2015).

of the stigma attached to such women. Since SW, themselves come from such societies, it was assumed that they shared similar outlooks. The perceptions of these women were contrary to the views of BO who indicated that quick exits were not the norm with sex worker. Due to the stigma from being labeled as "non-respectable" and "immoral," it is often difficult to leave sex work behind despite a desire to do so. There were women who openly accepted their realities by rationalizing that sex work is just like any other type of work. These women perceived sex work as their best alternative with one interviewee openly stating, *"I don't want to stop ... I just started and I am making money, when I have more friends coming to see me I will earn more" (SW 13).*

The women interviewed also discussed the attitudes of their family members toward sex work. On the one hand, some stated that their significant other and family members had no problem with them working in the sex industry because they are able to help their families financially. On the other hand, it was stated that family members would not allow it [sex work] because of the stigma or shame attached to it. In the latter case, sex work is considered taboo with women being labeled such as "loose" or "whores." For one sex worker, her narrative was as follows:

Figure 4: Thematic Network with Supra-Global Theme

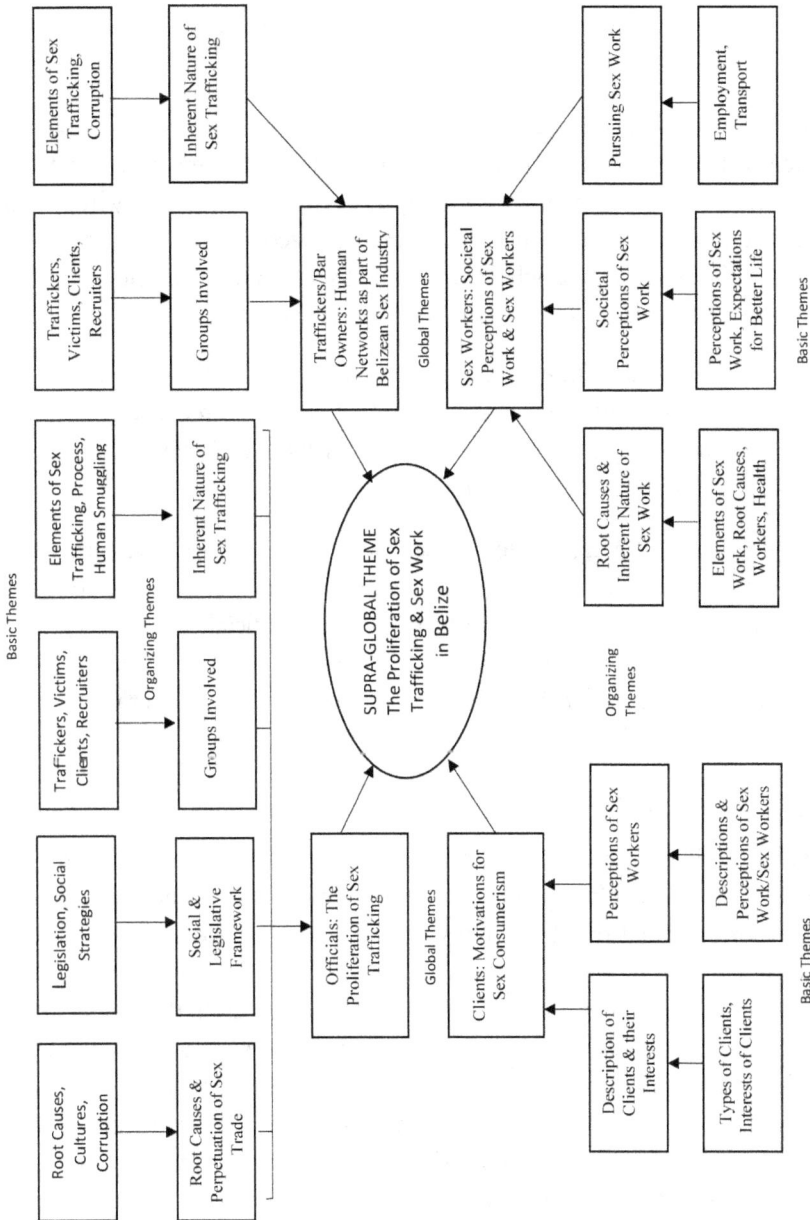

Source: Fieldwork (2014–2015).

> *My mother doesn't know, if she knew that I was working in a bar she would not take care of my children but so far she hasn't asked what I do, all she knows is that I am working and sending money. She would say I am a loose woman (SW12).*

Even if it is assumed that their families and friends know what work they do, they don't openly admit it. The main concern is the remittances they receive from them, not how it is earned. These women stated that sex work was temporary work, essentially a means to an end. Many hoped to save enough money to return to school or to become legitimate entrepreneurs. There was an overwhelming desire to return to the mundane world of work. For another sex worker, her narrative was

> *Sometimes I think about leaving here for any better job, it doesn't matter what kind of job, anything. I would like to go back to my family in Honduras and continue studying and get my education (SW8).*

However, this leaving Belize and sex work is not always possible as the "whore stigma" is a reality and its presence is continuous, more-so if the women want to leave the sex industry. BO and officials both agreed that women who enter the sex trade remain there for many years because they can no longer assimilate into ordinary life and that they adapt to the labels society places on them.

"Happy Hooker" and the "Pretty Woman" Syndromes

BO interviewed shared the common perception that they were helping SW to provide a better quality of life for themselves and their dependents. They often stated that the money these women earned in Belize far exceeded what they would have earned in their countries of origin. Importantly, traffickers further justified their actions by stating that the women had been previously involved in sex work in their own countries; one trafficker animatedly described SW as being "old meat" in their own countries but became "new beef" when they arrived in Belize. These women were perceived as "happy hookers" in the sense that they were earning far more for comparably "easy" work. This directly contradicts what the vast majority of the interviewed SW claimed. They were not "happy hookers" but were engaged in commercial sex work because of a lack of alternatives that could adequately support them, sex worker 1 stated:

*This is work, just like any other kind of work. I like it and I
don't like it, some days it is good and some days it is not so
good, it is work so it is something I have to do (SW1).*

The sex worker's worth is measured based on her physical characteristics
with the younger and more visually appealing women being able to earn
more money. SW reinforced their commoditization through significant,
continuous, and often ill-afforded investments in their appearances.

Clients shared similar beliefs to BO since they believed they were helping
these women financially. Such stigmatization further exacerbates the lack
of response to addressing the needs of SW while simultaneously increasing and somewhat, validating the demand for their services. Although the
vast majority of clients approached declined to be interviewed, the few
who did tended to similarly stereotype these women as "happy hookers."
According to clients, SW' intentions primarily involve payment for sexual
services, and so they are happy to work because more work means more
income. Although their reality is one based on financial responsibility and
a lack of opportunity, they remain "happy hookers" contented with their
high earnings in exchange for relatively "easy work." The "pretty woman
syndrome" reflects a bright, sunny side to the sex trade whereby SW, like
Julia Roberts' portrayal of Vivian in the 1980 film *Pretty Woman*, can mar-
ry a client and live a secured and respectable life. A believer in such possibilities, one client described his neighbor, a former sex worker and now
married to a Belizean man, as having a position of a "decent, respectable
woman." Interestingly, the SW interviewed displayed more independent
personalities preferring to leave on their own terms.

Powerless Victims

Officials generally perceived SW as powerless victims who were deceived
and coerced into the commercial sex industry and were in need of rescuing. An understanding of the lines between migratory sex work and sex
trafficking were, in most instances, blurred. Belize appears to have a problem of human trafficking based on various reports, the recent Trafficking in Persons report (2018, p. 98) stated that "sex trafficking of Belizean
and foreign women and girls ... occurs in bars, nightclubs, and brothels
... [they] migrate voluntarily to Belize in search of work and are often exploited by traffickers." This study reflects a different reality. These women
are not powerless victims, but rational decision makers who chose to en-

gage in sex work after weighing their financial needs and responsibilities and the availability and feasibility of alternatives.

Officials also stereotyped SW in Belize as being not simply impoverished, but as having a lack of education or labor conducive skills. Interviews with SW revealed that they possessed varying levels of education and training, some finished secondary school, while others had skills such as sewing, cooking, and child rearing. One sex worker, in particular, said that in Guatemala, she was a teacher, but she had left that "respectable" work because it could not financially provide for her family. Instead, she became a sex worker. According to this study's participant:

> I use to teach primary school, but the pay is too low. I found out about this work from a friend on Facebook, this friend she works in another bar and she is married to a Belizean. I wanted to update my lifestyle so I came for the money, back home as a teacher $1500 quetzal and here I make that in two weeks (SW19).

SW often claimed that they have a lack of alternatives, but this is not accurate. There are sometimes other opportunities that do exist, but these do not provide the economic relief that desired. The difference in the value of their currency, the quetzal (the local Guatemalan currency), for example, has a value of 1 USD to 7.50 GTQ, while the Belizean dollar has an average current rate of 1 USD to 1.9 BZD, means that many women choose sex work in Belize since they earn significantly more than they would have in their own countries not only because of the currency exchange rates but also the amount work as "new beef."

Stereotypes and stigmas have an active role in how SW are treated and their personal sense of self-worth. Instead of helping these women, these societal labels degrade them, restrict their potential and initiative, and damage their ability to adapt to a world outside of the commercial sex trade. The emergent supra-global theme, "the proliferation of sex trafficking and sex work in Belize" is reflective of a reality where the stigmatization and stereotyping of SW play a significant role in the well-being of SW and the overall proliferation of the sex trade. SW are faced with a multiplicity of labels—from whore to happy hookers and powerless victims in need of rescuing. This makes it increasingly difficult to leave the sex industry, thus ensuring that the supply side of the sex trade market is maintained.

Challenging Stigmas and Stereotypes

There are studies that focus on the stigmatization associated with sex work and SW (see Benoit, Jansson, Smith, & Flagg, 2018; Comte, 2010). However, there are but a few that examine these issues from the perspectives of SW themselves (Wong, Holroyd, & Bingham, 2011), and even less that focus on the perceptions of pimps, clients, and relevant officials as well as SW. The consequences of stigmatization and negative stereotypes faced by SW are far-reaching, affecting quality of life, access to social services, employment, and income (see Benoit, Jansson, Jansenberger, & Phillips, 2013; Link & Phelan, 2001). Links have also been established with physical and mental problems (see Green et al., 2005) and little accessibility to healthcare (see Link & Phelan, 2001; Pescosolido, Martin, Lang, & Olafsdottir, 2008; Stuber, Meyer, & Link, 2008). Hatzenbuehler, Phelan, and Link (2013, p. 814) noted that "[T]the accumulated literature makes a compelling case that stigma represents an added burden that affects people above and beyond any impairments or deficits they may have." Despite the apparent immutability of these social perceptions, there have been claims that challenges against stigmatization can be made through collective action by SW and their supporters, geared at influencing policies at the political, social, or legal levels (Parent, Bruckert, Corriveau, Mensah, & Toupin, 2013).

One example where sex worker stigma was successfully challenged was through New Zealand's implementation of the Prostitution Reform Act (PRA) in 2003 during which SW were included within the process of shifting from criminalization to decriminalization. As a direct consequence, SW reported feeling more protected by workplace health and safety regulations as well as a decrease in stigmatization. SW are able to:

1. access the criminal justice system if they are victims of crime;

2. have customers within the privacy of their own secured establishments;

3. be empowered to insist on condom use; and

4. refer to labor laws to negotiate working conditions.

Overall, as Mensah and Bruckert (2012, p. 9) point out, "decriminalizing sex work ... ensure sex workers are respected and have access to the same rights and protections as every other citizen." Another example that illustrates how sex work stigmas and stereotypes are being challenged is the Sonagachi Project in Kolkata, India, which prioritizes the mobilization of community participation. Sonagachi is India's largest red light district. The destigmatizing of SW aims at recognizing SW as respectable people who can bring about positive and effective change. The Sonagachi Project has focused its efforts on emphasizing the rights of SW, through claiming equivalence with other groups and via evidence of the successes of SW. Such successes include SW who were trained and now able to secure the release of a woman who has been arrested in a police raid, or can get the police to investigate cases of violence or abuse of SW. Committees of SW have been set up to resolve disputes and conflicts, and they can advocate on a sex worker's behalf in a dispute with a madam or landlady (see Ghosh, 2006; Nag, 2005).

This does not mean that the decriminalization of sex work has been fully supported. Some SW and advocates believe that decriminalizing the sex trade will not protect its workers from abuse (Vanwesenbeeck, 2017). Since SW have been subjected to profound and sustained exclusion and discrimination so, then, how can such a group not only challenge stigmatization but also develop positive understandings of their status? Looking at the New Zealand situation again, despite the noted benefits of decriminalization, there are also some failures within the system. Police powers, for example, have been reduced since they are unable to enter brothels despite having intelligence of illegal activities occurring as they would be accused of harassment by brothel owners (Bindel, 2017, as cited in Parmanand, 2018).

Decriminalization: A Direct Response to the Stigmatization and Negative Stereotyping of SW in Belize

The World Health Organization (WHO) defines prostitution as "a dynamic and adaptive process that involved a transaction between seller and buyer of a sexual service" and has openly recommended its decriminalization (Farley, 2004, p. 1089). Decriminalization has been advocated by the United Nations, the World Health Organization, Amnesty International, and peer-led sex worker organizations worldwide (Mano, 2018). It is recommended that Belize regulate its already rampant sex industry through the decriminalization of sex work. According to Albright and D'Adamo (2017, p. 122):

research shows that it is criminalization that creates condi-
tions of impunity and enhances sex workers' vulnerabilities
to violence and exploitation, including trafficking ... decrim-
inalization can also destigmatized sex work and help resist
political, social and cultural marginalization of sex workers.

It is submitted that the decriminalization of sex work in Belize would ensure that SW are legally protected from abuse, be paid fairly under the
labor laws, and work under satisfactory conditions. All four groups interviewed drew references to the various stigmas inherent in sex work.
SW saw themselves as tainted, and sex work as undesirable but also as the
best available financial alternative. Their low opinions of themselves are
reflected in their inability to maintain healthy personal relationships or to
make significant attempts to leave the sex trade despite having the desire
to do so. As a result, they remain working in conditions of exploitation
and sometimes, debt bondage with little or no access to health, social, or
legal aid.

While not referring directly to Belize, Abel (2014) effectively described
the nation's reality when she stated that the terms "sex work" or "prostitution" in most countries have been used synonymously with that of "trafficking" despite evidence suggesting that the issue of trafficking has been
greatly exaggerated. It is because of the perpetuation of such trafficking
discourse that SW are classified as victims, incapable of making the rational decision to enter the sex industry. Decriminalization is perceived
as a harm reduction strategy, "human rights are essential to health and
well-being, and decriminalization gives sex workers autonomy and the
capacity to protect themselves" (Abel, 2014, p. 583). Being migrant SW
in Belize and in a somewhat ambiguous situation, these women are vulnerable to arrest and deportation and have little recourse to justice. The
stigmatization these women face is not only enacted by others, but also
internalized by the SW themselves.

Advocates of the decriminalization of prostitution agree that "the primary harm of prostitution is social stigma against prostitution. Those on all
sides of the debate agree that women in prostitution are stigmatized. Socially invisible as full human beings, those in prostitution often internalize
toxic public and private contempt directed against them" (Farley, 2004, p.
1,092). Supporters of decriminalization believe that it will effectively remove the social prejudice against women involved in prostitution.

Authors such as Farley (2004) have noted that, "the shame of those in prostitution remains after legalization or decriminalization" (p. 1092). Bindel (2017) as cited in Parmanand (2018) also agrees and points to an interview with a sex worker in New Zealand, "I asked her if her situation had improved since decriminalization, and she told me no, because in her experience, the men who buy her feel entitled to do exactly what they want" (n.p.). It therefore cannot be claimed that the decriminalization of sex work will solve all the problems inherent within the sex trade, but it does have the potential to improve the overall quality of life for SW. Mensah and Bruckert (2012) discussed why the criminalization of sex work has failed to protect SW against discrimination, specifically identifying the following issues

1. The very existence of "prostitution" laws which reinforce the position that SW are different from "normal" citizens so discrimination against SW appears justified

2. Within a system that criminalizes sex work, the identity of the people who work in the sex industry is confused with the work they do. All other aspects of these individuals are negated and their behaviors and relationships are evaluated through the activity of sex work alone. This is stigmatization.

3. The idea that SW are powerless victims in need of salvation is often used to justify criminalization. This delegitimizes and silences SW while simultaneously renders their agency invisible.

CONCLUSION

SW are a highly vulnerable group characterized by a lack of feasible alternatives, familial responsibilities, poverty, and societal perceptions in the form of stigmas and stereotypes (Mano, 2018). These issues not only compel women to voluntary enter the sex industry, but significantly deters them from leaving, and as a consequence assures the continuing stability of the Belizean sex industry. A long-term approach is necessary, although it may be difficult for policymakers to agree to such change, this will have a more positive effect since the focus would now be shifted from unsuccessful "rescue missions." The reality remains that there is a continuous supply of available women to satisfy an increasing demand for commercial sex, and given the myriad of seemingly insurmountable factors which lend support to the perpetuation of the trade such as the involvement corrupt officials, migration practices, the vulnerability of the women, and sex tourism, it can be said with some certainty that the Belizean sex trade will escalate over time. Protecting SW against exploitation through decriminalizing sex work is therefore the most logical decision for policymakers.

It is recommended that Belize adapt to an approach that resembles the New Zealand model. It should encompass the main ideas of the model but simultaneously be guided by the country's specific realities. The decriminalization of sex work in Belize ought to safeguard the human rights of SW and protect them from exploitation, address their welfare and occupational health issues. It should also be conductive to public health access, prohibits the involvement of minors and informs the implementation of related policy reforms. The decriminalization of sex work is thus the most logical long-term solution geared at effectively protecting the rights and welfare of SW.

REFERENCES

Abel, G. M. (2014). A decade of decriminalization: Sex work "down under" but not underground. *Criminology and Criminal Justice, 14*(5), 580–592.

Albright, E., & D'Adamo, K. (2017). Decreasing human trafficking through sex work decriminalization. *AMA Journal of Ethics, 19*(1), 122.

Attride-Stirling, J. (2001). Thematic networks: An analytic tool for qualitative research. *Qualitative Research, 1*(3), 385–405.

Banach, L. M., & Metzenrath, S. (1999). *Unjust and counter-productive: The failure of governments to protect sex workers from discrimination.* Scarlet Alliance and the Australian Federation of AIDS Organisations.

Benoit, C., Jansson, M., Jansenberger, M., & Phillips, R. (2013). Disability stigmatization as a barrier to employment equity for legally-blind Canadians. *Disability & Society, 28*(7), 970–983.

Benoit, C., Jansson, S. M., Smith, M., & Flagg, J. (2018). Prostitution stigma and its effect on the working conditions, personal lives, and health of sex workers. *The Journal of Sex Research, 55*(4–5), 457–471.

Blume, S. B. (1991). Sexuality and stigma: The alcoholic woman. *Alcohol Research, 15*(2), 139–146.

Braun, V., & Clarke, V. (2006). Using thematic analysis on psychology. *Qualitative Research in Psychology, 3*(2), 77–101.

Brunovskis, A., & Tyldum, G. (2004). *Crossing borders: An empirical study of transnational prostitution and trafficking in human beings.* Norway: Institute for Applied International Studies.

Cohen, L. E., & Felson, M. (1979). Social change and crime rate trends: A routine activities approach. *American Sociological Review, 44*(4), 588–608.

Comte, J. (2010). Stigmatization of sex work and worker identity among female sex workers. *Déviance et Société, 34*(3), 425–446.

Demir, O. O., & Finckenauer, J. O. (2010). Victims of sex trafficking in Turkey: Characteristics, motivations, and dynamics. *Women & Criminal Justice, 20*(1–2), 57–88.

Farley, M. (2004). "Bad for the body, bad for the heart": Prostitution harms women even if legalized or decriminalized. *Violence Against Women, 10*(10), 1087–1125.

Fereday, J., & Muir-Cochrane, E. (2006). Demonstrating rigor using thematic network analysis: A hybrid approach of inductive and deductive coding and theme development. *International Journal of Qualitative Methods, 5*(1), 80–92.

Fontana, A., & Frey, J. (1994). Interviewing: The art of science. In N. Denzin (Ed.), *The handbook of qualitative research* (pp. 361–376). Thousand Oaks: Sage Publications.

Ghosh, S. (2006). Empowerment of sex workers: The Kolkata experience. *Economic and Political Weekly 41*(13), 1289–1291.

Goffman, E. (1963). *Stigma: Notes on the management of spoiled identity.* New York: Prentice-Hall.

Goldbart, J., & Marshall, J. (2014). Using thematic network analysis—an example using interview data from parents of children who use AAC. In M. J. Ball, N. Muller & R. Nelson (Eds.), *The handbook of qualitative research in communication disorders* (pp. 297–310). New York, NY: Psychology Press.

Green, S., Davis, C., Karshmer, E., Marsh, P., & Straight, B. (2005). Living stigma: The impact of labeling, stereotyping, separation, status loss, and discrimination in the lives of individuals with disabilities and their families. *Sociological Inquiry, 75*(2), 197–215.

Gubrium, J. F., & Holstein, J. A. (Eds.). (2008). *Handbook of constructionist research.* New York, NY: Guilford Press.

Guinn, D. E., & Steglich, E. (2003). *In modern bondage: Sex trafficking in the Americas, Central America, and the Caribbean.* Herndon, VA: Transnational.

Hannabuss, S. (1996). Research interviews. *New Library World, 97*(5), 22–30.

Hatzenbuehler, M. L., Phelan, J. C., & Link, B. G. (2013). Stigma as a fundamental cause of population health inequalities. *American Journal of Public Health, 103*(5), 813–821.

Karandikar, S., & Gezinski, L. B. (2012). "Without us, sex workers will die like weeds": Sex work and client violence in Kamathipura. *Indian Journal of Gender Studies, 19*(3), 351–371.

Kempadoo, K. (2005). From moral panic to global justice: Changing perspectives on trafficking. In K. Kempadoo, J. Sanghera, & B. Pattanaik (Eds.), *Trafficking and prostitution -reconsidered: New perspectives on migration, sex work, and human rights* (pp.7-34). Boulder, CO: Paradigm.

Kempadoo, K., & Doezema J. (Eds.). (1998). *Global sex workers: Rights, resistance and redefinition.* London, UK: Routledge.

LeCompte, M. D., & Schensul, J. J. (1999). *Designing and conducting ethnographic research.* Walnut Creek, CA: Alta Mira.

Link, B. G., & Phelan, J. C. (2001). Conceptualizing stigma. *Annual Review of Sociology, 27*(1), 363–385.

Mai, N. (2013). Embodied cosmopolitanisms: The subjective mobility of migrants working in the global sex industry. *Gender, Place & Culture, 20*(1), 107–124.

Mano, A. P. (2017). An innovative approach to sex trafficking research: The methodological advancement of Attride-Stirling's thematic network analysis. *International Annals of Criminology, 55*(1), 40–59.

Mano, A. P. (2018). *Hidden in plain sight: Examining the nature of migratory sex work in Belize from multiple perspectives.* (Unpublished doctoral dissertation). The University of the West Indies, St. Augustine, Trinidad and Tobago.

Mensah, M. N., & Bruckert, C. (2012). *Reasons to fight for the decriminalization of sex work.* Social Sciences and Humanities Research Council of Canada. Retrieved from http://maggiestoronto.ca/uploads/File/10reasons.pdf

Miller, J., & Schwartz, M. D. (1995). Rape myths and violence against street prostitutes. *Deviant Behavior, 16*(1), 1–23.

Murray, C. E., Crowe, A., & Overstreet, N. M. (2018). Sources and components of stigma experienced by survivors of intimate partner violence. *Journal of Interpersonal Violence, 33*(3), 515–536.

Nag, M. (2005). Sex workers in Sonagachi: Pioneers of a revolution. *Economic and Political Weekly, 40* (49), 5151–5156.

Overs, C., & Loff, B. (2013). Toward a legal framework that promotes and protects sex workers' health and human rights. *Health and Human Rights, 15*(1), E186–E196.

Parent, C., Bruckert, C., Corriveau, P., Mensah, M. N., & Toupin, L. (2013). *Sex work: Rethinking the job, respecting the workers.* Vancouver; Toronto: UBC Press.

Parmanand, S. (2018). Book review of Julie Bindel's "The pimping of prostitution: Abolishing the sex work myth." *Gender, Work & Organization, 25*(6), 734–737.

Pescosolido, B. A., Martin, J. K., Lang, A., & Olafsdottir, S. (2008). Rethinking theoretical approaches to stigma: A framework integrating normative influences on stigma (FINIS). *Social Science & Medicine, 67*(3), 431–440.

Pheterson, G. (1996). *The prostitution prism.* Amsterdam, The Netherlands: Amsterdam University Press. Retrieved from www.oas.org/atip/belize/belieze-%20petit.pdf

Raymond, J. G., D'Cunha, J., Dzuhayatin, S. R., Hynes, H. P., Rodriguez, Z. R., & Santos, A. (2002). *A comparative study of women trafficked in the migration process: patterns, profiles and health consequences of sexual exploitation in five countries (Indonesia, the Philippines, Thailand, Venezuela and the United States).* New York, NY: Coalition against Trafficking in Women.

Sallmann, J. (2010). "Going hand-in-hand": Connections between women's prostitution and substance use. *Journal of Social Work Practice in the Addictions, 10*(2), 115–138.

Sanders, T. (2007). Becoming an ex-sex worker: Making transitions out of a deviant career. *Feminist Criminology, 2*(1), 74–95.

Stuber, J., Meyer, I., & Link, B. (2008). Stigma, prejudice, discrimination and health. *Social Science & Medicine, 67*(3), 351–357.

Vanwesenbeeck, I. (2017). Sex work criminalization is barking up the wrong tree. *Archives of Sexual Behavior, 46*(6), 1631–1640.

Wahab, S., & Sloan, L. (2004). Ethical dilemmas in sex work. *Research for Sex Work: HIV Prevention and Health Promotion in Prostitution, 7*, 3–5.

Williams III, F. P., & McShane, M. S. (2010). *Criminological theory* (6th ed.). Upper Saddle River, NJ: Prentice-Hall.

Wong, W. C., Holroyd, E., & Bingham, A. (2011). Stigma and sex work from the perspective of female sex workers in Hong Kong. *Sociology of Health & Illness, 33*(1), 50–65.

CHAPTER VII

INCENTIVIZING CRIME PREVENTION THROUGH CITIZEN PARTICIPATION IN TRINIDAD AND TOBAGO

Ashaki Dore

The University of the West Indies, St. Augustine, Trinidad and Tobago

ABSTRACT

In Trinidad and Tobago, a number of strategies ranging from imposing harsher penalties to providing incentives to deter individuals from engaging in criminal activities have been undertaken. The use of monetary incentives has become a matter of concern, given the connection that has been established between the government and criminal elements, through the award of state funding of various initiatives geared toward crime prevention at the community level. The chapter problematizes the absence of a discourse surrounding the use of nonmaterial incentives such as education and participation by leveraging technology to incentivize and achieve sustained citizen participation in the state's crime prevention strategies. This qualitative study employed homogeneous sampling to engage Community Action Officers of the Citizen Security Programme through a focus group. The findings revealed that citizens that readily participate in crime prevention initiatives are those that engage in criminal activity and that their main motivation to participate in community initiatives are monetary incentives. Consequently, this chapter argues for a holistic approach to citizen participation in crime prevention, with a focus on engaging the law-abiding citizens of Trinidad and Tobago rather than rewarding those citizens who engage in criminal activity as a form of deterrence.

Keywords: Incentives, citizen participation, crime prevention, citizen security, Trinidad and Tobago

INTRODUCTION

Trinidad and Tobago is one of the wealthiest and most developed countries in the Caribbean (McCoy & Knight, 2017). However, it has been unable to control the high level of violence in recent years. The homicide rate increased from almost zero per 100,000 people in 1990 to almost 30 in 2010 and the figures have been increasing since 2011 (Williams, 2017, p. 263). Since 2007, gang-related violence has been considered the single most pressing security issue and Trinidad and Tobago has overtaken Jamaica as the Caribbean nation with the most gun-related murders (Townsend, 2009, p. 18). Gangs in Trinidad and Tobago differ from gangs in other parts of the region, given that most gangs in Trinidad and Tobago are transient, smaller, and are not as interconnected as the gangs located in Latin America and the United States (see Wallace, 2018 for support). While several of the large gangs in Latin America are multinational, with links to cousin gangs throughout the region and in cities of the United States, the majority of gangs in Trinidad and Tobago have a very local orientation (Townsend, 2009, p. 18).

The State's inability to control crime internally has also been affected by regional crime, given the effects of the drug trade, organized crime, and money laundering. Trinidad and Tobago is strategically located; due to its proximity to Venezuela and its porous borders, which enable drug traffickers to move cocaine and marijuana from South America on to markets in the United States and Europe. As a result, the poor urban areas of Trinidad, in particular, have become magnets for lawlessness as rival gangs vie for control of the territory where drugs are sold (Williams, 2017, p. 273).

The literature on participation in citizen security at the community level does not appear to problematize the issue of incentives; the positive and negative implications; and how they contribute to individualism; which counters collective action. As a result, this work seeks to identify the strategies that are utilized to mobilize citizen participation in the citizen security framework in Trinidad and Tobago. According to the Citizen Security Programme (2015), there appears to be a general perception of a lack of state commitment which has resulted in citizen frustration and has contributed to low levels of civic participation and social cohesion at the community level; this is in spite of the fact that in many instances, these communities are said to be the most heavily resourced with investment in infrastructural development, government housing, and recreational spaces all of which focus on unification exercises to allow rival communities to engage in organized recreation. Moreover, money characterizes the mode of engagement between the government and members of these rival communities; where money is accessed through government contracts (Vice News, 2014). This chapter will first discuss the mechanisms that are utilized to mobilize citizen participation in crime prevention, and will then discuss the implications for citizen security in Trinidad and Tobago.

CRIME PREVENTION INITIATIVES

Crime prevention in general is not a homogeneous area of policy orientation, but rather, it is ingrained with certain assumptions and political choices. It is a contentious policy field where people hold different perceptions of what should be the philosophical objectives. However, what remains true is that the politics of crime prevention determine the means adopted to achieve a safer place and how this is achieved at a practical level (White, 1996, pp. 98–99). In 2012, the Trinidad and Tobago Police Service (TTPS) launched the 21st Century Policing Initiative. This reform effort intended to expand police capacity and improve community involvement. In 2011, the Special Anti-Crime Unit of Trinidad and Tobago (SAUTT) was dissolved and this increased the resources available to the TTPS. As a result of the reforms in recruitment and training, the number officers assigned to the Organised Crime, Narcotics, and Firearms Bureau (OCNFB) increased by 10% (The International Security Sector Advisory Team, 2016). However, despite the progress community policing has had in some nations, in Trinidad and Tobago, the predominant policing model continues to focus on State security and not citizen security (UNDP, 2013).

The Citizen Security Programme (CSP) is a State-led initiative which commenced in 2008, as an initiative of the Ministry of National Security. The objective was to use preventative interventions to reduce violence and increase the perception of safety in 22 pilot high-risk communities. It involved collaboration between the government, nongovernmental organizations (NGOs), and community-based organizations. The government received a loan from the Inter-American Development Bank for the implementation of the initiative and its execution was based on the financing of three components:

1. The reduction in crime and violence through community-led collaborative initiatives.

2. Capacity building within the TTPS, focusing on their policing for people initiative.

3. Capacity building within the Ministry of National Security in the area of evidence-based policy building (Citizen Security Programme, 2015).

In terms of the reduction in crime and violence through collaborative initiatives, community-led initiatives such as Community Action Councils (CACs) were established in communities as an initiative geared toward improving community participation and providing guidance to the CSP on community issues. CACs were a broad group comprised of representatives from many sectors of the community including traditional, non-traditional, and emerging leaders. CACs also included local NGOs, activists, representatives from churches, schools, businesses, trade unions, civic organizations, children, parents, elders, persons with disabilities. Furthermore, it favored the participation of local residents who worked in that community rather than that of professionals. The community leaders who participated in the CACs played a significant role in the transmission of values and norms, associated with peaceful coexistence (Citizen Security Programme, 2015).

Moreover, the CSP promoted social inclusion and coexistence, by promoting recreational activities, sports, educational support in a number of areas. The program had at its core the desire to integrate the community. Consequently, the case of Trinidad and Tobago placed great emphasis on changing the perception of insecurity and improving trust at the community level. As a result, the (CSP) program aimed to increase community involvement in citizen security and to improve cooperation between communities and the government by financing activities aimed at improving the public's perception of the police, increasing positive police–public interaction, and institutional strengthening of the Ministry of National Security (The International Security Sector Advisory Team, 2016).

In an attempt to implement long-term strategies for dealing with violence and controlling gangs, prevention programs have been instituted aimed at keeping youths from joining gangs and helping gang members leave criminal groups to be reintegrated into society. One program which aimed to assist with the foregoing is the Caribbean Basin Security Initiative (CBSI). The CBSI is a U.S. government-funded program in which Trinidad and Tobago was a beneficiary. The CSBI initiative was aimed at increasing the capacity of its police through training programs and technical assistance (The International Security Sector Advisory Team, 2016). The government has engaged in modernizing the police service by training the police on how to deal with young offenders, and policing to engage the community as a whole to move toward a community policing model and improving public confidence in the law enforcement apparatus (Kirton, Anatol, & Brathwaite, 2010, p. 55).

In Trinidad and Tobago, the police service has been criticized by human rights organizations for the excessive use of force (Amnesty International, 2000). During the 2011 State of Emergency (SoE), there were reports of police killings and poor treatment of suspects and detainees. There has been minimal punishment of members of the security forces, and as a result, there is a widespread perception of impunity due to the slow pace of criminal justice proceedings. Additionally, many high-level officials of the People's Partnership (PP) administration have been accused of having ties to gang leaders; individuals who often lead parallel public lives as community leaders (The International Security Sector Advisory Team, 2016). However, the People's National Movement (PNM) administration has also been accused of supporting and sometimes relying on, suspected criminals. For example, the PNM government made several attempts to establish truces with heads of the largest gangs; their stated aim for meetings held in 2002, were intended to settle local gang wars. However, the meetings also served to cement a relationship between top gang leaders and government officials and the result was that the gang leaders were able to lead parallel public lives.

As a result, these behind-the-scenes interactions with gangs have not always resulted in public disclosure, and these private meetings have prompted suspicions of government complicity with the gangs' criminal agendas (Townsend, 2009, p. 22).

There is, therefore, a high level of cynicism among Trinidad and Tobago's populace as it pertains to the capacity of the state to effectively contain the security problem and the deteriorating police–citizen relationship (Kirton et al., 2010, p. 66). Instructively, the security forces play a significant role in securing and maintaining the confidence of the citizenry in the democratic process; however, there is low public confidence in the police, while citizens appear to be more confident of the Trinidad and Tobago Defence Force (Kirton et al., 2010, p. 55). In fact, in a 2010 survey, only 9.9% of the respondents in Trinidad and Tobago had confidence in the ability of the police to control gang violence, giving it the lowest ranking of the seven countries surveyed (The International Security Sector Advisory Team, 2016).

A Framework of Participation and Incentives for Crime Prevention

Citizen participation often rests on the belief that an engaged citizenry is better than a passive citizenry (Arnstein, 2011, p. 4). Consequently, there is the idea that citizenship is primarily about active participation where citizens are automatically willing and ready to participate and that citizen participation leads to better decision making (Church, et al., 2002, p. 14). Another assumption is that participation is necessarily beneficial and that the more participation there is, the better the outcomes which would be appreciated by all involved (Robins, Cornwall, & Von Lieres, 2008, p. 1,072).

The traditional model of crime prevention sees crime as a matter of incentives and deterrents. Consequently, the literature argues that the solution to crime lies in increasing the cost and reducing the opportunities for the commission of crime. These measures traditionally entail increased surveillance and reliance on the auxiliary role of members of the community in support of official law enforcement agencies (White, 1996, pp. 101–102). On the other hand, the liberal view of crime prevention understands crime as a social problem where people are seen as the starting point for change on the basis that these individuals display a greater propensity to engage in criminal activities (White, 1996, p. 103), as such, the solution is found at the individual level where opportunities are enhanced for "at-risk" individuals who may not have been exposed to work and educational opportunities.

General Incentives Model

The General Incentives Model states that actors need incentives to ensure that they participate in politics (Olson, 1965, p. 72). Consequently, individuals become politically active in response to incentives of various kinds. However, only "a separate and selective incentive will stimulate a rational individual in a latent group to act in a group-oriented way" (Olson, 1965, p. 72). Selective incentives emerged as an approach to the collective action dilemma (Whiteley & Seyd, 2005, p. 44). This view holds that participation is motivated by selective private incentives, because "individuals participate in collective action in response to salient offers of private benefits that disproportionately motivate them" compared to those who engage in nonparticipation (Ginges & Atran, 2009, p. 115). Selective incentives are distinguished from intrinsic incentives on the basis that selective incentives are external to the individual and intrinsic incentives are at times equated with civic duty; which implies an internal moral obligation to act civically (Kyriacou, 2010, pp. 824–826).

The general incentives model speaks of a separate incentive which would stimulate an individual to act in a group-oriented way (Olson, 1965, p. 72). Consequently, it argues that citizens are motivated to participate because of the benefit of gaining private or selective incentives. Thus, these incentives are not associated with a moral obligation to perform responsible citizenship and neither is it associated with citizens acting in solidarity. Consequently, according to the data, unless citizens can be provided with a monetary incentive, participation is not expected to occur. However, of all the incentives, monetary incentives are said to have an undermining effect on the individual's sense of civic duty (Frey & Oberholzer-Gee, 1997, p. 746).

There are three types of selective incentives to promote political participation: process, outcome, and ideology. The process incentive refers to motives that emerge from participating in and of itself; motives such as the entertainment value of being involved in a revolution or the cathartic value of involvement in political protest; regardless of the objectives or the outcome. Selective outcome incentives refer to motives concerned with achieving certain goals in the political process which are private rather than collective, such as well-paid jobs and elective office. Thus, in this context, activism is regarded as an investment to achieve private returns from participation. A third type of incentive is ideology, where motivation lies in the ability to interact with like-minded individuals and where membership allows for the expression of deeply held beliefs (Whiteley & Seyd, 2005, p. 44). However, in a purely individualistic world, people do not think in solidarity terms and as a result, they do not want to contribute to a collective effort and may instead let others do the work to advance policy goals unless they are offered selective incentives (Whiteley & Seyd, 2005, p. 44). This is because citizens need a material basis, not just social capital or civic virtue to act as an active citizen (Honohan, 2002, p. 191).

According to Frey and Oberholzer-Gee (1997, p. 746), monetary incentives tend to undermine an individual's sense of civic duty. Notwithstanding the pronouncement by Frey and Oberholzer-Gee (1997), the literature states that economic incentives are not the only incentives. For as Olson (1965, p. 60) cogitate, people are also motivated by a desire to win prestige, respect, friendship, and other social and psychological objectives. Other incentives can take the form of legal penalties (fines or incarceration), social sanctions (ostracism), and social rewards (status and respect). Social sanctions and social rewards are among the kinds of incentives that may be used to mobilize a latent group. Moral attitudes determine whether or not a person will act in a group-oriented manner, the crucial factor being that the moral reaction serves as a selective incentive as it relates to the sense of guilt that occurs when a person feels he has forsaken his moral code. Consequently, moral attitudes could mobilize a latent group only to the extent they provided selective incentives, given the adherence to a moral code which demands the sacrifices to obtain a collective good (Olson, 1965, p. 60).

It is in the nature of social incentives that individuals can be distinguished from each other in such a way that the unwilling individual can be ostracized, and the cooperative individual can be invited into the center of the charmed circle (Olson, 1965, p. 61). Thus, selective incentives can be either negative or positive, given that they can either coerce by punishing those who fail to bear an allocated share of the costs of the group action or they can be positive inducements offered to those who act in the group interest (Olson, 1965, p. 72). Consequently, private incentives reward those who cooperate within the action or punish those who do not (Oliver, 1980, p. 1356). However, mobilization differs significantly between developed and developing societies, given that the problem of participation in a developing nation involves the mobilization of apolitical parochials to active citizens (Verba, Nie, & Kim, 1978, p. 98). As a result, in the current context, mobilization is the result of a number of forces such as changes in the social structure and the psycho-cultural predisposition of the individual such as level of literacy and education and development of the economy as it relates to increases in the number of those employed. Consequently, as people become more aware of the wider world of politics, and more involved in political life, citizens become psychologically mobilized and also undergo behavioral mobilization and adopt a more active political role. Consequently, these changes provide motivation and resources for development, while citizens learn the norms of citizen participation and develop the cognitive skills needed for political activity (Verba et al., 1978, p. 21).

NONGOVERNMENTAL ORGANIZATIONS ROLE IN CITIZEN SECURITY INITIATIVES

The provision of citizen security has become a "crowded market" (Muggah & Aguirre, 2013, p. 10). Multilateral and bilateral agencies have been financing citizen security initiatives through grants and loans since the 1990s and, as a result, have become the most important funding agencies. There have been more than 1,300 interventions across the region since the late 1990s, and up to 2013, multinational and bilateral cooperation and development agencies together represented 71% of total spending (Muggah & de Carvahlo, 2014, pp. 7–8). The most important funding agencies in the region include multilateral agencies and financial institutions such as the IADB, World Bank, and EU and bilateral agencies such as U.S. aid agencies, the U.S. State Department, and the U.S. Agency for International Development (USAID) (Muggah & de Carvahlo, 2014, p. 8).

Muggah and de Carvahlo (2014, p. 8) point out that "in spite of the apparent appetite for investing in citizen security, there is a surprising lack of clarity about what it is and what it is not." Consequently, this has led to overlapping and competing conceptions of citizen security, given that the different institutions mobilize different visions and methodologies. As a result, they tend to interpret citizen security differently in spite of some agreements on broad concepts, which generates contradictions, given that there is no consensus on how it is defined which leads to an uneven application of the concept "The fact is that different entities; whether federal ministries, police and judicial departments, mayors' offices, international financial institutions, development agencies or citizen action groups, understand citizen security differently" (Muggah & Aguirre, 2013, p. 4).

The different conceptions of the concept of citizen security also highlight that different agencies prioritize different issues; which includes strengthening of norms and policies, evidence generation and sharing and technical assistance, social and situational prevention, preventive policing and rehabilitation; and policy framework, capacity support, and best practices. Consequently, multilateral agencies dominate the field of citizen security and the various initiatives; although their mandates do not allow for their engagement in defense and intelligence-related matters (Muggah & Aguirre, 2013, p. 4).

Unequal Security Responsibility

The literature highlights that everyone is not thought to occupy the same status in society and as a result does not share the same level of responsibility (Stewart, 1995, p. 67). It is argued that people living in the marginalized peripheral communities are differentially held responsible for increased insecurity. This places uneven responsibility on citizens living in the urban areas which are seen as being ground zero for the level of insecurity experienced in society. As a result, these populations are differentially expected to participate in solving these urban problems by participating in direct security activities, such as night patrols (Cattelino, 2004, p. 115). On the one hand, there is the case of Peru in which citizens in the periphery engaged in night patrols. This activity is also linked to the notion of "civilian policing/patrols" which were once enacted in Honduras in the late 1990s but were quickly disbanded when it led to violence (Arias & Ungar, 2009, p. 114). On the other hand, the people in the city engaged in indirect security activities, which placed a greater value on attending official activities. As a result, they participated by being merely present (Marquardt, 2012, pp. 176–177).

The contention regarding the unequal responsibilization of citizens is linked to a debate concerning the political economy of citizenship, in which it is argued that civic access through crime prevention is differentially distributed among neighborhoods and participants. Consequently, it brings to light that citizenship practices tangibly affect the distribution of state resources, the safety of neighborhoods and communities, and the concrete economic and political shape that difference takes (Cattelino, 2004, p. 122). The differential distribution of responsibility is also linked to the differential distribution of resources which can vary from granting more resources to crime prevention organizations which maintain close ties with institutions to police granting less time to small tenant's associations or groups of parents working on their own to keep children out of crime; which presents a challenge to motivating citizens to participate in the public realm (Cattelino, 2004, p. 124).

Another example is the case of England and Wales, where by 1993, there were over 130,000 neighborhood schemes in which neighborhood schemes were encouraged to engage active citizens in patrols in order to foster voluntary collective action. Neighborhood watch; usually associated with the success of community policing, is primarily concerned with crime prevention partnerships. They seek to encourage individuals to be more security conscious in two fundamental aspects as it relates to their own responsibility for personal crime and in terms of their role in community surveillance, to promote shared concerns in matters related to crime (Crawford, 1999, p. 50). However, similar to the notion of unequal security responsibilization experienced in Peru, citizen patrol, connoted "policing on the cheap," and vigilantism (Crawford, 1999, p. 51). Thus while, the idea is that the role of the government is to activate and facilitate individuals into performing their duties of citizenship, there is also a popular view among citizens, that the government should not transfer more functions onto the individual, and that it should continue to do the things for which it accepted responsibility (Crawford, 1999, pp. 82–85).

While placing responsibility on the citizen is viewed negatively as it relates to the unequal distribution of security responsibility, it is also viewed as an incentive to participation. It has been argued that sharing responsibility for self-safety in society is in fact a primary motivator for citizen participation in community crime prevention activities (Choi, Lee, & Chun, 2014, p. 295). As a result, another critical element found in citizen participation literature refers to incentives and personal interests. In the Peruvian experience, the young men who formed part of the urban patrols could count two years of service in the patrols as fulfillment of obligatory military service. However, once military service became voluntary, the incentive for participation in the patrols disappeared. As a result, participation is significantly determined by the existence or lack of incentives (Marquardt, 2012, p. 178). Consequently, it brings to light the role incentives play in encouraging sustained participation; whether these incentives are selective, collective, symbolic, or material (Föhrig & Pomares, 2007, pp. 22–24).

When participation cannot be sustained over time, and if it remains limited to small groups, it runs the risk of co-optation by individual interests (Smulovitz, 2006, p. 234). Thus, in spite of the engagement aspect found in the processes of community partnership, there is a tendency to exclude and include, as organization is a paramount requisite and as a result groups that are disorganized are excluded. Inclusion may have more to do with personal relations with key agency personnel, noted activism or previous good service in other fields of voluntary community work, rather than representativeness. In addition, inclusion is also bound up with powerful agency definitions of the respected and respectable, where traditionally, groups that are viewed as troublesome are excluded, marginalized, ignored, or overlooked (Crawford, 1999, pp. 169–171).

METHODOLOGY

In the conduct of the study, a qualitative research design is used to gain in-depth insights as "The idea of acquiring an 'inside' understanding—the actor's definitions of the situation, is a powerful central concept for understanding the purpose of qualitative inquiry" (Patton, 2002, p. 51). Qualitative research design involves the purposeful selection of participants and material that will best help the researcher to answer the research problem. The strength of the purposeful sampling strategy lies in its selection of information-rich cases for in-depth study (Patton, 2002, p. 447).

A homogenous sampling approach was utilized in the selection of a focus group, which brought together people of similar backgrounds and experiences to discuss major issues that affected them (Patton, 2002, p. 236). As a result, 16 Community Action Officers (CAOs) out of 22 at-risk communities where CSPs were established were interviewed in a focus group. This involved open-ended questions which focused specially on targeted issues at the community level, where the CAOs were able to share their insights and experiences. This sampling strategy was useful because it minimized variation and facilitated group process. Moreover, executive interviews were conducted with key officials from the CSP at both headquarters in Trinidad and Tobago, respectively.

Ethical considerations were taken into account to respect the rights of the participants. Consequently, informed consent was obtained from the participants, the research objectives were articulated verbally and in writing and a description of how the data would be used was provided to ensure that the participants clearly understood the nature of the research project. After obtaining informed consent, the focus group and executive interviews were recorded and transcribed, and detailed records of transcripts and questionnaires were maintained in order to ensure transparency. The participants decided to remain anonymous, and as a result, it was agreed that their confidentiality would be maintained by not using their names or any other personal means of identification (Cohen, Manion, & Morrison, 2011, p. 91).

The study employed data triangulation as it leads to more reliable, valid, and diverse findings which consequently helped corroborate the findings and minimize researcher bias by employing more than one method of data collection. First, rich, thick description allows the reader to formulate his or her own decisions based on the transferability of the study, where the reader will be able to apply the information to different settings and thus determine the validity or trustworthiness of the study. Second, data triangulation was employed with the objective of obtaining a "true fix" on the notion of citizen participation by combining different ways of looking at findings (Patton, 2002, p. 247). Third, reflexivity was used to identify the researcher's preconceptions, theoretical foundations, motivation, and personal experiences, given that a researcher's background can affect what is investigated, the angle of the investigation, the methods judged most adequate for this purpose, the findings considered most appropriate, and the framing and communication of conclusions. Reflexivity involves rigorous self-scrutiny by the researcher throughout the research process. Subjectivity arises when the effect of the researcher is ignored and it asserts that it will be an illusion to ignore the fact that the researcher can affect the process. Objectivity requires the recognition that knowledge is partial and situated and to account adequately for the effects of the positioned researcher.

In Vivo coding was selected to refer to the "terms used by the participants themselves," who belong to a particular culture, subculture, or micro-culture (Saldaña, 2016, p. 105). Consequently, their unique expressions were extracted in order to honor the participant's views. In the context of crime prevention, this is important given the view that the voices of ordinary citizens are often marginalized; they are "almost never consulted on crime prevention initiatives" (Wallace, 2012, p. 65). Consequently, citing their words in the text provides the reader with the opportunity to deepen their understanding of the participant's condition.

INCENTIVIZING CITIZEN PARTICIPATION

A major theme which emerged in this study of crime prevention in the context of Trinidad and Tobago referred to the important role incentives play in encouraging individuals to participate in crime prevention. According to the literature, people do not naturally become involved because the practice of citizenship is considered an unnatural practice for human beings. However, this does not mean that human nature is unfitted to do so (Oldfield, 1990, p. 187). This view is supported by the General Incentives Model, which states that people become politically active in response to various kinds of selective incentives in order to achieve certain personal goals and these incentives encourage prolonged participation (Föhrig & Pomares, 2007, p. 33).

Selective outcome incentive refers to motives associated with achieving private goals. Moreover, the literature argues that only selective incentives are said to be able to stimulate a rational individual to act in a group-oriented way; that is, to act collectively. This is because people do not think in terms of solidarity and do not engage in collective efforts (Whiteley & Seyd, 2005, p. 44). Consequently, the citizen that participates expects to benefit more than those who engage in nonparticipation. The concept of incentives coming out of participation theory also supports this view to the extent that it advances that individuals participate as a means to an end. Consequently, the various types of incentives that emerged in the data entail, monetary incentives, education as an incentive.

In Trinidad and Tobago's context, financial compensation or monetary incentives have been used as a mechanism to foster citizen participation. According to the data, this practice has been encouraged by the State through various initiatives geared toward crime prevention at the community level which is further worsened, given the connection that has been established between the government and criminal elements through state funding. It is argued that community leaders use the money obtained from the State to purchase weapons and to pay young people to carryout nefarious activities. Money characterizes the mode of engagement between these two parties; where money is accessed through government contracts. This is said to have fueled community (in)security, where so-called community leaders are seen as the head and protector of the community. This, subsequently, separates the people from the State (Vice News, 2014).

The culture of participation which has emerged from this practice is what respondents have characterized as the idea of "getting through" which refers to the notion of receiving personal interests because it refers to doing something in exchange for personal benefits rather than for the common good of all. Consequently, the notion of "getting through" has led to what has been termed a "real 'me-me' culture" (personal communication, June 27, 2015). However, the idea of getting through is directly linked to financial incentives, and as a result, this has developed into a tendency to expect financial compensation for participating. This is evident in the following statement by a CAO in Trinidad and Tobago, who was a part of the focus group discussion for this study. The CAO explained the challenges she had experienced in encouraging persons to attend meetings outside of their own communities:

> When I try to get persons from Caledonia to come to Paradise Heights, the person in Caledonia is wondering what I can get out of it, the only time they were able to come across Caledonia to come to Paradise Heights and forget border lines was because of their interest in LifeSport ... people was getting through!

In the quote above, the individual refers to a previous government sporting initiative, the LifeSport program. This program was conceptualized as one part of a comprehensive approach to address crime in Trinidad and Tobago. LifeSport was launched in 2012 and was specifically geared toward positively impacting the future of young men who needed to be protected from being preyed by criminals. It was argued that they would benefit greatly from becoming involved in this initiative; even to the extent of leaving the safety of their communities to enter a community that was considered to be hostile. Consequently, participation in the CSP relied heavily on what benefit it entailed for the individual rather than the community. Another CAO expressed similar sentiments as it pertained to the financial incentives that participation in government programs entailed by submitting the following:

> *In my community they had what they considered a very prof-*
> *itable LifeSport Programme. So with CSP coming in now,*
> *the entire place was like, so what are we getting? That was so*
> *from the beginning because of what existed before.*

This assertion highlights that the way citizens participate depends largely on the culture of participation that had been engendered by precursor programs. Another CAO echoed similar views by highlighting what motivated many citizens to participate:

> *As a hustler my idea of living and existing is to hustle and*
> *make money .... In the CSP meeting what they are saying is*
> *that, "what we had existing here was working for us. We were*
> *getting money, we was relaxing home, I had no reason to go*
> *and shoot up the place and at the end of the day, all yuh dis-*
> *rupt the scene here and now I can't eat ah food .... Now that*
> *that is gone, what happens now?"*

Similar to the notion of getting through is the concept of "to eat ah food" which again refers to making financial gains. The assertions presented in the data support what has been highlighted in the literature; as it relates to interests. It states that a number of interests inform why individuals participate and argues that different participants participate to achieve different objectives (White, 2011, p. 144). Consequently, through these lenses, participation for monetary incentives could be understood as participation as a means to an end.

As a result, in an attempt to curtail the culture of dependency and individualism which has been engendered as a result of the state's interaction with the community, the CSP in Trinidad and Tobago removed the option of providing financial compensation in order to engender a culture of citizen participation for the collective good of all. This is evidenced in the following statement made by an official:

> *We do not deal with finances ... they know that there is no*
> *financial gain here. We know the culture we are dealing with*
> *.... You give to get. [However] we would not pay people to*
> *attend. We don't want to feed into the notion that somebody*
> *owes you something .... Community work has no thanks.*

However, the findings present a dichotomy, given that people are preoccupied with the lack of financial resources which is continuously highlighted as a major concern which keeps people away from engaging collectively. A CAO expressed her views regarding, the provision of financial incentives which she felt had a debilitating effect on the individual's will to participate collectively, rather than for their own personal gain:

> *What is happening in their personal life is not left outside while they continue to serve. We have to collaborate the two, we have to find ways to mesh the two ... because people cannot serve from a place of not "having." You understand what I am saying?*

What this highlights is that collective participation and personal gain are not mutually exclusive concepts, given that collective participation does not signify that individuals do not also seek personal benefits as well. This is aligned with the literature, in two aspects; firstly, on the basis that economic status is a catalyst to participation, where the assumption is that those who have the resources are able to participate in public life. Secondly, it confirms the argument that it is unlikely that citizenship would become the primary consuming passion because of other competing factors which draw citizens away from the public realm (Walzer, 1989, p. 215).

The issue of monetary incentives as a way to prevent crime through citizen participation in Trinidad and Tobago highlights an interesting finding as it pertains to the perception of fear. While there is a claim that citizens are fearful of entering rival communities, monetary incentives succeed in mobilizing individuals sufficiently to overcome fear and become active participants, albeit for personal gains. This became evident when participants stated that individuals would leave their communities to participate in activities located inside of rival or hostile communities, because of the promise of monetary gains. Another mechanism that functions as an incentive, to a lesser extent, is education. In Trinidad and Tobago, efforts are geared toward educating citizens to take responsibility. An official from the CSP in Trinidad submitted the following: "citizens have to trust each other, respect each other ... to be actively involved ... They have to learn to take responsibility." This includes training processes designed to empower citizens with the objective of enabling citizens to make more responsible decisions that would have a positive impact on security.

DISCUSSION

The research sought to examine how citizens are mobilized to participate in crime prevention initiatives in Trinidad and Tobago. The findings revealed that a number of initiatives were introduced in an attempt to mobilize citizens and what is interesting is that regardless of the program; whether it was the LifeSport Programme or the CSP, incentives were a key feature, which could be accessed in the form of monetary incentives, access to funding, or other benefits. According to the literature, participation in the area of security is problematic because it is a public good which can be enjoyed by free-riding, and as a result, there is the view that participation yields insignificant results (Smulovitz, 2006). This may account for the states' reliance on the use of monetary rewards to incentivize citizen participation in crime prevention initiatives.

The findings revealed that the individuals who readily participate in these initiatives are those that engage in criminal activity. These findings are consistent with White's (1996) discussion of the liberal view of crime prevention which views crime as a social problem in which at-risk individuals are provided with enhanced opportunities in an attempt to discourage them from engaging in criminal activity. However, this short-term solution has instead created a culture of dependency, and one can argue, it has led many to develop a sense of entitlement to the extent that a reward is expected for refraining from criminality. This can be discerned from the views expressed by former recipients of monetary rewards "what we had existing here was working for us. We were getting money, we was relaxing home, I had no reason to go and shoot up the place."

This is further supported by the General Incentives Model which argues that incentives are needed in order to mobilize people to participate. However, monetary incentives are not sustainable and effective in the long term; particularly, since there is no guarantee that these individuals would truly abstain from criminal activity. The literature argues that gang leaders have been able to successfully lead parallel lives, and whether the rewards provided by the state and other initiatives funded by NGOs are enough to prevent these individuals from engaging in criminality in the face of better monetary opportunities resulting from criminal involvement, remains to be seen.

Moreover, the implementation of CSPs in at-risk communities presents a paradox, given that the idea behind the CSP is to promote social inclusion and coexistence, and generally achieve a more engaged and civic-minded citizenry that would contribute to citizen security. However, rather than seeking the active involvement of the law-abiding citizens, efforts have instead centered on rewarding particular groups of individuals who engage in criminal activity.

RECOMMENDATIONS

An analysis of the findings suggests that the incentives must be dual in nature to the extent that while there may be a measure of personal gain, incentives should also entail a collective dimension that can contribute to the good of the wider society. It is recommended that opportunities be created at the community level to encourage citizens to exercise responsible citizenship. The state must strike a balance between empowering citizens and avoid becoming overly intrusive to the extent that it engenders a culture of entitlement and dependency which would lead to an erosion of their sense of civic responsibility.

CONCLUSION

This chapter discussed the view that the government, throughout various administrations, has focused solely on preventing crime by engaging citizens who engage in criminal activity or are predisposed to engage in crime because they reside in what has been characterized as an at-risk community. However, it argues that there needs to be a more holistic approach to citizen participation, which engages the wider citizenry of Trinidad and Tobago. Moreover, it discussed how the use of material incentives has failed to achieve sustained citizen participation in crime prevention initiatives. The current economic climate in Trinidad and Tobago may provide policymakers with the opportunity to employ new, innovative, and sustainable incentives to foster and maintain active citizenship as a mechanism of crime prevention and subsequently, increased citizen security. This could be achieved by levering the use of technology and the technological capabilities citizens already possess and by engaging citizens to participate in the various virtual spaces. This can provide citizens with a space in which they could express their concerns, increase their awareness about government initiatives on crime prevention, collaborate on crime prevention initiatives, and communicate on a greater level on matters of active citizenship.

REFERENCES

Amnesty International. (2000). A summary of concerns. Briefing for the Human Rights Committee, Session 70. Geneva: UNHCR.

Arias, E. D., & Ungar, M. (2009). Community policing and Latin America's citizen security crisis. *Comparative Politics, 41*(4), 409–429.

Arnstein, S. (2011). A ladder of citizen participation. In A. Cornwall (Ed.), *The participation reader* (pp. 3–18). London: Zed Books.

Cattelino, J. R. (2004). The difference the citizenship makes: Civilian crime prevention on the lower east side. *American Anthropological Association, 27*(1), 114–137.

Choi, K., Lee, J., & Chun, Y. (2014). Why do citizens participate in community crime prevention activities? *Revija za Kriminalististiko in Kriminologogijo/Ljubljana, 65*, 287–298.

Church, J., Saunders, D., Wanke, M., Pong, R., Spooner, C., & Dorgan, M. (2002). Citizen Participation in Health Decision-Making: Past Experience and Future Prospects. *Journal of Public Health Policy* 23(1), 12-32. Retrieved from https://www.jstor.org/stable/3343116

Citizen Security Programme. Retrieved July 21, 2015, from http://www.csp.gov.tt//.

Cohen, L., Manion. L., & Morrison. K. (2011). *Research methods in education*. London: Routledge.

Crawford, A. (1999). *The local governance of crime: Appeals to community and partnership*. Oxford: University Press.

Föhrig, A., & Pomares, J. (2007). "El impacto de las policitas participativas de seguridad de la Argentina: Estudios de caso." In J. Varat (Ed.), *Seguridad Ciudadana en las Américas: Proyecto de Investigación Activa*

(Vol. 18, pp. 11–37). Washington, DC: Woodrow Wilson Center Reports on the Americas.

Frey, B., & Oberholzer-Gee, F. (1997). The cost of price incentives: An empirical analysis of motivation crowding-out. *The American Economic Review, 87*(4), 746–755.

Ginges, J., & Atran, S. (2009). What motivates participation in violent political action: Selective incentives or parochial altruism? Values, empathy, and fairness across social barriers. *Annals of the New York Academy of Sciences, 1167,* 115–123.

Honohan, I. (2002). *Civic republicanism: The problems of philosophy.* New York, NY: Routledge.

Kirton, R., Anatol, M., & Brathwaite, N. (2010). *The political culture of democracy in Trinidad & Tobago: Democracy in action.* Institute of International Relations, The University of the West Indies, St. Augustine.

Kyriacou, A. P. (2010). Intrinsic motivation and the logic of collective action: The impact of selective incentives. *The American Journal of Economics and Sociology, 69*(2), 823–839.

Marquardt, K. (2012). Participatory security: citizen security, participation and the inequities of citizenship in urban Peru. *Journal of the Society for Latin American Studies, 31*(2), 174–189.

McCoy, J. & Knight W.A. (2017). Homegrown violent extremism in Trinidad and Tobago: Local patterns, global trends. *Studies in Conflict and Terrorism, 40*(4), 267–299.

Muggah, R., & Aguirre, K. (2013). Mapping citizen security interventions in Latin America: Reviewing the evidence. *Norwegian Peacebuilding Resource Centre.* Retrieved from https://igarape.org.br/wp-content/uploads/2013/10/265_91204_NOREF_Report_Muggah-Aguirre_web1.pdf

Muggah, R., & de Carvahlo, I. S. (2014). Changes in the neighbourhood: Reviewing citizen security cooperation in Latin America. *Igarape Institute.* Strategic Paper 7. Retrieved from https://igarape.org.br/wp-content/uploads/2014/03/AE-07-Changes-in-the-Neighborhood_10th_march.pdf

Oldfield, A. (1990). Citizenship: An unnatural practice? *The Political Quarterly, 61*(2), 177–187.

Oliver, P. (1980). Rewards and punishments as selective incentives for collective action: Theoretical investigations. *American Journal of Sociology, 85*(6), 1356–1375.

Olson, M. (1965). *The logic of collective action: Public goods and the theory of groups.* Cambridge: Harvard University Press.

Patton, M. Q. (2002). *Qualitative research and evaluation methods.* London: Sage Publications.

Regional Human Report 2013–2014. Citizen security with a human face: Evidence and proposals for Latin America. *United Nations Development Programme* 2013. Retrieved from hdr.undp.org/sites/.../citizen_ security_with_a_human_face_-executivesummary.pdf.

Robins, S., Cornwall, A., & Von Lieres, B. (2008). Rethinking "citizenship" in the postcolony. *Third World Quarterly, 29*(6), 1069–1086.

Saldaa, J. (2016). The coding manual for qualitative researchers. Los Angeles: Publications. Sage.

Smulovitz, C. (2006). Citizen participation and public security in Argentina, Brazil and Chile: Lessons from an initial experience. In J. S. Tulchin & M. Ruthenburg (Eds.), *Toward a society under law: Citizens and their police in Latin America* (pp. 206–242). Washington, DC: Woodrow Wilson Center Press.

Stewart, A. (1995). Two conceptions of citizenship. *The British Journal of Sociology, 46*(1), 63–78.

The International Security Sector Advisory Team. (2016). Trinidad and Tobago country profile. *The Geneva Centre for the Democratic Control of Armed Forces.* Retrieved from issat.dcaf.ch/Learn/Resource.../Trinidad-and-Tobago-Country-Profile.

Townsend, D. (2009). No other life: Gangs, guns and governance in Trinidad and Tobago. *Small Arms Survey, Graduate School of International and Graduate Studies.* Retrieved from http://www.smallarms-survey.org/fileadmin/docs/F-Working-papers/SAS-WP8-Gangs-Guns-Governance-Trinidad-Tobago-2009.pdf.

Verba, S., Nie, N. H., and Kim, J. (1978). A seven nation comparison: participation and political equality. Chicago: The University Press.

Vice News. (2014). Corruption, cocaine and murder in Trinidad. Retrieved from http: bit/subscribe-to-Vice-News.

Wallace, W. C. (2012). Findings from a concurrent study on the level of community involvement in the policing process in Trinidad and Tobago. *The Police Journal, 85*(1), 61–83.

Wallace, W. C. (2018). Understanding the evolution of localized Community-based Street Gangs in Laventille, Trinidad. The Journal of Gang Research, 26(1), 1-16.

Walzer, M. (1989). Citizenship. In T. Ball, J. Farr & R. L. Hanson (Eds.), *Political innovation and conceptual change* (pp. 211–219). Cambridge: Cambridge University Press.

White, R. (1996). Situating crime prevention: models, methods and political perspectives. Retrieved from https://www.researchgate.net/publication/242214868_SITUATING_CRIME_PREVENTION_MODELS_METHODS_AND_POLITICAL_PERSPECTIVES

White, S. (2011). Depoliticizing Development: the Uses and Abuses of Participation. In A. Cornwall (Ed.), *The Participation Reader* (pp. 57-69). London: Zed Books.

Whiteley, P. F., & Seyd, P. (2005). *High-intensity participation: The dynamics of party activism in Britain.* Michigan: University of Michigan Press.

Williams, D. (2017). An assessment of Trinidad and Tobago as a fragile state. In J. D. Rosen & H. S. Kassab (Eds.), *Fragile states in the Americas* (pp. 259–276). New York: Lexington Books.

CHAPTER VIII

"We Reduce It in Writing": Exploring the Status of Kwéyòl in the Criminal Justice System in St. Lucia

R. Sandra Evans

The University of the West Indies, St. Augustine, Trinidad and Tobago

Abstract

In many multilingual postcolonial societies across the globe, one of the most patent colonial hangovers or corollaries of European colonization, is the use of an ex-colonial language as the sole "official language" of the state. This type of official monolingualism in a former colonial language is generally the norm, even though it is seldom the native or dominant language of the majority of the citizens of these societies. In the case of St. Lucia, English is the sole official language of all state institutions, including the criminal justice system, notwithstanding the fact there are many native St. Lucians who lack competence in this language. These persons speak Kwéyòl, which is a creole language that is lexically related to the French language but is not mutually intelligible with either the French or English language. Drawing on data from St. Lucia's criminal justice system, this chapter employs a rational choice approach to explore the status of Kwéyòl and its implications for the participation and treatment of Kwéyòl monolingual and Kwéyòl-dominant speakers in the system. It underscores the urgent need for both legal and language policy reform that will provide specific language rights and ultimately, better access to justice for Kwéyòl speakers in St. Lucia.

Keywords: St. Lucia, Kwéyòl, criminal justice system, status of Kwéyòl, rational choice approach

INTRODUCTION

Although in many postcolonial multilingual societies across the globe, official language status is accorded to more than one language for use in public formal domains such as education, the courts, and public administration, there are others that continue to rationalize the use of one language in these domains. The Caribbean region is a typical example of the latter, where, despite its complex multilingual situation, only one language, usually the language of the ultimate colonizing power, is institutionalized as the sole official language of most of the states. According to Brown-Blake (2014), institutionalization concerns the degree of use and acceptability of a language in a given domain so that it is "taken for granted" rather than through legitimization or laws arising from legislation or judicial opinion (p. 53). In other words, there is no legislation that spells out the meaning and consequence of the term *official language* or specifically deals with the practical implementation of official language status in Caribbean jurisdictions. Therefore, official language status in the Caribbean has traditionally been accorded on a predominantly social, rather than legal basis, where the language of last colonizing power was simply retained as the socially, culturally, and economically prestigious and dominant language by the political, cultural, and economic élite (Alleyne, 1961).

Of the 70 surviving languages of the Caribbean, only 6 function in an official capacity; 4 of which are European-born, nonindigenous languages, namely Spanish, English, French, and Dutch, and the remaining 2, Ayisyen/Haitian and Papiamentu, officialized in 1987 and 2003, respectively (Ferreira, 2012), are the only two Caribbean-born official languages. They are also the only two official languages that were actually legitimized in the Caribbean. However, unlike the European-born languages, they do not enjoy sole official language status. In Haiti, Ayisyen shares the rank with French, while in Aruba and Curacao Papiamentu shares it with Dutch and English.

In Commonwealth Caribbean societies in particular, which share a common legacy of British colonialism, English was instituted as the exclusive official language of all the states. Even after the attainment of political independence from Britain, the plantation linguistic structure remained dominant in these societies and the language of power and prestige remained unchanged. Another marked feature of the language situation in these societies is the coexistence of English with one or more creole languages, which are the native languages of the mass of the population. These native languages may be subdivided into two groups based on their lexical relationship and intelligibility with English. The first group comprises those that are lexically related to and mutually intelligible with English, and have wide local currency in the majority of the territories. The second group comprises those that are lexically related to French and only have considerable local currency in Dominica and St. Lucia.

These creole languages are all products of a historical language-contact situation involving a European language and various West African languages brought by slaves to the Caribbean during the slave trade (Alleyne, 1971). An inherent feature of this language-contact situation was the complete dominance of the European languages as the languages of power and prestige, while the creole languages were generally regarded as broken, deformed versions or corruptions of these "higher" European languages (Holm, 2000), even by their own speakers. The colonially imposed negative language ideologies and social perceptions of creole languages in slave societies have transcended time and "everywhere in the Caribbean, creole remains subordinate to the language of the former European colonizer" (St- Hilaire, 2003, p. 68). In stark contrast to English, they only have wide local currency in informal contexts, and they are typically disrespected, unwritten vernaculars that have not undergone standardization or been formally admitted to public use in institutional discourse even in their home settings (Patrick & Buell, 2000). In addition, Patrick and Buell (2000) contend that many of their own native speakers are uncertain whether they exist as "real languages" (p. 1), and they often dismiss them as badly spoken English or French.

Another crucial factor that continues to contribute to the low status of creole languages is their customary oral usage, which is compounded by the fact that many of them do not have an official orthography. It is interesting to note that even in territories where orthographic systems are available, Caribbean people are not competent in the use of these systems, mainly because they are not used as a language of instruction in schools, where writing in any language is normally taught. The absence of writing has had far-reaching implications for these languages and their speakers, particularly with regard to their participation in public formal domains, such as the criminal justice system, where writing as well as language status play such a central role.

This chapter is concerned with the current status of a local creole language, commonly referred to as Kwéyòl, in the criminal justice system in St. Lucia. Kwéyòl, which is lexically related to French, found its roots in early French-colonial periods. It is the native language of many St. Lucians and still has wide local currency on the island. In contrast to the majority of the other creole languages of the Commonwealth Caribbean that coexist with their lexifier language, English, Kwéyòl can be found in a more peculiar situation, where it is coexisting with English, instead of its lexifier, French. Midgett (1970) asserts that the negative valuation placed upon Kwéyòl seems to be perhaps more intense in St. Lucia than in other islands where creole and standard are lexically derived from the same language (Midgett, 1970).

Kwéyòl's status in St. Lucia has always been patently subordinate to that of English in terms its perceived utility and its functions in the society. It is the local language of the country that is principally the vehicle for informal, elemental aspects of life. Similar to the linguistic situation in the other Commonwealth Caribbean territories, English enjoys a more elevated status in terms of its utility, functions, or what it is used to do. It is the vehicle for very formal and artificial occasions; it is the medium through which all official, national, and inherited institutions function (Alleyne, 1961). A case in point, is the exclusion of Kwéyòl from an important legal document, the St. Lucia Criminal Code Act (2004), which applies to jury service. Act 925 reads as follows:

Qualification

925. A person is qualified to serve as a juror if he or she is

(a) A citizen of St. Lucia; or

(b) A citizen of a CARICOM member State ordinarily resident in St. Lucia for 2 years;

(c) A Commonwealth citizen ordinarily resident in St. Lucia for not less than 2 years.

Act 926, however, disqualifies (1) A person who (a) cannot speak, read, and write English. It reads,

Disqualification

926. (1) A person who

(a) cannot speak, read, or write English;

This Act specifically targets and discriminates against Kwéyòl monolingual and Kwéyòl-dominant St. Lucians, who are normally the ones who lack competence and literacy skills in English and it automatically disqualifies and excludes them from serving as jurors. Examples such as this one make St. Lucia a germane site for exploring the question of language status in postcolonial criminal justice systems. It has the potential to inform other postcolonial jurisdictions, which use an ex-colonial language as the sole official language at the expense of local languages and their speakers.

Language Status and Local Languages in Postcolonial Criminal Justice Systems

Generally, the term language status is used to refer to social, cultural, and political classifications of languages and speakers. In its most common use, it describes the legal and/or social standing of a language in a given jurisdiction (Porter, 2018). The status of a language also depends on its potential or what people can do with it. This is supported by Mackey (1989), who defines status as the sum total of what you can do with a language legally, culturally, economically, politically, and demographically (Mackey, 1989, p. 4). The concept is also used to refer to the social standing of a language or attitudes toward a language and its speakers in a given setting (Porter, 2018), and its use requires a consideration of language ideologies, or practices and interpretations through which a given language becomes socially significant (Canagarajah, 2013).

In recent years, researchers have intensified focus on language issues in criminal justice systems particularly in postcolonial, English-dominant countries. There is a growing body of scholarly work on the status and functions of local languages in criminal justice systems in inherently linguistically diverse settings that preserve a "dominant institutional bias towards monolingualism" (Eades, 2003, p. 114) or continue to rationalize the use of one language as the sole official language of the system. There is also a growing body of research on postcolonial initiatives to introduce local languages into inherited criminal justice systems, which were once dominated by one language. Some of these include the use or inclusion of local or nonofficial languages in courts in Africa (for example, David & Powell, 2003; Powell, 2008; Thekiso, 2001; Yahya-Othman & Batibo, 1996). Other states in Asia have established official bi-or multilingual judicial systems (Hang Ng, 2009; Leung, 2008; Powell, 2008). There are a few rare cases where the criminal justice system has undergone comprehensive language shift, from the use of the exoglossic language to an endoglossic one. For example, Indonesia has evolved into a monolingual vernacular system, and in Myanmar, Burmese is the language of all new legislation and nearly all proceedings (Powell, 2008).

With regard to the Commonwealth Caribbean, very little research has been conducted into the language status and its impact in the criminal justice system. This is surprising, given that the criminal justice system is one of the institutions of the state where language status plays a crucial role. The literature on the status of creole languages has traditionally examined two features of their presence in Caribbean societies: first, the functional distribution of languages in various social domains, and second, the attitudes of various categories of users to the use of the languages (Carrington, 1999). Carrington (1999) further states that the social domains of use have, by and large, been determined by assumptions that place the languages of the society into competing relationships (p. 41).

As a result, research on the status of creole languages in the Commonwealth Caribbean has mostly been with reference to their coexistence with English. More specifically, their status has been ascertained by their degree of penetration into those areas of the public domain that have traditionally been the preserve of English. The domains used as measures of penetration are frequently the following: politics and government, education, the media, and the performing arts (Carrington, 1999, p. 41). The criminal justice system, which constitutes the functioning and relatedness of police, courts, and corrections (Burns, 2007), has rarely been used as a measure of penetration, although it is perhaps the public formal domain that is most strictly dominated by English, which was inherited as the language of the law along with rules and traditions of the English Common law. According to Antoine (1998),

> "Since the English Common law system originated in England in form, character, substance, [and language], it should be of little surprise to learn that it was imposed, through the

> *process of colonisation, upon the former conquered territo-*
> *ries, some of which now make up the Commonwealth Carib-*
> *bean. They continue to exhibit perhaps excessive tendencies*
> *of reliance on form, structure, substance, content, [and lan-*
> *guage] of the law as expressed in England" (p. 39).*

The criminal justice system is in essence a linguistic institution. Speech and writing, the two principal modes of human communication, are the lifeblood of the system in literate societies. Criminal justice processes such as police investigations, court cases, and the management of prisoners, take place predominantly through spoken and written language. Given that this system is also one of the most profoundly significant and impactful in contemporary societies, it is important to understand how its use of language impacts people whose dominant language is different from the one in which it operates. If the criminal justice system is to actually work for all people irrespective of language differences, it is important to identify, understand, and eliminate any disparities in how speakers of non-dominant languages are treated. The question of language status and its impact on justice administration is, therefore, crucial to any discourse on Caribbean criminology and criminal justice.

DATA AND METHODS

The data for this chapter are taken from the data pool of a larger study, which examined the language use patterns and practices of the legal system in St. Lucia. A range of data collection procedures was used to collect the data for this study. These included questionnaires, interviews, observation, field notes, and document analysis. A written, open-ended questionnaire was used to elicit data from the police. This method of data collection allowed the researcher an efficient means of gathering a relatively large number of responses from police officers. Questionnaires were administered to police officers at all the police stations in St. Lucia and a total of 81 were collected. They were analyzed quantitatively using frequency counts and percentages.

Informal interviews (semi-structured and open-ended) were also used to elicit additional data from police officers and to corroborate the information provided in questionnaires. Semi-structured interviews were also conducted with lawyers, magistrates, and clerks of the court who work in the criminal justice system in St. Lucia. A total of 20 interviews were conducted. Directed systematic observations in magistrates' courts were used to produce field notes that informed the study. Official written documents of all kinds are accumulated in modern institutions including police departments and courts. These institutional documents were analyzed within the practical social contexts of everyday life, within which they are constructed and used. These documents provided an invaluable source of information for the study. They include, the St. Lucia Constitution (1978), the Criminal Code (2004), the St. Lucia Evidence Act (2002), the Police Ordinance (1965), and the District Court Ordinance (1888). The analysis in this chapter is centered around the questionnaires and interviews with the police, the field notes, the constitution, and the criminal code.

THEORETICAL APPROACH

As mentioned previously, this chapter employs a rational choice approach to assess the status of Kwéyòl in the criminal justice system in St. Lucia. This approach, which is rooted in the field of economics, has become more visible and influential in many of the social sciences and in related disciplines such as law and philosophy. Rakner (1996) contends that rational choice cannot be presented as one single theory as most practitioners of rational choice agree to some, but not all, features present in a definition of rational choice theory (p. 9). However, some theoretical features are generally shared by all rational choice theorists and may therefore described as *the core* of rational choice theory (Rakner, 1996, p. 9). Therefore, at the core of orthodox models of rational choice is the notion that all action is fundamentally "rational" in character and people calculate the likely costs and benefits of any action before deciding what to do (Scott, 2000). In other words, social interaction is guided by rational choice between alternative outcomes that are considered in terms of costs and benefits (Coleman, 1990).

Also basic to all forms of rational choice theory is the assumption that complex phenomena can be explained in terms of the elementary individual actions of which they are composed (Scott, 2000). This adherence to the individual as the unit of analysis, in other words, methodological individualism holds that,

"The elementary unit of social life is the individual human action. To explain social institutions and social change is to show how they arise as a result of the action of and interaction of individuals" (Elster, 1989, p. 22).

One of the major criticisms of rational choice theory is its heavy focus on individual behavior. Hindess (1988) and Jordan (1989) argue that the theory inadequately addresses the context in which individuals make choices. However, some rational choice models contain specifications of social structures, which serve both as the social and material context for individual action (Coleman, 1990). Those features of social life that are conventionally called "social structures" are, for rational choice theorist, simply chains of interconnected individual actions (Scott, 2000). Since norms and other kinds of institutions enter the models both as contexts for and as outcomes of action, rational choice theories do not rest on premises pertaining exclusively to individuals (Hechter & Kanazawa, 1997). They regard both individual values and structural elements as equally important determinants of outcomes.

Although language status in postcolonial societies has been researched, there is a lacuna in the literature that considers language status as the outcome of rational choice or purposive action of criminal justice stakeholders. This chapter draws on rational choice theory to explore the status of Kwéyòl in St. Lucia's criminal justice system and to frame a critical discussion about the potential implications of the language's low status for its speakers who participate in the system. It proposes that language status can be the subject of free choice of rational individuals. The chapter also localizes the stakeholders or actors in a broader sociolinguistic context that sometimes go beyond individual choice or preference. By modeling language status as a product of individuals' choice, the chapter offers new insight into the nature of rationality in according and maintaining language status.

The Status of Kwéyòl in St. Lucia's Constitution: A Rational Choice?

St. Lucia's constitution is the defining source of law of the country, which determines the shape of the criminal justice system. Therefore, any understanding of language status in this system must be rooted in the statutory provisions or laws (or the lack thereof) in the constitution that pertain to language. A careful study of St. Lucia's constitution revealed a stark absence of constitutional provisions that specifically deal with language issues in the state and its institutions. Also noteworthy is the absence of constitutional provisions to outlaw discrimination on the grounds of language or to include language among the grounds upon which discrimination is constitutionally prohibited in the Bill of Rights. Chapter 1 (1) of the constitution states that,

> Whereas every person in St. Lucia is entitled to the fundamental rights and freedoms, that is to say, the right, whatever his or her race, place of origin, political opinions, colour, creed or sex ...

This omission of language is particularly glaring, given that at the time that the constitution was framed and instituted in 1979 as a product of St. Lucia's independence (Antoine, 1998, pp. 4–5), there had already been a deep-rooted stigma attached to Kwéyòl. Persons whose linguistic competence was largely confined to Kwéyòl were regarded as inferior, as belonging to the lower strata of society, not because it was poorly developed or structured, but it was the language of the African slave, the black man and woman (Lubin & Serieux-Lubin, 2011). Therefore, language marginalization and discrimination issues would have already been an inherent part of this sociolinguistic context, which would have warranted the inclusion of language in the Bill of Rights in the constitution.

The omission of Kwéyòl and the implications for its status in the criminal justice system can be explained using a rational choice framework, which holds that individuals are seen to make rational decisions based on the extent to which they expect to maximize their benefits and minimize costs (Gül, 2009, p. 38). I argue that the framers of the constitution made a rational choice, which was most in line with their personal preferences, to ignore Kwéyòl and omit it from the constitution. They were the local, political élite, a small minority of expatriate Englishmen, headed by the Governor (Alleyne, 1961, p. 6) who moved into the social and political void created by the gradual diminution in numbers of English colonials (Midgett, 1970) and they were also "English-speaking." This is supported by Alleyne (1961) who states that the advent of English-speaking people as a political élite and their later development into a cultural and economic élite have been attended by the introduction of English as the language of social, cultural, and economic prestige (p. 4). Prior to independence, St. Lucia had been a British colony for 165 years after the British gained ultimate control of it from the French in 1814. Therefore, during that period, its laws were anglicized and English became institutionalized as the socially dominant as well as the most valuable language in the society. Therefore, at the time of independence, English was already established as the language with the greater political, economic, educational, and legal utility, and the language of prestige with exclusive formal functions, none of which were fulfilled by Kwéyòl. One could argue that the framers of the constitution did not make a rational choice to omit Kwéyòl and that its exclusion was enabled and constrained by the preexisting, broader sociolinguistic context in which the language was situated. This supports Elster's (1989) view of rationality in which he refers to structural constraints as "All the physical, economic, legal, and psychological constraints that an individual faces" (p. 14). Recast in linguistic terms, Elster's structural constraints are the social context and situational factors (Myers-Scotton & Bolonyai, 2001, pp. 13–14) that affect linguistic choices. However, Myers-Scotton and Bolonyai (2001) warn that although they impinge on choices, they do not ordain the actual choices and choice comes AFTER (sic) structural constraints have had their effects. Similarly, Cruickshank (2000) posits that,

> Social structures may exert a causal influence over individuals, but this means that they only condition, but do not determine, the activity of individuals. Thus, over time, individuals may affect changes in structures (p. 81).

Therefore, even though the choice of the framers of the constitution may have been constrained by the broader sociolinguistic milieu, it did not determine their agency. They could have made a rational choice to change the status of Kwéyòl if they wanted to, instead of choosing to perpetuate the dominant negative ideologies and the colonially imposed language values on Kwéyòl. In addition, given that independence afforded them an opportunity to make independent decisions, without seeking acceptance from England, they could have made a rational choice to change the function of Kwéyòl, as well as its status. After independence, they made no attempt to alter the legal or the social status of English, even though as mentioned previously, it was not the language that was most widely spoken by St. Lucians at the time. Therefore, it is quite evident that although St. Lucia became politically independent, it remained linguistically dependent on the colonial language.

With specific regard to the criminal justice system, the English jurisprudence was retained and maintained along with its language, and the relevant authorities exhibited failure in their ability to put the island's own linguistic stamp on its justice. Rational choice also considers individual behavior to be a function of preferences of individuals (Hetcher, 1986, p. 268). In the case of the St. Lucian elite, I argue that the elite made a rational choice to keep Kwéyòl in its place because of their preferences and benefits that were to be derived from this choice. English was used by the elite to delineate social group membership in a social context where the speakers of English were in the minority. This is supported by Alleyne (1961) who submits that in St. Lucia, people who have great facility in speaking English pay considerable attention to the preservation of this index of separation from the uneducated poorer masses. Some, we have seen, even disclaim any linguistic ability in French creole [Kwéyòl] (p. 8).

In addition to the maintenance of the linguistic status quo, the choice to promote English over Kwéyòl also had economic benefits, as a means of bettering St. Lucia's trade position with other English-official neighbors and English-speaking countries and Kwéyòl would have been regarded as limiting the scope of the island's trading capacity. Another factor that may have influenced the choice of English is that the written constitutions of the Caribbean borrowed heavily from international human rights instruments, and were constructed with much less indigenous input than is usually expected of such defining documents (Antoine, 1998). The use of English as the language of these instruments reinforced the preeminence of English in St. Lucia's constitution.

THE STATUS OF KWÉYÒL IN THE LANGUAGE PROCEDURES AND PRACTICES OF THE POLICE

Although the constitution does not spell out the meaning and consequences of language status in St. Lucia, it contains statutes about language matters, most of which pertain to the criminal justice system. More specifically, the first two pertain directly to the preliminary phases of criminal case processing, which falls under the remit of the police, and the third one pertains to the courts. The first one, found in Chapter 1(3)(2) states,

> (2) Any person who is arrested or detained shall with reasonable promptitude and in any case no later than 24 hours after such arrest or detention be informed in a language that he or she understands of the reasons for his or her arrest or detention ...

The second one found in Chapter 1 (8)(2) (b) mandates that,

> (2) Every person who is charged with a criminal offence

> (b) shall be informed as soon as reasonably practicable, in a language that he or she understands and in detail, of the nature of the offence charged;

Given that the act of arresting and charging suspects falls within the ambit of the police, the statutes place an added language responsibility on the police officers. In other words, they are constrained by the law to inform persons of their arrest and the nature of the offense charged in "a language that they understand." Despite this constraint, the law enables them to exercise rational choice in its enactment, within the limited scope of their choices. This is supported by Cruickshank (2000) who contends that structure and culture are "more than" individuals and individual agents with free will are both enabled and constrained by culture and structure, which includes the law. Therefore, in their attempt to adhere to the law, the police officers can make a rational choice to take on the language responsibility themselves or they can choose to employ an independent party. According to the data, 76% of the police officers surveyed listed English and Kwéyòl as the two languages that they speak. Only four respondents (5%) recorded English as the only language that they speak. The data also revealed that 69% of the police officers claimed to inform Kwéyòl speakers, who are not competent in English, of the reasons for their arrest in Kwéyòl, "the language that they understand."

With regard to the second statute, which relates to charging suspects, 69% of the police officers also claimed to charge English speakers in English and Kwéyòl speakers in Kwéyòl. However, in order to charge foreign language speakers, they seek the assistance of an independent party such as a teacher or an embassy employee who speaks relevant language. Even though there may be police officers who speak a foreign language, they would still seek outside assistance to deal with a foreign language speaker. This is because, the foreign languages such as French, Spanish, or German are languages with official language status and must be dealt with in an "official" manner. Kwéyòl, on the other hand, receives a different treatment because of its status. It is regarded as just a local language that many St. Lucians speak that does not require any "special" or "official" treatment. Thus, although police officers can make a rational choice to outsource assistance for Kwéyòl speakers, it has become the norm for them to deal with Kwéyòl speakers themselves. They make this choice mainly because many of them consider themselves to be competent in Kwéyòl by virtue of being St. Lucian. For instance, during a personal interview, an inspector stated that "All police officers are bilingual, they speak English and Kwéyòl." However, contrary to the inspector's proclamation, the data showed that while all of the police officers are St. Lucian, 24% of them did not name Kwéyòl as one of the languages that they speak. These officers indicated that when they encounter a Kwéyòl speaker, they normally seek assistance, from a Kwéyòl-speaking police officer, to deal with them on their behalf.

The data has shown that police officers in St. Lucia willingly provide "in-house" assistance to Kwéyòl speakers in the execution of their language-related duties in accordance with the law, despite its low status in the society. This practice can be viewed as an instance of rational choice their part, in which they have calculated costs and benefits. It is beneficial to them to use Kwéyòl themselves for a number of reasons. First, it allows them to fulfill of some of their language duties and also enables them to adhere to the law. Second, it is timesaving, as it allows them deal with Kwéyòl speakers immediately or on-the-spot, rather than having to deal with delays that can occur when waiting for outside assistance. Third, it is more economical for them to provide in-house assistance as opposed to paying persons, who are untrained as they are, to do a job that they can do themselves, since they normally have to pay for interpreting services. Given these benefits, they have embraced the language as an inevitable part of their practices, even when the law does not require them to do so, for example, when taking reports and statements. However, researchers have expressed concern about the absence of clear-cut demarcations between police officers' policing and interpreting roles that could have a negative impact on justice administration. These include, inter alia, issues of false confessions, impartiality and conflict of interest, and interpreter training and qualifications (Berk-Seligson, 2000).

As far as the status of Kwéyòl is concerned in criminal case processing in St. Lucia, it enjoys the same standing with English on an oral level, in that they are both spoken by police officers when necessary. However, with regard to its written status, it is still subordinate to English as all writing is done in English. The data revealed that the standard procedure used by police officers to record any statements made in Kwéyòl is to record them in English rather than in Kwéyòl. However, this practice cannot be adequately described as an outcome of the rational choice of the police officers. This finding is supported by Elster (1983) who states that action is not always rational and individuals cannot always choose a course of action that is in line with their personal preferences. Hindess (1988) also contends that actors do things that are not the result of any decision, and they must be explained in some other way. Therefore, the police officers do not choose to record Kwéyòl discourse in English and even though it may be their individual preference to record it in Kwéyòl, they do not have the ability to do so. Their ability to write Kwéyòl has been constrained by the broader social structure, which excludes it from the formal education system.

Social structures are, for rational theorists, chains of interconnected individual actions. They are the "patterns that result from individual actions" (Scott, 2000). Although there are orthographic systems for writing Kwéyòl, many St. Lucians, including police officers, are not competent in the use of these systems. Consequently, anything that is spoken in Kwéyòl that must be recorded is interpreted by the attending Kwéyòl-speaking police officer, and written in English. This is encapsulated by one police officer who states, "We try to speak to them [Kwéyòl speakers] in Creole...well we translate it ourselves and we reduce it in writing in English and when we read it over to them we read it in Creole."

There are several notable issues that this practice could pose for the proper administration of justice to Kwéyòl speakers. As soon as spoken Kwéyòl is "reduced in writing in English," it is instantly lost. Monolingual English transcripts, that are subsequently (back-)translated in to Kwéyòl, as stated by the police officer above, can be fraught with problems when, as is commonly the case, the court has no access to the original recordings and relies solely on the police transcript, which may in turn be inaccurate or incomplete. Kredens and Morris (2010) warn that in such cases, due to the almost infinite number of linguistic permutations available, the back-translated version in the suspect's language is highly likely to differ, perhaps significantly, from the actual words they uttered (p. 463). Additionally, given that records of police interviews could become important evidence in court, the total absence of Kwéyòl in records of verbal interactions with Kwéyòl speakers could have serious implications for access to and delivery of justice, particularly in cases that go to trial. This is because the court has no way of verifying the accuracy or veracity of the recorded information, and the police officer's record, which may or may not be accurate, becomes the only record. It is quite evident that the reduction of spoken Kwéyòl to written English, makes it difficult for the language to have any "real" status in criminal case processing and it also gives police officers way too much power over the recorded evidence.

THE STATUS OF KWÉYÒL IN THE MAGISTRATES' COURTS

The third statute, which is found in Chapter 1 (8) (2) (f), mandates that,

(2) Every person who is charged with a criminal offence

> (f) shall be permitted to have without payment the assistance of an interpreter if he or she cannot understand the language used at the trial

In contrast to the first two statutes, this one does not provide an accused person with the right to be tried in "a language that he understands." If this were the case, then Kwéyòl speakers, after having been cautioned and charged in their language by the police, would have to be tried in Kwéyòl, in the courts. However, instead of allowing St. Lucian citizens who are not competent English to use their own language freely in their defense, the law permits them to have an interpreter, free of charge. This constitutional language-related right is neatly couched within the framework of an accused right to a fair trial, which spans a number of rights designed to prevent the arbitrary exercise and use of excess power by a state in the criminal trial process and, at the same time, promote trial fairness for an accused (Brown-Blake, 2006). However, an inherent flaw in the statute is that it does not spell out the nature and function of an interpreter. Another notable shortcoming is that there is an underlying misconception in the law that assumes that interpretation is only needed for an accused in order to ensure a fair trial as it is not extended to witnesses who do not speak the language of the court. Therefore, if there is a Kwéyòl-speaking witness who comes to testify on behalf of the defendant, the law does not require him or her to be provided with an interpreter. How, then, does this promote trial fairness for an accused? Hale (2004) asserts that if one participant cannot understand or be understood, it is the legal process itself that suffers and justice cannot be done (pp. 440–441).

In spite of these language-related constitutional constraints, magistrates in the magistrates' courts in St. Lucia make a rational choice to provide "interpreters" for anyone (for example plaintiffs, witnesses) who cannot understand the language used at the trial. The findings revealed that the court provides different interpreters for persons of different language backgrounds. However, there is a difference in the quality of the interpreters that are provided. For instance, when the need for an interpreter for a foreign language speaker arises, the court normally appoints a teacher (from the secondary or tertiary level) or an employee from the relevant embassy who has formal training in the relevant language, although they are not trained in court interpreting. This person also has to be sanctioned by the prosecution and defense, before he or she is appointed. However, Evans (2011–2012) notes that in the case of the Kwéyòl speaker, the function of interpreter, is normally fulfilled by the clerk of the courts, who does not have to be sanctioned by the prosecution and defense. This means that he or she is appointed by the court in addition to his or her normal duties, as the "resident interpreter" for Kwéyòl speakers and interprets for them when called upon to do so by both local and foreign magistrates.

The reduction of spoken Kwéyòl to written English, continues in the magistrates' courts where all cases are formally recorded in English. English speech is, in turn, interpreted into Kwéyòl for Kwéyòl speakers by the clerk, but it is not recorded in writing. As a result, where interpreters are used in courtrooms, the official transcript records only the English utterances, so that the original utterances, in a language other than English, have no legal status (Eades, 2003). Similar to the case of the police, the use of English to record court proceedings is not an outcome of the rational choice of the magistrates, who are responsible for recording court proceedings.

Although some local magistrates speak Kwéyòl, they do not have written competence in the language, and foreign magistrates have no competence in the language. However, in contrast to the practices of the police, where police officers interpret and record for themselves, the clerk of the courts interprets for the courts, even in cases where the magistrates and lawyers are all local and are competent in Kwéyòl. Thus, local magistrates, who are competent in Kwéyòl, make a rational choice to allow a third party, who is not trained in interpreting to do it for them, instead of doing it for themselves. These interpretations become the facts of a case and since the official transcript records only English utterances, the actual utterance of a Kwéyòl-speaking defendant during trial has no legal status and is completely unavailable in an appeal case. It is the interpreter's English version, which is the basis of any legal argument or decision (Eades, 2003). Although one could argue that these local magistrates are adhering to the law by providing interpreters for Kwéyòl speakers who do not speak English, the interpreters that are provided are not trained in interpreting and they sometimes provide inaccurate interpretations. It is ironic that although the local magistrates and lawyers do not speak Kwéyòl in the courts, some of them are able to correct inaccurate interpretations provided by the clerk. This practice is, therefore, highly ceremonial and does not benefit the court in anyway, except to maintain the dominant status of English, and to perpetuate language practices that are essentially Eurocentric and classist. It also shows that 40 years after independence, the courts have failed to evolve, to become more inclusive, and to provide fair and equal justice for all St. Lucians.

CONCLUSIONS AND RECOMMENDATIONS

Language plays a crucial role in the processes of the criminal justice system, particularly in postcolonial multilingual situations where official language status is accorded to one language in the system. St. Lucia, is a typical example of such a situation, where English is the only language that has de facto official standing in the criminal justice system. Using a rational choice model, this chapter sought to examine the status of Kwéyòl in the practices and processes of the system to find how they impact the administration of justice to Kwéyòl speakers. The findings revealed that its absence in the constitution has played a significant role maintaining its low status, and its traditional, static, unofficial position in the criminal justice system in St. Lucia.

With regard to its status in police procedures, although it is used by the police to speak to Kwéyòl speakers in criminal case processing, they are unable to use it in writing. A major consequence of their inability to write Kwéyòl is that everything that a Kwéyòl speaker says to the police in Kwéyòl, is "reduced" in writing in English, rather than in Kwéyòl, for the record. The problem for Kwéyòl-speaking suspects is that the written English transcripts that are produced by the police, which contain no trace of their actual utterances, could become crucial evidence if they are charged and the case goes to trial. This practice places them in at a severe disadvantage in the court where the judge or the magistrate will only hear or read the words of the police, instead of their own words. Kwéyòl speakers cannot be receiving fair justice if their language, which they used to speak to the police, is wholly debarred from entering the courts through writing.

In terms of its status in the courts, Kwéyòl continues to occupy markedly lower status than English and its use is even more restricted than it is in the first phase of the system. While it is used willingly by police officers in the course of their duties, its use in the court is restricted to Kwéyòl speakers and the clerk of courts, who is the most junior member of the court. A notable finding is that local magistrates and lawyers, who proclaim to be competent in Kwéyòl, make a rational choice to not use the language in court. Despite their competence in the language, they choose to rely on clerks of the courts who are not trained in interpreting, to interpret from Kwéyòl to English. Instructively, this practice only serves to reinforce the dominant status of English as the language of choice in St. Lucia's courts.

Although Kwéyòl has wide local currency, and its speakers have been participating in the criminal justice processes in St. Lucia for more than a century, the relevant authorities have made a rational choice to maintain its status, despite the disadvantage to its speakers, in a system that purports to provide justice for all. Therefore, this chapter calls on the relevant authorities to make a new, long overdue set of rational choices, which must be based on calculations of the costs and benefits for proper justice administration, instead of on their personal language preferences. The first choice that must be made is the inclusion of language among the grounds upon which discrimination is legally prohibited in the Bill of Rights in the constitution. This will legally prohibit language discrimination in all public formal domains.

Another crucial decision must be made to change and elevate the current status of Kwéyòl and allow it to perform official language functions in all domains. However, this can only be done if it is acknowledged in the constitution as one of the legitimate languages of the country and is accorded official language status. If Kwéyòl is constitutionally legitimized as an official language, then Kwéyòl speakers will have a right to use their language in all state institutions. When this right is protected by law, interference by anyone with their exercise of that right will be constrained by the authorities. The support of the law is absolutely critical and without it the status of Kwéyòl in St. Lucian society will remain as stagnant as it has always been and Kwéyòl speakers will inevitably continue to experience unjust treatment and no protection from language discrimination, on account of the status of their language.

REFERENCES

Alleyne, M. C. (1961). Language and society in St. Lucia. *Caribbean Studies, 1*(1), 1–10.

Alleyne, M. C. (1971). Acculturation and the cultural matrix of creolization. In D. Hymes (Ed.),

Pidginization and creolization of languages (pp. 169–186). Cambridge: Cambridge University Press.

Antoine, R. B. (1998). *Commonwealth Caribbean Law and legal systems* (2nd ed.), New York: Routledge-Cavendish Publishing Limited.

Berk-Seligson, S. (2000). Interpreting for the police: Issues in pre-trial phases of the judicial process. *Forensic Linguistics* 7(2), 213–237.

Brown-Blake, C. (2006). Fair trial, language and the right to interpretation. *International Journal on Minority and Group Rights*, 13, 391–412.

Brown-Blake, C. (2014). Expanding the use of non-dominant Caribbean languages: Can the law help? *The International Journal of Speech, Language and the Law, 21(1),* 51–82.

Burns, R. G. (2007). *The criminal justice system.* New Jersey: Pearson Prentice Hall.

Canagarajah, A. S. (2013). *Translingual practice: Global Englishes and cosmopolitan realities.* London: Routledge.

Carrington, L. D. (1999). The status of creole in the Caribbean. *Caribbean Quarterly,* 45(1/2), 41–61.

Coleman, J. S. (1990). *Foundations of social theory.* Cambridge: Belknap.

Constitution of St. Lucia. Statutory Instrument 1978 No. 1901, (U.K.), Schedule 1.

Cruickshank, J. (2000). Social theory and the underclass: Social realism or rational choice individualism. In S. Archer & J. Q. Tritter (Eds.), Rational choice theory: Resisting colonization. (pp. 71–92). London: Routledge.

David, M. K., & Powell, R. (2003). *Constraints on language choice in postcolonial legal systems: Comparing Kenya and Malaysia.* Symposium on language, law and life, 30th International Systemic Functional Linguistics Conference, Lucknow.

Eades, D. (2003). Participation of second language and second dialect speakers in the legal system. *Annual Review of Applied Linguistics* 23, 113–133.

Elster, J. (1983). *Sour grapes.* Cambridge: Cambridge University Press.

Elster, J. (1989). *Nuts and bolts for the social sciences.* Cambridge: Cambridge University Press.

Evans, S. R. (2012). Language rights and legal wrongs: Examining the right to an interpreter in Magistrates' courts in St. Lucia. *Sargasso: Language rights and language police in the Caribbean,* 2011–2012 (2), 53–67.

Ferreira, J. S. (2012). Caribbean languages and linguistics. In B. Reid (Ed.), *Caribbean heritage* (pp. 130–148). Jamaica: University of the West Indies Press.

Gül, S. K. (2009). An evaluation of rational choice theory in criminology. *Girne American University Journal of Social and Applied Sciences,* 4(8), 36–44.

Hale, S. (2004). *The discourse of court interpreting.* Amsterdam/Philadelphia: John Benjamins.

Hang Ng, K. (2009). *The common law in two voices: Language, law & the post-colonial predicament in Hong Kong.* California: Stanford University Press.

Hetcher, M. (1986). Rational choice theory and the study of ethnic and race relations. In J. Rex & D. Mason (Eds.), *Theories of ethnic and race relations* (pp. 264–279). Cambridge: Cambridge University Press.

Hechter, M., & Kanazawa, S. (1997). Sociological rational choice theory. *Annual Review of Sociology, 23,* 191–214.

Hindess, B. (1988). *Choice, rationality, and social theory.* London: Unwin Hyman.

Holm, J. (2000). *An introduction to pidgins and creoles.* Cambridge: Cambridge University Press.

Jordan, B. (1989). *The common good: Citizenship, orality and self-interest.* Oxford: Blackwell Publishers.

Kredens, K., & Morris, R. (2010). "A shattered mirror?" Interpreting in legal contexts outside the courtroom. In M. Coulthard & A. Johnson (Eds.), *The Routledge handbook of forensics linguistics* (pp. 455–472). New York: Routledge.

Leung, E. S. M. (2008). Interpreting for the minority, interpreting for the power. In John Gibbons and T. Turell (Eds.), *Dimensions of forensic linguistics* (pp. 197–211). Amsterdam/Philadelphia: John Benjamins Publishing Company.

Lubin, I. A., & Serieux-Lubin, L. K. (2011). Reviving indigenous language and culture in post-colonial Sent Lisi (St. Lucia). *International Journal of Humanities and Social Sciences, 1*(9), (267–274).

Mackey, W. F. (1989). Determining the status and functions of languages in multinational societies. In U. Ammon (Ed.), *Status and function of languages and language varieties* (pp. 3–20). Berlin: Walter de Gruyter.

Midgett, D. (1970). Bilingualism and linguistic change in St. Lucia. *Anthropological Linguistics, 12,* 158–170.

Myers-Scotton, C., & Bolonyai, A. (2001). Calculating speakers: Code-switching in a rational choice model. *Language in Society, 31,* 1–28.

Patrick, P., & Buell, S. (2000). Competing creole transcripts on trial. *Essex Research Reports in Linguistics*, 32, 103–132.

Porter, C. (2018). Language status. In J. I. Liontas (Ed.), *The TESOL encyclopedia of English language teaching* (pp. 1–6). New Jersey: John Wiley & Sons, Inc.

Powell, R. (2008). *Motivations for language choice in Malaysian courtrooms and implications for language planning.* Kuala Lumpur: Universiti Malaya.

Rakner, L. (1996). Rational choice and the problem of institutions. A discussion of rational choice institutionalism and its application by Robert Bates. *Working paper*, Chr. Michelsen Institute, Development Studies and Human Rights, Bergen Norway.

Scott, J. (2000). Rational choice theory. In G. Browning, A. Halcli & F. Webster (Eds.), *Understanding contemporary society: Theories of the present* (pp. 671–685). Sage Publications.

St-Hilaire, A. (2003). Globalization, urbanization, and language in Caribbean development. *New West Indian Guide/Nieuwe West-Indische Gids* 7, 1(2), 65–84.

Thekiso, E. (2001). *A sociolinguistic analysis of communication processes in a bilingual court of law in Garborone, Botswana.* (Doctoral Dissertation). University of Warwick.

The St. Lucia Government Gazette Extraordinary. (2004). Vol. 173 Issue 15.

Yahya-Othman, S., & Batibo, H. (1996). The swinging pendulum: English in Tanzania, 1940–1990. In J. A. Fishman, A. W. Conrad & A. Rubal-Lopez (Eds.), *Post-imperial English status change in former British and American colonies, 1940–1990* (pp. 373–399). Berlin: Mouton de Gruyter.

CHAPTER IX

ASSESSING THE JUDICIARY IN TRINIDAD AND TOBAGO: VIEWS FROM A LEADING JUDICIAL OFFICER

Wendell C. Wallace

The University of the West Indies, St. Augustine, Trinidad and Tobago

ABSTRACT

The judiciary in Trinidad and Tobago is an integral component of the island's criminal justice system. The structure and operation of Trinidad and Tobago's judiciary generally mirrors that of its former colonial master, the UK, due to the island's past attachment as a former colony of England. However, while many aspects of the English judiciary have been contemporized, certain aspects of the judiciary in Trinidad and Tobago are outdated, antiquated and mired in controversy. While there is available literature of the criminal justice system in Trinidad and Tobago, research focusing solely on the judiciary is rare and even rarer is qualitative research with leading functionaries from the jurisdiction's judiciary. As a result, the current research effort was conducted to fill that lacuna. The findings indicate a convoluted judicial system that is in dire need of reform. Other key findings and recommendations are also discussed.

Keywords: Judiciary, criminal justice system, judicial officer, post-colonialism, Trinidad and Tobago

INTRODUCTION

In order to assess the state of the Judiciary in Trinidad and Tobago, the researcher decided to utilize a qualitative approach. This approach was chosen as qualitative research tends to elicit rich contextual data which may not be so succinctly obtained through quantitative methods.

Qualitative data also provides a rich, detailed picture about the operation of systems, the individuals who are employed within the system and their feelings about the system. In the current research effort, the qualitative approach is premised on a host of separate, yet, inter-related factors. For example, the aim of this research is to have real-world application that can assist the Judiciary in Trinidad and Tobago. With this in mind, the qualitative approach used in this research afford the researcher the following: (1) content that is useful for practical application, (2) a chance to develop specific insights into the workings of the Judiciary in Trinidad and Tobago, (3) conversion of individual, practitioner experiences into usable data, and (4) the opportunity to probe deeper into convoluted issues (see Atieno, 2009). Keeping in mind the aim of the research, the researcher decided to interview Senior Counsel Mrs. Pamela L. Elder, President of the Criminal Bar Association of Trinidad and Tobago.

Mrs. Pamela L. Elder is an Attorney-at-Law (Senior Counsel) in Trinidad and Tobago and is the Head of Chamber at Guerra, Elder and Associates. She is the holder of a Law degree (LLB) and a Legal Education Certificate (LEC) from the University of the West Indies and the Hugh Wooding Law School (HWLS), respectively. Mrs. Elder is a respectful, humble, and motherly individual whose approach is premised on that of an educator, having taught for many years at a family-owned educational institute, Elders and Associates.

As a child, Mrs. Elder was raised in Belmont, on the outskirts of Port-of-Spain with her father and mother until she was a teenager; however, she credits her mother as her real inspiration and influence. She considers her status as that of the poor class during her childhood and credits her successful upbringing to the strengths of her parents who instilled within her strong spiritual and family values as well as the importance of education. She attended the Belmont Girls RC primary School and later the St. Francois Girl's College before pursing tertiary education. She is the middle child of three children and is the only female. SC Elder's route to becoming an Attorney-at-Law is quite interesting and is based on a calculated decision. In fact, Mrs. Elder SC had no real childhood desire to become an Attorney-at-Law, but was largely due to her weakness in Mathematics which precluded her from entering the field of Mathematics or Science. She therefore made a calculated decision to pursue Law as she had to operate within her limitations in order to achieve academic success.

Mrs. Elder, who is married, is the mother of three adult children, one male and two females; however, none of her children followed her career path. At the time of the interview, her son was completing his Doctoral studies in Petroleum Engineering in Edinburgh, Scotland, while one daughter had recently completed her Master of Science Degree in Computer Science at University of Aberystwyth, Wales, and her youngest daughter was a 4th year medical student at the Royal College of Surgeons (RCSI) in Dublin, Ireland.

THE RESEARCH CONTEXT

The Republic of Trinidad and Tobago is a unitary twin-island, archipelagic Republic state in the Southern Caribbean. The country consists of two main islands: (1) Trinidad, and (2) Tobago, as well as numerous smaller landforms. Trinidad is the larger and more populous of the main islands, comprising about 96 percent of Trinidad and Tobago's 1.3 million citizens, while Tobago is the smaller island. Its neighbors include Venezuela to the south-west and Grenada to the north. Trinidad and Tobago shares maritime boundaries with Barbados to the northeast, Guyana to the southeast, and Venezuela to the south and west. Trinidad and Tobago has a bicameral parliamentary system based on the Westminster System and the Head of State is the President, currently Her Excellency Paula-Mae Weekes. The Head of Government is the Prime Minister, currently Dr. Keith C. Rowley.

In 1498, Spain claimed Trinidad as a Spanish colony while Tobago changed hands on numerous occasions between Spanish, British, French, Dutch, and Courlander colonizers. In 1802, Trinidad and Tobago was ceded to Britain under the Treaty of Amiens. The two colonies were amalgamated in 1889. Thereafter, Trinidad and Tobago was part of the British Empire and was ruled in the name of the Queen by a Governor. Independence from Britain was attained in 1962 and on August 1, 1976, Trinidad and Tobago ceased to be a part of Her Majesty's dominions and became a Republic within the Commonwealth. The Queen was replaced as the Head of State by a President and a new Constitution was put in place via the Constitution of the Republic of Trinidad and Tobago Act 1976 (1976/4) (Trinidad and Tobago).

Politically, Trinidad and Tobago is divided into Municipal Corporations and the Tobago House of Assembly. Presently, there are 14 Municipal

Corporations in Trinidad with responsibility for infrastructure and local governance, while the Tobago House of Assembly (THA) is the local government body responsible for Tobago. The THA is responsible for local government functions in Tobago as well as carrying out some of the responsibilities of central government within Tobago (*Tobago House of Assembly Act, 1996, Schedule Five*); however, it cannot conduct several functions of Central Government such as collection of taxes, creation of local laws, and/or the imposition of zoning regulations (*Tobago House of Assembly Act, 1996, Schedule Six*). The THA is enshrined within the constitution of the Republic of Trinidad and Tobago for the "... purpose of making better provision for the administration of the Island of Tobago and for matters connected therewith" (*Constitution of the Republic of Trinidad and Tobago, Legal Supplement, Part A*).

THE JUDICIARY OF TRINIDAD AND TOBAGO

In Trinidad and Tobago, the Judiciary is the third arm of the State, established by the Constitution to operate independently from the Executive and the Legislature as a forum for the resolution of legal disputes. The Judiciary is independent of the other branches (Executive and Legislature) and is free from outside interference. According to Zimmermann, Lawes, and Svenson (2012, p. 117), "The long shadow of colonialism has exerted an indelible influence on the cultures and institutions of the Caribbean for centuries" and Trinidad and Tobago is no exception. Indeed, Trinidad and Tobago's past colonial attachment to the UK has influenced its judicial system as it follows the UK's judicial model, with some local variations. With this in mind, the laws in Trinidad and Tobago consist of a mixture of English common law and statute law. The prosecutorial system is utilized in the island, the doctrine of precedent is applicable and judgments of the Supreme Court of Judicature of Trinidad and Tobago and of the Judicial Committee of the Privy Council are binding, while those of the UK and the Commonwealth are highly persuasive.

Quite notably, there is the Caribbean Court of Justice which was established in 2001 to "provide for the Caribbean Community an accessible, fair, efficient, innovative and impartial justice system built on a jurisprudence reflective of Caribbean history, values and traditions, while maintaining an inspirational, independent institution worthy of emulation by the courts of the region and the trust and confidence of its people" (http://www.caribbeancourtofjustice.org/). Instructively, though the seat of the CCJ is located in Port of Spain, Trinidad and Tobago, and has both original and appellate jurisdiction, Trinidad and Tobago does not subscribe to this court and the island's final appellate court is the Privy Council that is based in England.

The Constitution of Trinidad and Tobago provides for a Chief Justice to be appointed by the President after consultation with the Prime Minister and the Leader of the Opposition. Other Supreme Court Judges are appointed by the President acting in accordance with the advice of the Judicial and Legal Service Commission. The Chief Justice is the Head of the Judiciary and has overall responsibility for the administration of justice in Trinidad and Tobago. The Chief Justice is President of the Court of Appeal and is the Chairman of the Judicial and Legal Service Commission. He is also ex-officio, a judge of the High Court and can therefore sit in that Court. The current Chief Justice is The Honorable Mr. Ivor Archie. The court system in Trinidad and Tobago has three levels. They are:

1. The Magistrates' Court;

2. The Supreme Court of Judicature, which consists of the High Court of Justice and the Court of Appeal, the second level; and

3. The Judicial Committee of the Privy Council (the final Court of Appeal).

The Magistrates' Court

The Magistrates' Court has limited jurisdiction and presides over minor cases related to criminal, civil, and youth offender crimes. The Magistracy exercises original jurisdiction in relation to summary criminal matters. The Magistrates' Courts also facilitates Preliminary Inquiries into serious indictable criminal matters to determine whether a prima facie case has been established against an accused person before he or she can be indicted for trial at the High Court Division of the Supreme Court. The Petty Civil Court Division of the Magistracy deals with civil matters involving small money claims of less than $50,000.00 (http://www. ttlawcourts.org/). There are thirteen (13) magisterial districts in Trinidad and Tobago, namely: St George West (covering Port of Spain and environs), Tunapuna, Chaguanas, Couva, San Fernando, Point Fortin, Arima,

Sangre Grande, Princes Town, Rio Claro, Mayaro, Siparia, and Scarborough (Tobago). For the Magistracy, there is a Chief Magistrate who is supported in the 13 magisterial districts by a Deputy Chief Magistrate, 13 Senior Magistrates, and 42 Magistrates. More than one Magistrate's Court operates in some of these districts and a Clerk of the Peace is attached to each of the courts.

The Supreme Court

The Supreme Court of Judicature consists of the High Court of Justice and the Chief Justice and 10 puisne judges. Its jurisdiction, practices, and procedures follow closely those of the High Court of Justice in England. Civil actions and proceedings are usually heard by only one High Court judge but may be tried by a jury of nine members, while a High Court judge with a jury of 9–12 members tries criminal offenses. The Supreme Court includes the Court of Appeals which is the country's highest Court and consists of the Chief Justice and three other justices. The Supreme Court has unlimited jurisdiction over appeals of criminal and civil matters. The Judicial Committee of the Privy Council in London decides final appeal on some matters. There are other judicial bodies (specialized courts) such as the Industrial Court and the Tax Appeal Board in Trinidad and Tobago's legal system.

Though the Judiciary in Trinidad and Tobago is independent of the Executive and the Legislature, and is generally viewed as being strong, there exist several flaws in its operations. That there are serious flaws within the Judiciary in Trinidad and Tobago is no secret and has been complemented by the views expressed by High Court Judge, Justice Mr. Malcolm Holdip as cited in Wallace (2017). The major flaw of the Judiciary in Trinidad and Tobago appears to be the immobile manner in which cases move through the system. In other words, the system appears to have ingested the tranquilizing drug of gradualism (King, 1964) as some serious criminal matters take an inordinate length of time from arrest to trial and conviction or acquittal and also seems slow to adapt to the modern realities of life.

This situation has led to inmates spending many years on remand, in some instances between 8 and 12 years (Al-Rawi, 2016; Wallace, Hill, and Rosales, forthcoming). The end result is that there have been riots by remand inmates protesting the inhumane condition of the Remand Yard at prisons in Trinidad and Tobago as well as inmates escaping from prison and highlighting their plight on social media. The most recent of those escapes being eight inmates who escaped from the Remand Yard at Golden Grove Prison in Arouca in May 2019 (Dowlat, 2019). In recognition of the inordinate delays in trial and the length of time inmates spend on remand in Trinidad and Tobago, Justice Rajendra Narine in the matter of Walter Borneo v. The State Cr. App. No. 7 of 2011 held that any time spent in pre-trial custody should be fully taken into account by means of an arithmetical deduction when imposing sentences on convicted offenders in the jurisdiction.

The Interview

The interview with Defense Lawyer, Mrs. Pamela L. Elder SC was conducted on Thursday, June 9 and August 2, 2016 at the conference room of her chambers at Guerra, Elder and Associates at No. 40 Alfredo Street, Woodbrook, in the island of Trinidad. This location is an urban area on the outskirts of the capital Port-of-Spain and is a hub of social and other activities. The interviews were conducted in a very permissive atmosphere which was devoid of any interruptions and were cordial and pleasant in keeping with the personality of Senior Counsel Pamela L. Elder. As the head of her Chamber, Mrs. Elder is responsible for the supervision of eleven (11) junior Attorneys and was clearly delighted to be interviewed for this project and spoke glowingly, openly, and frankly on a wide range of issues inclusive of her challenges as a female in a male-dominated profession as well as her experiences of being an Attorney, the importance of values and humility, the role of Defense Counsel in the local (contemporary) criminal justice systems, challenges to the Judiciary and sentencing options.

Mrs. Elder is a motherly, nurturing individual who is very eloquent in speech and who appears very passionate about her profession. She is desirous of seeing reforms within the legal system and was very compassionate, understanding, and empathetic to the woes of persons in the underprivileged class who she often represents with verve and vigor. Quite interestingly, Mrs. Elder (SC) spoke about the need for holistic reforms of the criminal justice system in Trinidad and Tobago inclusive of joint efforts with all stakeholders, especially the educational sector. Senior Counsel Elder's passion for legal reform is reflected in her comments to the People's Partnership Government (2010–2015) on amendments to the controversial Preliminary Enquiries Act. SC Elder also spoke in passionate terms about the desire for an informed, preventative-based judicial system in the island which looks at the full circumstances of persons brought before the local courts. At the completion of the interview, Mrs. Elder thanked the researcher for his persistence in keeping abreast of her busy schedule which made the interview possible and considered it an honor and a privilege to have been a part of the project.

CAREER

WCW: Tell me a little bit about your career?

PLE: I attended The University of the West Indies, St. Augustine campus where I completed my Law degree and went onto the HWLS and was called to the Bar in Trinidad and Tobago in 1987. I have also acted as a Temporary Judge for six (6) months as I was appointed to the position on December 4, 2002, and assumed duty from January 1, 2003 until July 2003. I am also the present President of the Criminal Bar Association of Trinidad and Tobago since 2010.

I started off my career by being trained by deceased Theodore "Teddy" Guerra (SC) as in 1987, he requested permission from the Principal of HWLS to have me assist him in defending the then Commissioner of Police Randolph Burroughs who was on trial for corruption. Permission was granted and I was trained by Theodore Guerra (SC) and worked under his tutelage early in my career. On entering private practice as a defense Attorney, I did not specialize initially and worked on Family, Civil, and Criminal matters; however, after 8 years of practice I realized that I had to specialize in one area of law and I choose Criminal Law. I chose to specialize in one area of law, Criminal Law, based on my ever-increasing family responsibilities as well as my belief that being a generalist compromised the quality of my work. Additionally, I do not like to depend on anyone to conduct research on my behalf so I decided to focus on Criminal Law so that I could give full focus on this one area while conducting my own research for my matters. In addition to the practice of Criminal Law, I also enjoy teaching and at one time I lectured Advanced Level Law at a family-owned educational institute, Elders and Associates between 1987 and 2012.

WCW: As your career as a defense lawyer developed what has surprised you?

PLE: As my career as a defense lawyer developed, I was surprised by the level of respect that I have been afforded by my clients. I have always been honest and respectful as well as motherly on some occasions to my clients and that has been translated in respect from my clients. In fact, I have never been disrespected by my clients. Also, on entering the legal profession in 1987, there was an inherent, ingrained, and perhaps institutionalized bias against female Attorneys and the respect and faith shown to me by hardened male criminals strengthened my resolve to excel. In fact, I remember a male client who I got acquitted on a murder charge returning to my office years after as he wanted someone to talk to and he came to me because he was being harassed in his community and felt like killing the individual who was harassing him. He remembered me and he remember my word to him on being acquitted that "you have been given a golden opportunity, walk the straight and narrow road." I respect them and conversely they respect me.

WCW: Has your work as a defense lawyer proved as interesting or rewarding as you thought it would when you first started?

PLE: Yes. Indeed, my work as a defense lawyer has proven to be interesting, rewarding, exciting, fulfilling, and satisfying. The job consists of extremely hard work and can take a toll on individuals, especially in criminal trials where the consequence is the death penalty or loss of liberty and that's why I strive for excellence at all times. Interestingly, though there have been some minor disappointments, there have been more interesting and rewarding aspects.

PHILOSOPHY OF LEGAL ADVOCACY

WCW: What do you think should be the role of the public defense counsel in society?

PLE: The role of public defense counsel is to use all the tools of their profession to ensure that their clients receive a fair trial. This does not necessarily mean seeking an acquittal for all clients at every trial as the circumstances of the alleged offense might dictate otherwise. For example, the person might have committed the offense and is deserving of some punishment; however, defense counsel must ensure that the trial is not biased against the offender. Therefore, defense counsel can use advocacy tools via a stirring plea in mitigation to ensure that a harsh punishment is not imprisoned on the client.

WCW: What should be their job, functions, and responsibilities? What should be left to others?

PLE: The defense counsel is there to ensure that clients receive a fair trial. Similarly, the role of the prosecution is to prosecute and not to persecute. Their jobs, functions, and responsibilities are wide ranging but should be confined to that of a defense lawyer. I am not a pastor, neither I am here to massage the ego of clients. I am as honest as possible with them. Though at times I may give counseling to persons who are traumatized or victimized (for example, as a female I may empathize, console, and counsel a client who is a victim of domestic violence) that is not my function and I refer many of my clients to the psychological experts as I am not an expert in that field. Defense counsel must avoid getting too close to their clients, as a client is a client and not a friend and I have seen many Attorneys being embarrassed by their clients due to familiarity. Whatever is not the job, function, and responsibility of the defense counsel should be left to those individuals holding the responsibility.

WCW: What organizational arrangements work and which do not?

PLE: The legal system in Trinidad and Tobago is a failed system, the system of transportation of prisoners is a failed system which exposes the traveling public to dangers. In fact, in my estimation, nothing works in the justice system in this island. There have been no improvements in the system in this island since 1987. A sense of frustration and hopelessness pervades the justice system due to a chronic lack of improvements and I am of the view that on my retirement, the justice system would be just as was back in 1987 when I entered practice. Most of the Courts are in need of improvements to their infrastructure and technological capacity. There are inordinate delays in trials which should not occur and could never be justified. If an accused person cannot be tried within a reasonable time, they should be granted bail, but this is not done and some persons spend many years awaiting trial because they have no bail.

There are failures at all levels of the justice system in Trinidad and Tobago's legal system and this includes the Magistrate's Court, the High Court, and the Court of Appeal. For example, the High Court is scheduled to start at 9 am and jurors are required to be there before 9 am, probably by 8.30–8.45 am; however, the prisoners usually arrive at 10.00 am and this is done on a continuous basis without any consideration for the jurors time. In fact, the jurors remain locked in the jury room from the time of their arrival at approximately 8.30 am until Court starts at 10.00 am. Furthermore, a great majority of the Jury rooms are "less than desirable" in terms of their physical conditions with inadequate and oftentimes insanitary conditions.

At the Magistrate's Court, Magistrate can spend a very long time reading charges to defendants (sometimes 100 charges). This serves no real purpose besides delaying the Court's time. The defendant/accused can simply be given a copy of the charges if literate or if represented by Counsel. Forensic analysis is sorely deficient and leads to great delays as well. At the High Court, the time period between committal proceedings and trial can take YEARS. For example, committal proceedings can take 3–4 years. After being committed to stand trial, committal papers from the Magistrate's Court to the Director of Public Prosecution (DPP) can take as much as two (2) years. When the committal papers get to the DPP, it can take as much as two to three (2–3) years for the indictment to be filed. The next step, placement on the Cause List (to determine the readiness of the parties to proceed), can take as much as one to two (1–2) years and this become even more complicated when there are multiple accused. The movement from the Cause List to the Trial List is another delay as Defense Counsel must wait for the Court to be cleared, so that there is an available Court to hear the matter and this can take two (2) years on average. With that in mind, how do you charge your clients in light of those delays?

This is the current state of affairs in the Judiciary in Trinidad and Tobago. This has been consistently occurring over a long period of time as we keep doing the same things over and over, even though it's a failure because we have been doing it since time immemorial. For instance, I have an ongoing matter at the 1st Criminal Assizes involving a father and son who were charged for Murder in November 2008 and committed to stand trial in 2009. I have had to write to the DPP on several occasions to have the indictment filed as the family members have become frustrated with the delay and so am I. This trial was only started earlier this year (2016). Another example of the current sorry state of affairs in our judicial system involves a male who was charged with corruption in 2008 and was brought before the magistrate's Court in 2008. This indictment was only signed by the DPP in 2014, the first Cause List hearing was in March 2016, and the second Cause List hearing took place in June 2016. This is unacceptable as justice delayed is justice denied.

WCW: How difficult is it for defense counsel to relate to the living and social conditions of those from economically deprived backgrounds who appear before them?

PLE: It should not be difficult for defense counsel to relate to the living and social conditions of those from economically deprived backgrounds who appear before them. For me, it is not difficult at all as I am able to relate well with these individuals. This is due to my upbringing as a child in a poor neighborhood of Belmont as well as the values that were instilled in me by my parents. This helps me to connect with those individuals from economically deprived backgrounds who appear before me.

It is also quite important to never to lose touch with the common man, jurors etc. as well as their views, feelings, and language used by the man in the street. However, some Attorneys are arrogant, cocky and proud, and out of touch with those individuals. I remember having to inform one of my junior Attorneys to apologize to a client for being late as the client had been waiting in the Chamber for 30 minutes and the Attorney rushed in and started the interview without even apologizing to the client.

WCW: How can a legal advocate develop empathy for those from the lower rungs of the social division in society from which they can derive a degree of understanding why that person before them did what is alleged?

PLE: The background of the advocate is important. Defense lawyers must never lose their humility and must remain conscious to the fact that they are being paid to represent clients, no matter their [clients] station in life. They must also remember that clients give them their hard earned monies and they [lawyers] should be patient, listen attentively to their clients, develop empathy, and do the research. Empathy can be developed by legal advocates by being humble and shedding their arrogant and proud feelings which are often façades for their incompetence as these are impediments to the development of empathy to their clients; more-so, those from the lower rungs of the social division in society.

WCW: How should the criminal legal system in your country be performing? What should be the preferred priorities and strategies; hard-edged crime control, prevention, services, order work, what mix for which types of problems, etc.?

PLE: The criminal legal system in Trinidad and Tobago should be performing at a level (optimum) which is very different to what exist at the moment. First and foremost on the minds of persons within the criminal legal system should be prevention as a main strategy. We must address the offender when offenses are committed; however, a wider range of sentencing tools should be made available to magistrates and Judges.

The system should include preventative measures and must be educational-based. Because of my personal experiences and interactions with a host of offenders, I have seen both sides. Most of the offenders are not depraved, they are deprived of a moral home life, proper education, they are often neglected, possess a host of learning impediments in the early stages of development and just went through the [education] system. We must strive for proactive preventative measures; however, when crime occurs we must not be blinded by the crime but must also look at the antecedents and circumstances of the crime and find a solution which is suitable for that specific individual. Punishment is not just simply incarceration. There are other measures and we must seek alternative sentencing measures. In fact, I once recommended suspended sentences and intermittent custody for minor offenses as punishment should serve as a deterrent as well as assist with rehabilitation.

SUCCESSES AND PROBLEMS EXPERIENCED

WCW: In your experience what policies or programs have worked well and which have not? And can you explain for what reasons? (e.g., if someone has to plead guilty to enter drug court? What about "Probation before judgment" programs, with no criminal record if you complete them successfully?)

PLE: Based on my experience in the legal system in Trinidad and Tobago, I am of the view that not much has worked. For example, the probation system is ineffective, there is no proper plea bargaining system; however, the Drug Court is a step in the right direction. Presently, the Court system is clogged and we must start encouraging persons who are genuinely guilty to start pleading guilty by putting a proper plea bargaining system in place. All matters cannot go to trial and there must be some compromise but persons must be able to derive some benefits from plea bargaining. The system in Trinidad and Tobago cannot continue to incarcerate persons from lower rungs of society for possession of small quantities of marijuana while white collar crime continues unabated by individuals in the higher echelons of society.

WCW: What do you consider to be the greatest problems and issues facing the criminal courts at this time? (e.g., caseload, plea bargaining, misdemeanors never tried, preliminary dispositions; presumption of guilt; leniency, unlimited, or preventive detention, etc.)

PLE: There are many problems which plagues the criminal courts (Magistrate's, High, and Court of Appeal) in Trinidad and Tobago at this time; however, collectively, the greatest problems and issues are that, for example, Magistrates have too many matters (caseload) to deal with on a daily basis and this promulgates a system of lengthy delays. Additionally, the system of adjournments is very problematic and should be improved as the public's time is wasted just sitting in the Court awaiting an adjournment. Other problems include the lack of video recording of ID parades, reading of numerous charges by magistrates and Judges, inordinate delays in the filing of witness statements, the late arrival of prisoners at Court which leads to the late start of Court, inordinate delays in accessing Court transcripts, and delays in forensic analyses. The criminal Courts in Trinidad and Tobago is also plagued by the problems such as delays in trials, lack of video recording of interviews with suspects, protracted and irrelevant questioning by Lawyers, lack of technology in the Courts such as video/audio recording of Judges and Magistrates, poor facilities for jurors as well as inadequate facilities, and the frustratingly long wait for judgments emanating from the criminal courts.

WCW: What problems in courts do you find the most difficult to deal with?

PLE: There are many problems which I have been faced with since being called to the Bar in 1987 and which I still face up to today. The problems in courts in Trinidad and Tobago which I find most difficult to deal with are the inordinate delays in starting trials, especially for persons who are in custody awaiting trial. In fact, I am deeply embarrassed by this. Another problem with which I have difficulty with is the representation of non-nationals who speak a foreign language and who are before our Courts and speaking through an interpreter. The process is tedious, embarrassing, faulty, and antiquated and present grounds for appeals. The lack of technology in some Courts is also very frustrating and difficult to deal with. For example, in this day and age, our Judges and magistrates are not voice recorded and I am irritated and greatly impatient by this lack of technology. Further, the Judges notes, for example, must be transcribed and this takes a while. Added to that is the exorbitant cost of attaining court transcripts. For me, another problematic issue is the filing of witness statements which also takes a very long time in our jurisdiction.

WCW: What would be easy to change? Internal problems (culture of the organization, managerial deficiencies, allegations of corruption, or gender-related problems, etc.) or externally generated problems (resources, community support, etc.)? Is anything easy?

PLE: In light of the myriad of problems in the system which has been in existence for a very long time, in order to properly answer that question, we would first have to approach it at different levels of the hierarchy. So, for example, you look at the criminal justice system, what is causing the delays there and what could be changed, then we would consider the High Court where trial are conducted, then we would also have to go the Court of Appeal. If I could start with the Court of Appeal, I have been of the opinion for a very long time that the time has come for us to structure the Court of Appeal in terms of having a Division that deals specifically with criminal matters so you are going to have expert Judges, Judges with the expertise in Criminal Law matters and I think this in some way could ease the delays in the delivery of judgments in the Court of Appeal because we also have delays in the Court of Appeal.

Also the paperwork, we have to find a way to reduce the amount of paper that is used with respect to the filing of Appeals in the Court of Appeal. When I started off practice and an Appeal was being done, what we did with respect to the authorities was that we just prepared a list of authorities for the Judges and this list was sent to the library and the library would provide the Judges with the authorities. Now what we have to do is to copy the entire case and make about five copies for filing. So you see the paperwork involved there. So in light of the technological advances, I am sure that IT persons could find a way to reduce that dependency on paperwork. This would also impact on the cost factor.

Dr. Wallace, at the High Court, there are so many problems. We could start with little ones like the prisoners being brought to Court late on an almost daily basis. What could be done to address that? How could we have prisoners in Court on time? I have been thinking that if we are building new Courts then we should consider having facilities at the Court itself, so that prisoners could be brought at nights. So they stay in the building at night and in the morning they are just ushered up a staircase or elevator and they are in the Court promptly, okay. Then we also have to look at prolix cross-examination questioning by Counsels and unmeritorious and lengthy legal submissions. Could these things be addressed prior to the empaneling of the Jury so that when the Jury is empaneled the trial could proceed without frequent and long interruptions for legal matters to be addressed?

It is frustrating because as Attorneys we are expected to be in Court on time, so we would generally arrive in Court at about 8.45 am (start time for Courts in this jurisdiction is 9.00 am). I would usually arrive to Court by 8.45 am and time you put down your papers and organize yourself and your thoughts and then you find yourself sitting there from 9.00 am to 10.00 am waiting on prisoners. And then one has to consider the impact this delay is having on the jurors who may have left their homes very early to come to Court to perform their civic duty of jury service and they are there locked away in a little room waiting on the prisoners to arrive for the trial to commence. I cannot see any difficulty in having these things changed. You see, I am a utilitarian and I always consider what is the utility of doing something? What are we achieving, what are the benefits? Don't only focus on it has always been done in this manner. It is not working. It is not working. So what changes can be implemented and I see no problems in, for example, bringing the prisoners to Court overnight.

THEORY AND PRACTICE

WCW: What should be the relationship between theory and practice in legal advocacy?

PLE: Of course, there should be a marriage of both. It should not be disjunctive. That is the only way you are going to have a fair and efficient system. Because what is justice? It is achieving a fair result based on the particular circumstances of the offense and the offender. So one cannot ignore all relevant factors pertaining to the offender which may have contributed to the commission of the crime and if these factors are not addressed then it is quite likely that that offender may become a recidivist offender because the underlying problems have not been addressed. For example, you get a young child on the street, loitering. Should that child be brought to Court and charged with loitering? What is hoped to be achieved by charging a young offender with loitering? There has to be a reason that child was on the street unsupervised. So what we need there, we need the guidance counselors, we need the psychologists, we need to address even the parents, consider the factors operating in the home. There should be a marriage between legal theory and the advocate's practice. In fact, both are inextricably interwoven. Because a person does not get up suddenly one morning and say look, I want to go and shoot a man, or I want to go and loiter on the streets. What are the causative factors?

WCW: What can legal practitioners learn from theory, and what can theory builders learn from legal advocates?

PLE: Legal practitioners can learn from theory and theorists, and theory builders learn from legal advocates. Those who practice the criminal law, it calls not just for legal qualifications. It calls for maturity. It calls for experience. Because from my experience in speaking to a client, sometimes I am able to assess whether the client telling me the truth and also from my experience, I am able to speak to a client in a manner in which he is able to repose trust in me.

WCW: What is the relationship right now? Does it exist? Does it work?

PLE: I am aware that there is an existing relationship between legal practitioners and theory builders in a global context and certainly, it has been working for a long while. Yes, indeed, there is a relationship and what would happen there is that it would not amount to a legal excuse but it would go toward mitigation. It would be a mitigating factor which would guide the sentence in the determination of the appropriate sentence. So, the legal theory could be relevant to both things. One, have you committed the offense, or two, if it's irrelevant to the commission of the offense, it may be relevant to mitigating factors. Because, certainly a man's conduct cannot be regulated in all respects by law, man has to regulate himself by his conscience. However, each person's conscience is different (laughter).

WCW: What holds back collaboration or interactions?

PLE: To the best of my knowledge nothing holds back this collaboration or should act as a restraint to collaborations and/or interactions.

WCW: What kind of research, in what form, on what questions would you find most useful for legal advocacy practice? If not very useful, what could or should theory builders do to make their findings more useful to you?

PLE: I have a passion for research and I am not dependent on my juniors for research. I do my own research, which is unusual for a Senior Counsel, but all my juniors would attest to that. I do my research, I would give them the authorities and then I would tell them to do further research on it such as comparative analysis and so forth. I feel comfortable doing my research and with the available technology, it is so much easier. It contributes to the lack of sleep because with the touch of a button, you can move from one jurisdiction to another, but I have a passion for research. I would look at everything, once it is relevant to the matters I am doing. You see the practice of law is so demanding that it restricts the extent of the reading one can do. Yes, I would like to look at all other interesting matters, but it's a question of time. For example, if I have a heavy matter on sentencing, yes then I would try to read a lot articles on sentencing, on the basic concepts rehabilitation, reformation, deterrence, and protection of society. Sometimes when you read other articles, you get a different view. So if I get an interesting article, then I would say okay, I would bring this to the attention of the Judge.

WCW: Where do you find theory-based information? Where do you look? What journals, books, publications, reports?

PLE: For theory-based information I look at journals, books, publications, reports, everything. Sometimes, it's necessary to go the Journals because the Journals could give you an understanding, a deeper understanding of the principles. So Journals and articles are interesting. If you limit yourself in that manner to case reports, for example, you are depriving yourself of educational material, of knowledge. Because by reading a Journal, you may even learn a word, a manner of expression. Sometimes, I am reading an article and I am blown over by the way in which the author has expressed himself and I would say "he certainly has the gift of the gab."

For example, I think I did one of the first cases in Trinidad on DNA (Deoxyribonucleic Acid), this was the Khoury's kidnaping where Dr. Edward Khoury was kidnaped and beheaded in 2005 and there was DNA evidence. I did not learn anything about DNA in Law School and I had to teach myself and I couldn't just go to the cases which were applying the principles. I had to first understand the principles and where would I get that knowledge. Sometimes, the text books were a bit too challenging for me, so I had to go basic, to authors, articles. In fact, during that case, the Magistrate stated in open Court that she knew nothing about DNA. The only thing she knew about DNA is what she learnt from watching OJ Simpson (a renowned murder trial in the United States). The research is critical. I have just completed a Commission of Enquiry into the Las Alturas where I was lead Counsel to the Commission and this deals with Civil Engineering. I knew nothing about Engineering, but again the Internet, a wealth of knowledge. Then the articles and I took an ABC course in Engineering.

WCW: Do you conduct supplementary research (beyond legal research required) for pending cases? If so, what are the areas, issues, or questions of law researched?

PLE: I have never seen anything, any writing, and I don't know of anything written by members of our local Judiciary outside the writing of judgments which takes such a toll on them. I don't know whether they would have time to do this other writing. Remember we have some Judges now who have a real backlog with respect to judgments; however, I conduct research outside of the scope of required legal research for my matters and this encompasses a wide range of legal questions as well as non-legal research as mentioned earlier.

TRANSNATIONAL RELATIONS

WCW: Have you been affected by, and how, in the work of your organization, by developments outside your country (human rights

demands, universal codes of ethics, practical interactions with legal practitioners from other countries, personal experiences outside the country, new crime threats, etc.)? (e.g., ACLU, Amnesty International, environmental crimes, trafficking, social science and law, expected relapses in drug court, etc.).

PLE: Well, I won't look at England as we generally rely on England for precedent. I have relied a lot on the American jurisdiction with respect to developments in electronic searches of computers and cell phones. For example, a police stops someone in a roadblock, searches him and takes his cell phone, in light of the massive material this is contained now in a cell phone, is the police entitled without the requisite Court Order to go through that person's cell phone and look at all his contacts, his messages, and so forth. Can a police officer come into your workplace or your home and just access the material you have on your computer? And to guide me in this area I have relied greatly on the American jurisprudence and they are very vigilant with respect to the privacy rights of individuals and they are like a computer is not to be considered just as a box which would store limited information because of the variety of information, the volume of information stored in computers and electronic devices, certain restrictions should be put on police officers when going through these pieces of equipment.

WCW: Have those interactions been beneficial or harmful? What kind of external international influences are beneficial and which ones less so?

PLE: These interactions have generally been more beneficial than harmful to me in respect of the developments outside of the Trinidad and Tobago's jurisdiction which impact on the local Judiciary.

WCW: How have developments since the terrorist attack in the United States on September 11, 2001, affected your work?

PLE: No, No. The developments since the terrorist attack in the United States on September 11, 2001, have not affected my work.

GENERAL ASSESSMENTS

WCW: Are you basically satisfied or dissatisfied with developments in criminal law and criminal procedure in your system?

PLE: Dissatisfied would be an anodyne expression. (Shake of head; smirk and look of disgust from Mrs. Elder SC.). I am frustrated, I am unhappy. I feel that we do not have the necessary developments in our laws, in our procedures, in the accommodation. Our criminal justice system is in shambles ... ... and we need to put together a think tank of persons who are really interested in the Criminal Law to develop and to find a way forward, because I sometimes feel that I have more years behind me in the criminal justice system than ahead and I think that I will leave the system without seeing any progress and that saddens me. It really, really saddens me.

WCW: What are the most likely developments you see happening and which would you like to see happening?

PLE: Well I think it would be easier for me to start with what I would like to see happening in the criminal justice system. I would like to see technology being incorporated in the system. Something as simple as the recording of evidence! Presiding officers and Attorneys should not have to be struggling to capture each word of a witness. It should be electronically recorded and at the end of the day's proceedings, Counsel should be provided with a copy of the transcript of evidence and this transcript of evidence should be sent electronically. Also, another thing we have to consider is that we have non-nationals coming into the country and allegedly committing crimes, they do not speak English. This old procedure we have of having an interpreter standing next to them and translate; that belongs to a past age. There should be some software or technological device that could be used and it is going to speed up the procedure. Because could you just visualize every question asked, there has to be a pause for the interpreter to the answer given. He has to lean over and ask the person questions and interpret the answers for the Court. We need that, so we need the technology. It makes no sense going and having all these elaborate principles of law and we don't have the technology to expedite the criminal justice system.

WCW: What is most needed now to improve legal advocacy and the justice system?

PLE: That is a difficult question. You know what we most need? We need to clearly and objectively identify the problems. We have to stop pouring blame on persons and institutions. Be honest to recognize that the system is in need of help and we can only go forward if we are willing to ascertain what are the problems; and as I keep saying, we need to have as structured approach to it. We cannot just say what are the problems affecting the criminal justice system. You have to look at what are the problems affecting each level of the criminal justice system, because if you address the problems in the High Court without addressing the problems in the Magistrate's Court, it may aggravate the situation.

Indeed, one must remember that the first door through which an accused person enters is the Magistrate's Court. An accused person does not start off in the High Court or the Court of Appeal, right, his entry point is the Magistrate's Court. Even if you don't fix level by level, because some problems may be linked, so we have to identify the problems. If we don't identify the problems, how could we find the necessary solutions? How could we? And we must bring together all the stakeholders. You cannot have lawmakers just looking to make law. They may have noble intentions, they may think that this may well be the solution, but you have to speak to the people who work the system.

CONCLUSION

This chapter set out to understand the Judiciary in Trinidad and Tobago, the challenges faced, nuanced situations, setbacks, and what can be done to reform the apparently broken system. Based on the discourse by Mrs. Pamela Elder SC, there appears to be no doubt that the Judiciary in Trinidad and Tobago is riddled with a multiplicity of issues. As discussed by Mrs. Elder, these problems are not insurmountable and can be rectified; however, there appears to be a lack of will to have these issues alleviated as they may impinge on the maintenance of the status quo. As part of her discourse, Mrs. Elder SC has made several recommendations and suggestions aimed at improving the system of justice in Trinidad and Tobago's jurisdiction.

It is the author's desire that the recommendations and suggestions of Mrs. Elder will be implemented at some point in time in an effort to contemporize the system of justice on the island. Instructively, it is the future generation of criminologists, lawyers, judicial officers, legislators, policymakers, and even the criminal element who would be judge the implementation of these succinct suggestions and recommendations. The extent to which they are made will be reflected in our judicial history; however, history may be unkind toward those with responsibility for contemporizing the Judiciary if the system remains broken and immovable from its current state.

Some of the recommendations and suggestions garnered from the narrative of Mrs. Pamela Elder SC are as follows:

1. Widening the range of available sentencing options to include Suspended Sentences of Imprisonment and Intermittent Custodial Sentences. These would allow guilty persons a chance at rehabilitation as well as reducing the cost of incarceration on the state while allowing the individual a greater chance at rehabilitation by remaining in touch with family members as well as providing financially for them (Elder, 2016a).

2. The implementation of a system of plea bargaining. This would serve to reduce the number of matters going to lengthy trials (Elder, 2016b).

3. Conveying prisoners to the Court on the night before their trials so as to ensure a prompt start to Court on the following day (Elder, 2016b).

4. An electronic system of adjournment of criminal matters (Elder, 2016a).

5. Increased use of technology within the criminal justice system which would lead to a reduction in the quantum of paper used, for example, to file Appeals (Elder, 2016a).

REFERENCES

Al-Rawi, F. (2016). Paper presented at the Prison Reform Public Consultation, Port-of-Spain City Hall, Port-of-Spain, Trinidad and Tobago, April 6, 2016.

Atieno, O. P. (2009). An analysis of the strengths and limitation of qualitative and quantitative research paradigms. *Problems of Education in the 21st Century*, 3, 13–18.

Caribbean Court of Justice. (n.d.). "Our Mission, Our Vision." Port of Spain, Trinidad and Tobago.
Retrieved from http://www.caribbeancourtofjustice.org/.

Dowlat, R. (May 15, 2019). 8 inmates escape from Golden Grove. Trinidad and Tobago Guardian. http://www.guardian.co.tt/news/8-inmates-escape-from-golden-grove-6.2.845967.20a391dc36.

Elder, P. L. (2016a). Interview conducted on June 9th, 2016 at the conference room of Guerra, Elder and Associates, Woodbrook, Trinidad and Tobago.

Elder, P. L. (2016b). Interview conducted on August 2nd, 2016 at the conference room of Guerra, Elder and Associates, Woodbrook, Trinidad and Tobago.

King, M. L. (1964). Excerpt from the Speech "I Have a Dream," Delivered in Washington, DC.

The Judiciary of the Republic of Trinidad and Tobago. (n.d.). Retrieved from http://www.ttlawcourts.org/.

Wallace, W. C. (2017). Interview with the Honourable Justice Mr. Malcolm Holdip—High court judge, The Judiciary of Trinidad and Tobago (Book Chapter). In D. Lowe & D. K. Das (Eds.), *Trends in the Judiciary: Interviews with Judges Across the Globe* (Vol. 3, pp. 173–196). Boca Raton, FL: Routledge.

Wallace, W. C., Hill, B., & Rosales, A. R. (Forthcoming). Remanded in custody and punished without trial: The Criminal Justice System and Remand Populations in Trinidad and Tobago.

Zimmermann, R., Lawes, C., & Svenson, N. (Eds.) (2012). *Caribbean human development report 2012: Human development and the shift to better citizen security*. United Nations Development Programme. UN Plaza, New York, NY, USA.

CHAPTER X

CHARACTERISTICS OF YOUNG FEMALES IN NEED OF STATE SUPERVISION IN TRINIDAD AND TOBAGO

Kevin Sean Peters

College of Science, Technology and Applied Arts of Trinidad and Tobago, Trinidad and Tobago

ABSTRACT

Issues surrounding females in criminology and criminal justice have received growing attention since the 1970s. This is based on the philosophy that females display deviancy that is different from their male counterparts. In the context of twenty-first-century criminological research, studies on females are less common when compared with the research attention placed on males. This research attention is even lower among the subset of female juvenile delinquents and holds true for Trinidad and Tobago, even though the juvenile justice on the island is currently undergoing one of the most consequential revolutions in the country's post-colonial history. This paper seeks to examine specific aspects of the sociological lives of girls deemed by the courts to be in need of supervision, and thus housed at the St. Jude's Interim Rehabilitation Centre for Youthful Female Offenders (SJIRCYFO) over a period of 2 years with two separate cohorts. A quantitative approach was used to attain sociological factors from the entire population at SJIRCYFO in 2015 (N=39) and again in 2017 (N=35) when the population of the home changed and there was a new cohort of girls. Aspects of their lives included institutionalization history, abuse, gang activity, substance abuse, and mental disposition. The results provide a profile that can assist in understanding the social anatomy of female juvenile delinquents in Trinidad and Tobago and these features can assist in shaping policy and meaningful interventions in the lives of at-risk female juveniles in the jurisdiction.

Keywords: Children in Need of Supervision (ChINS), female juvenile delinquency, deviance, parens patriae, Trinidad and Tobago

INTRODUCTION

This research paper is based on the criminological philosophy that female juveniles express a behaviour of deviance that is different from their male counterparts and as such, there is a need to construct an empirical understanding of their lives and the factors present in them if interventions are to be effective (Adler, 1975; Baptiste et al., 2002; Cauffman, 2008; Mullis, Cornille, Cornille, Mullis, & Huber, 2004; Shepherd, 2002). The latter is the focus of this research on female juveniles in Trinidad and Tobago who run afoul of the law are placed in the care of the state.

In her seminal work, Adler (1975) drew cognizance to the rising criminality among females in the United States and stood at the boundary of a new understanding in feminist criminology; even forecasting an increased focus on female penology. Future studies would vindicate her position. She attributed this new phenomenon to the liberation of women in the twentieth century, who, like their male counterparts, were seeking to improve their socio-economic position in society and thus utilized crime as one of means to attain it. Thus, if the authorities are to make meaningful interventions, then a comprehensive understanding, with an increased input by academia, is not only essential but mandatory. The juvenile female population represents the smallest group under state supervision in Trinidad and Tobago (Seepersad & Williams, 2016). Despite this, there is a need to understand the factors which are present in the lives of the female juveniles in the local juvenile justice system.

This study attempts to understand the underlying social conditions present in the lives of the female juveniles housed at the St. Jude's Interim Rehabilitation Centre for Young Female Offenders (SJIRCYFO), located in Belmont, a community on the fringes of Port of Spain. Local and international literature revealed several risk factors that permeate the lives of girls under *parens patriae* of the state in Trinidad and Tobago. They were thus used to investigate the extent of their presence in the lives of the girls housed locally at SJIRCYFO. It is understood that there are multiple pathways to detention. Indeed, Miller and Mullins (2009) allude to "gendered pathways" (p. 37) which speaks to indigenous characteristics that girls may experience on their pathway to deviance. It is in understanding these pathways that the first steps are taken to create and implement meaningful policy interventions. The factors under consideration are the institutionalization history of themselves and immediate family who dwell with them (Cauffman, 2008; Mullis et al., 2004; Phillips, 2013; (Zahn et al., 2010), history of abuse (physical and sexual) (Slowikowski, 2010), gang and violent activities (Arnull et al., 2005; Farrington & Painter, 2004; Mullis et al., 2004; Shepherd, 2002; Slowikowski, 2010; Youth Justice Board, 2009), substance abuse (Baptiste et al., 2002; Mullis et al., 2004), and mental disposition (Cauffman, 2008; Mullis et al, 2004). The research questions (RQs) derived from these issues are as follows:

1. What is the nature and history of detention of the girls under the care of the state?

2. What is the nature and history of detention of the immediate families of the girls under care of the state?

3. What is the extent of physical and sexual abuse among the girls housed under the care of the state?

4. To what extent have girls housed at the home engaged in gang and/or violent activities in the past?

5. What is the nature and extent of substance abuse among the girls housed under the care of the state?

6. What is the nature of the mental history of the girls housed under the care of the state?

7. What is the profile of an average female juvenile under supervision by the state in Trinidad and Tobago?

HISTORY OF FEMALE JUVENILE INSTITUTIONALIZATION
IN TRINIDAD AND TOBAGO

Female juvenile institutionalization and rehabilitation in Trinidad and Tobago has its historical antecedents in an initiative by Governor Sir Henry
Irving (1875–1889) during the period of colonialism. In league with the
archbishop at that time, an institution was established in on February 4,
1890, in Belmont Port of Spain to house female youths. It was the product
of a combination of religious determinism with aid from the state which
saw the need at that time to house females in need of "intense motherly
care and guidance" (Xavier, 1990, p. 3). The establishment of this home
represented a revolutionary policy locally as it recognized juvenile deviancy as separate from their adult counterparts. It was a philosophy im-
mersed in an early nineteenth-century approach by the Quakers and their
"House of Refuge" in the United States which sought to address the issue
of at-risk youth with the idea that re-socialization within a quasi-family
setting represents a pro-social step toward evoking rehabilitation in the
lives of juveniles (Fox, 1970).

At the time of its inception, the institution was named the "Catholic Girls
Reformatory" or colloquially as the "Girls Industrial School." This name
then evolved into the "St. Jude's School for Girls" under the ownership
of the Roman Catholic Church and managed by the Corpus Christi Carmelites (Abdulah, Moses, Shivaprasad, Ottley, & Mieres, 1980). The philosophy mirrored that of the global perspective of the time which saw the
need for interventions in the lives of female youth to prevent the growing
nexus to crime and criminality. Moreover, the basis of the rehabilitation
was faith-based and saw the need for spiritual rehabilitation in addition
to a social, moral, academic, and physical reform of the young female. At
that time, the facility housed females between the ages of 10 and 18 who
were sent by the courts and included those remanded in custody awaiting
the resolution of their hearings, those sentenced by the courts for various
offenses, those brought to the courts by parents or guardians for being
"beyond control," and those under the protection of the state for various
reasons (Wallace, 2013).

Presently, there are a collection of legislation which are geared toward the
care and protection of children in Trinidad and Tobago and they attempt
to address many spheres in the life of the child. For example, the Children

Act of 2012 represents an important legislative step to address juvenile justice and clearly outlines the procedures involved in the management of Industrial Schools. After 125 years of management by the Catholic church, the central government in Trinidad and Tobago assumed management of the institution and it became the St. Jude's Interim Rehabilitation Centre for Young Female Offenders (SJIRCYFO).

The Children Act of 2012 defines the institution in the following manner: "A school for the industrial training of youthful offenders, in which youthful offenders are lodged, clothed, and fed, as well as taught" (p. 33). In May 2015, the state officially took control of the SJIRCYFO and sought to bring the facilities and management in compliance with the new requirements of the legislation. As part of the process, the Government of Trinidad and Tobago issued a joint select committee on human rights and equality which sought to investigate the current paradigm pervading the treatment of child offenders. As such, the committee identified the role of the SJIRCYFO as providing accommodation to female children under two broad categories: those in need of care and protection and those deemed by the courts to be "beyond control." As part of the new paradigm, the center provides rehabilitation to females between the ages of 12 and 18 who have come into conflict with the law both in remand and convicted (Gadsby-Dolly et al., 2017). In addition to the SJIRCYFO, young female offenders can also be housed at the juvenile wing of the Golden Grove Women's Prison in cases where they have contravened the rules of the SJIRCYFO. Changes have also been realized in classification of children who interact with the courts at this level. The term "beyond control" has been replaced with the description of "a child in need of supervision" (ChINS) (Judiciary of Trinidad and Tobago, Children Court Rules, 2018).

Prior to state takeover of the SJIRCYFO, juvenile females aged 16–18 and 15 and under in need of supervision were remanded and even sentenced to a detention period at the Golden Grove Women's Prison (Laurent, Barnes, Chambers, & Gray, 2011). This was an egregious issue with lasting implications since it facilitated the social melding of the female youth with their senior counterparts. One of the first publications to acknowledge this was the Cabinet-appointed task force on prison reform (2002) which highlighted the policy as a problem to be addressed even prior to legislation-led enforcement. Though the Task Force of 2002 was vociferous in highlighting the illegal state of affairs surrounding female juveniles being held at the Golden Grove Women's Prison, knowledge of this outlandish act did not manifest into actionable changes. The foregoing was conducted despite studies highlighting that the mixing of juveniles with their adult counterparts increases the probability of recidivism and contributes to the increased vulnerability to a number of negative experiences at the hands of older and oftentimes influential adult convicts (Bishop, 2000).

Local newspaper reports attest to the latter in the form of alleged instances of violence against juveniles by prison officers while at the Women's Prison. For instance, an article in the Trinidad and Tobago Newsday reported that 10 female teenagers were allegedly beaten by prison officers (Seelal, 2015). Instances like these have acted as a catalyst for reimagining the segregation of adult and juvenile females in Trinidad and Tobago and the current paradigm under the new legislation warrants this orientation. The latest progress made in local juvenile justice is the introduction of the Juvenile Court System of Trinidad and Tobago which is a court dedicated to hearing children matters (Judiciary of Trinidad and Tobago, Children Court System, 2018). This was officially opened in 2018.

THE CURRENT CONTEXT OF FEMALE JUVENILE
OFFENDING IN TRINIDAD AND TOBAGO

Statistics for the 10-year period 2006–2015 show that the male juveniles in Trinidad and Tobago have been charged far more than their female counterparts for both minor and serious offenses (Crime and Pubic Analysis Branch, TTPS, 2017). Statistics from the Crime and Problem Analysis (CAPA) Branch of the Trinidad and Tobago Police Service shows that females represent 6% of all charges for the period 2006–2015. Disaggregating for types of crimes, they represent 10% of minor crimes and 4% for serious offenses. Unfortunately, a number of juveniles found guilty and subsequently sentenced are not yet recorded by the authority. This data nevertheless offers insight into the current landscape of juvenile offending in Trinidad and Tobago.

For the period 2006–2015, there were a total of 1,621 charges for minor offenses by male juveniles. Their female counterparts had 178 charges. There is an even greater difference for charges for serious offenses as juvenile males registered 2,485 charges compared to 104 for females. Indeed, statistics presented above does lend to the focus in policy direction and intervention for males, yet the argument of this paper is that there should be more emphasis on female juvenile interventions to address their needs. For example, upon closer scrutiny of the data, it is evident that there are crucial issues relating to the types of delinquent acts that female juveniles commit in Trinidad and Tobago. The data reveals that the minor offense of possession of narcotics was the most popular offense for which charges against female juveniles were laid. For the period 2006–2015, a total number of 112 charges were proffered against female juveniles for the possession of narcotics. This offense outnumbered the closest offense (possession of firearms and ammunition) by a factor of 3.

Concomitantly, charges for serious crimes showed a similar trend over the 10-year period in that the most charges against female juveniles were for the possession of narcotics for the purpose of trafficking. In this instance, there were a total of 48 charges brought against juvenile females. This also outnumbered the second most popular offense by a factor of 3 times that of breaking offenses. Moreover, in both instances of minor and serious offenses, the charge under scrutiny was the highest in occurrences for every year between 2006 and 2015. Instructively, the same can be said for male juveniles of the same period under inquiry. The conclusion one can draw from such statistics is that despite the small number of charges for minor and serious offenses when compared with their male counterparts, female juveniles in Trinidad and Tobago display a distinct pattern as it pertains to nonviolent drug offenses and this provides an important foundation when considering female juvenile interventionist strategies.

REVIEW OF LITERATURE

In order to critically analyze and understand the phenomenon of female juvenile behavior and ultimately the social underpinnings, one must understand that it is a multi-dimensional and multifaceted issue. Therefore, there is no one factor present in their lives to which their institutionalization is pinned. Indeed, female offenders are a heterogenous group and like their male counterparts, the implications for their delinquency and subsequent institutionalization hold a lot of implications for both their lives and the wider society.

It must be noted that research on the phenomenon of delinquent female juveniles is miniscule in comparison to their male counterparts. As a result, most of the measures, policies, and interventions have been designed with the aim of making interventions in the lives of males and thus, these measures have been imposed on their female counterparts with little to no thought of gender-specific issues (Adler, 1975; Patton, 2008; Shepherd, 2002; Slowikowski, 2010). Other research has noted that in cases where females are the focus of research, they are geared toward adult women. Additionally, due to their smaller numbers when compared with their male counterparts, their offending is seen as homogenous (Youth Justice Board, 2009).

As it pertains to the female juvenile and familial issues present in their lives, research has found that inter-generational instances of arrest and institutionalization have been a major factor (Mullis et al., 2004). Cauffman (2008) asserts that this can facilitate further patterns of institutionalization in their offspring along the life course. The results imply a continued cycle of criminality and institutionalization among multiple generations of the family. This will have negative implications for the status of the family and its ability to provide an environment that promotes pro-social skills, safety needs, and socio-economic progress. Moreover, girls exposed to violence within the family are more likely to be violent than those exposed to nonviolent families (Arnull et al., 2005; Farrington & Painter, 2004; Youth Justice Board, 2009). Other studies have linked this to previous victimization encounters, drug use, and associations with negative groups (Di Napoli, 2003 as cited in Youth Justice Board, 2009).

Goodkind and Sarri (2006) note in their study that most of the charges brought against females were for assault and drug charges. They link this behavior to abuse suffered by the juveniles. The California Justice System reported that physical and sexual abuse was one of the main features present in the lives of juvenile females. They noted that 92% reported some form of physical, emotional, and sexual abuse (U.S. Department of Justice, 1998). Mullis et al. (2004) note that substance abuse is quite prevalent among gang activity and is an integral part of the fabric of the subculture.

In the 1990s, female juvenile gang activity and by extension, the violence associated with such associations increased in the United States (Shepherd, 2002). This represented a new phenomenon among girls of this cohort. Slowinowski (2004) in his meta-analysis concluded that aggression in young females was a symptom of other issues that can be best understood within the context of their school, family, and by extension the community. Association with deviant peers has facilitated gang participation as a by-product of the links made in these groups (Mullis et al., 2004). They concluded that these negative associations germinated relationships of a negative and unproductive nature. Moreover, they eventually created schisms between them and pro-social groups which furthered the resolve and motives of the subculture and further perpetuated antisocial beliefs that are different than those of the mainstream society.

Cauffman (2008) conducted a meta-analysis of 20 studies which analyzed the adult lives of antisocial adolescent girls and found a variety of psychiatric issues, dysfunctional, and violent relationships which have ultimately led to higher mortality rates among cohorts (Hawkins, Cantalano, & Miller, 1992). Other studies have shown that juvenile females experience mental illness more than their nondeviant counterparts and deviant males (McWey & Mullis, 2005).

In summary, when building a profile, Shepherd (2002) attempted to present the narrative of the typical female offender with the use of empirical data. He defined her as 16 years old, residing in an urban setting with a single parent home. She is a high school dropout with little social skills and limited employment opportunities. The typical juvenile female is a victim of abuse; namely of a physically or sexual nature and being a woman of color. Mullis et al. (2004) constructed a similar dossier and concluded that a young female offender is between the ages of 14 and 16 with a low socio-economic status in a high crime community. They are likely to belong to a minority group and possess a poor academic history. Like Shepherd (2002), Mullis et al. (2004) assert that the female juvenile will most likely have a history of abuse but point out that this abuse also includes exploitation. Further, the female delinquent is also an abuser of narcotics and alcohol with unmet mental health needs and a negative disposition on life and her possible life chances.

Presently, the literature on female juveniles in Trinidad and Tobago comprise periodic reports compiled by the state and primarily focuses on juvenile boys (Abdulah et al., 1980; Baptiste et al., 2002; Sampson et al., 1994); independent research on both juvenile boys and girls (Cain, 1996; Seepersad & Williams, 2016; Sumter, Monk-Turner, & Rougier, 2013;

Wallace, 2013); and a report on juvenile girls (Phillips, 2013). Of these studies, two reports characterize the features of juvenile females (Baptiste et al., 2002; Phillips, 2013). Instructively, Baptiste et al. (2002) point out that local juvenile females are characterized by status offenses and are arrested for nonviolent crimes such as drug offenses. They posited that juvenile girls enter the juvenile justice system with mental ilnessess, issues involving substance abuse, high-risk sexual behavior, and are victims of abuse. The findings of Phillips (2013) showed that the juvenile girl is characterized by a "stepfather like family complex arrangement" (p. 17), either unrealistic or no future goals and deviant behavior like running away from home.

THEORETICAL FRAMEWORK

In presenting a theoretical explanation for deviancy among young females, the feminist school of thought can provide avenues to understanding the behavior. It is based on the principle that women (and by extension girls) are a point of central focus all by themselves and should not be an intellectual by-product of male-centered academic inquiry (Miller & Mullins, 2009). By providing a feminist perspective, the data on the girls are brought to the fore and their indigenous contexts highlighted (Kathleen & Chesney-Lind, 1988). There are some fundamental underpinnings that first must be understood about the use of feminist theory to explain deviancy among young female cohorts.

Under a feminist paradigm, no one theory exists that can explain deviance among girls (Carrington, 2013). Indeed, the means by which knowledge is constructed is the product of men, which is done in many cases for men. A feminist view can germinate analyses that are poignant to their demographic and thus presents a catalyst for focused social change (Daly & Chesney-Lind, 2006). Moreover, it presents an explanation from the point of women and girls that is counter to overly simplistic explanations that present females in a context that is sexualized (Carrington & Pereira, 2009). When feminist theory is then merged with theories of delinquency, the product is a gender-based explanation of deviancy that is focused and fits the paradigm under scrutiny far better than a generic explanation that is tailored toward young males (Daly, 1998).

The ideas presented in the adolescent-limited versus life-course persistent taxonomy is adequate ground for discourse and application in presenting a feminist perspective of deviance. It also lends the added benefit of predicting life trajectories. Temporary versus permanent deviance of a juvenile provides a potent predictor of life chances and an understanding to whether a deviant youth today will continue their antisocial behavior into adulthood (Moffitt, 1993). However, the findings by Moffitt (1993) presented the taxonomy with a focus on deviant boys. A subsequent study examined adolescent-limited versus life-course persistent deviance in both boys and girls. Moffitt, Caspi, Rutter, & Silva (2004) conducted a longitudinal study on the "continuous measure of adolescent antisocial behaviour" and "lifetime diagnosis of conduct disorder" (p. 161) in both boys and girls in Dunedin, New Zealand. The longitudinal study looked at a cohort periodically as they progressed between 13 and 21 years. Importantly, the research by Moffitt et al. (2004) did not find any support to the hypothesis that deviancy during adolescence has fewer consequences for girls than boys. Their results revealed that girls involved in deviant behavior were more likely to have a "truncated education" (p. 169) in which they were less likely to have a college or university education.

Young women also moved out of their parental homes earlier than their counterparts who did not engage in deviancy. They did not participate in the labor force as much as their male counterparts and the researchers attributed this absence to childbirth. They were also significantly more likely to use illicit drugs than nondeviant female counterparts. Young females were more likely to be associated with deviant peers and displayed dispositions that promoted such. It was a finding that they deemed to be a predictor of self-reported criminal offending. The study also revealed that antisocial behavior among young women is "significantly more likely" (p. 182) to be correlated with problems surrounding relationships, mental issues like depression, and a propensity to suicide than their male counterparts by the age of 21.

When blended with Moffitt's taxonomy, the feminist perspective on deviancy among girls reveal that there is ground for deeper exploration of the characteristics involved in the lives of females that encounter the criminal justice system. The premise is that their need for supervision by the state is a symptom of events that occurred before, and a possible trajectory of continued antisocial behaviors if effective interventions are not made. Discovering these factors is thus important.

METHODOLOGY

The research methodology was quantitative in approach and sought to collect data from every girl housed at the SJIRCYFO related to the five aspects of their lives outlined in the introduction. The data were collected at two separate times, in February 2015 and again in February 2017. At that time, all of the girls from the first round in 2015 were no longer present at the home. If any were present from that time, they would not have been administered another questionnaire to avoid double counting of responses. The number of females housed during the first round of data collection was 39 and all of the female juveniles were administered the instrument (N=39). During the second round of data collection, there were 35 students and the questionnaire was administered to every female juvenile housed at the facility (N=35). The questionnaire primarily comprised closed-ended questions with a limited number of open-ended questions in instances where opinions were warranted.

The administration of the questionnaire was conducted by the researcher and a teacher of the SJIRCYFO. The respondents were questioned on an individual basis and responses recorded on the respective questionnaire. This method of administering the questionnaire reduced the chances of respondent misinterpretation of questions and removed any ambiguities that may be experienced if they were self-administered. In order to protect the confidentiality of the respondents, the questionnaire did not capture any personal identification data, for example, names. Questionnaires were each given an indigenous number in order to track the data entry in Statistical Package for the Social Sciences (SPSS) version 20 and they were selected at random during data collection to reduce the chances of connecting a respondent with a specific questionnaire.

The questionnaire captured the juvenile's offense history and those of their family, the perceived relationship with their parents and siblings, school history, drug and alcohol abuse history, and history of mental health. The descriptive statistics gained from the exercise gave a clearer idea as to factors present in the lives of female youths under state supervision in Trinidad and Tobago, as well as the way they engage parents, siblings, and peers in their social settings thereby charting a path to understand the underpinnings in a lives more vividly. The data generated provided descriptive statistics; particularly the percentages of juveniles in the home who would display, possess, or have a history of a certain feature in their lives. The statistics was generated with the use of the (SPSS 20) as it provided an efficient avenue to derive tables and charts necessary to the analysis. It is envisioned that this data would provide the basis for more studies including research that will attempt to find strengths of relationships between important variables in the lives of female youths under state supervision. It must be noted that at the time of the data collection, no student was housed for the purpose of protection and this removed the possibility of skewing the data as the attempt was to capture those remanded and committed for alleged or criminal behavior and those deemed by the courts to be in need of supervision.

RESULTS

The number of females at the SJIRCYFO in 2015 was 39 with the average age being 15 years old. In 2017, the number of girls was 35 with the average age also being at 15 years.

Institutionalization History

In 2015, the percentage of female juveniles who were committed versus being on remand was 57% and 43%, respectively. In 2017, the percentage of female juveniles who were committed declined to 34%, while the remanded population increased to 66%. Based on 2015 data, the findings indicated that most of the girls or 54% were held under supervision of the state, while in 2017, 69% reported being there for the same reason (supervision of the state). Nine percent of the female juveniles in the 2017 cohort indicated that they were sentenced due to fact that they were in contravention of the law, 9% were at the SJIRCYFO for safety, and 12% for "other" reasons, which would have implied that they were likely there under protection of the state.

Most of the population in 2015 or 56% reported that this was not their first time at the SJIRCYFO. In 2017, 22% of the study's participants indicated that they had previously spent time at the institution, a decrease of 34% over the 2-year period. This reduction cannot be considered within a silo as a follow-up question asked if they have ever spent time at another institution. To this, 43% indicated that they have spent time at another institution in 2017. In 2015, the percentage reporting this was 44%. When asked about institutionalization of family members, 63% of the girls reported having a family member with at least one prison sentence. In 2017, 49% of the girls noted that they had at least one family member with at least one prison sentence. When disaggregated for the member of the family with an institutionalization record, 5% of the female juveniles in the 2015 cohort indicated that it was their father who was incarcerated, compared to 9% in 2017. When asked about their mothers, 25% of the respondents in the 2015 cohort and 11% of the 2017 cohort indicated that their mother had an institutionalization record of at least one prison sentence. As it relates to siblings, in 2015, 25% of the girls citied a sibling with a prior or an ongoing prison sentence, while in 2017, this percentage decreased to 17%. In 2015, 43% of the respondents indicated some other member of their family being incarcerated, when compared with 11% in 2017. In 2015, 35% of the respondents indicated that their family members did not have any history of institutionalization. In 2017, this percentage increased to 49%.

Abuse

Another characteristic of young institutionalized females in Trinidad and Tobago is abuse. In this context, 33% of the 2015 cohort of girls reported that they had been physically abused in the past, while among the 2017 cohort of girls, the figure was 57%. As it pertains to self-reported sexual abuse, 44% of the girls in 2015 answered in the affirmative, while in 2017, the number of self-reported sexual abuse by girls institutionalized at the SJIRCYFO increase to 46%. As it relates to domestic violence (DV), 35% of the respondents in 2015 indicated that they witnessed DV in some form at their home. In the 2017 cohort, the number increased to 74%. In 2015, 18% of the study's participants reported a combination of having been physically abused and having witnessed physical violence at their home, while for the 2017 cohort of girls at the SJIRCYFO, the figure was 49%, an increase of 31% when compared with the 2015 cohort.

The data emanating from the survey instrument completed with the female juveniles in 2015 indicated that 22% of the girls suffered from a combination of sexual abuse and having witnessed physical violence in their home, while in the 2017 dataset, the corresponding figure was 34%. In 2015, 44% of the girls reported that they were bullied in the past, with 23% stating that they had been victims of gang violence. In 2017, 37% of the girls self-reported being a victim of bullying, with 26% reporting having been a victim of gang violence.

Gang and Violent Activities

On the issue of gang activity, the data for 2015 indicated that 30% of the girls at the SJIRCYFO indicated that they either belong to or have been a member of a gang and have carried out gang-related activities involving the use of violence. The corresponding figure for 2017 was 51%, representing an increase of 21% from 2015. For the category of carrying a concealed weapon, 47% of the study's participants in 2015 reported that they had carried a weapon on their person at a previous occasion and in 2017, 60% of the girls reported the same (carrying a concealed weapon in the past). Of this population, when disaggregated for the type of weapon carried, 36% of the girls in the 2015 cohort reported carrying a gun, 50% a knife, and 14% reported carrying other types of weapons. In 2017, 9% of the institutionalized female juveniles reported carrying a gun, 20% a knife, 20% both a gun and a knife, and 6%, a knife and a scissors.

Substance Abuse

Another key and consistent characteristic that emanated from both datasets was the use of alcohol, as a major form of substance abuse by the juvenile girls. The data highlighted that in the 2015 cohort of institutionalized girls, 74% indicated that they consumed alcohol and in 2017, the figure was 97%. This data must be interpreted in the context that legal alcohol consumption is restricted to persons 18 years and older in Trinidad and Tobago's jurisdiction. The data also indicated that in 2015, 37% of the girls reported consuming alcohol often and in 2017, 34% reported frequent usage. In 2015, 63% of the study's participants reported occasional alcohol usage, while in 2017, the figure was 54%. As it pertains to marijuana usage, in 2015, 42% of the girls indicated that they had smoked marijuana, while in 2017, 49% indicated previous marijuana usage. With regard to frequency of marijuana usage, in 2015, 58% of the girls who smoked marijuana had used the drug often, while only 28% reported often usage in 2017. Reports of cocaine usage were comparatively small with 14% of the girls in the 2015 dataset indicating its usage in the past and 9% in 2017. With regard to drug and/or alcohol evaluation, 13% of the participants in the 2015 cohort and 14% in 2017 cohort reported being evaluation for drug and/or alcohol, with 11% in 2015 and 3% in 2017 accessing some type of drug intervention in the past.

Mental Disposition

A key component of the characteristics of the institutionalized young female juveniles was related to their mental disposition. On the issue of mental disposition, 21% of the female juveniles in the 2015 study indicated that they had been diagnosed with a mental illness in the past and 17% reported being diagnosed with a mental illness among the 2017 cohort of girls. As it pertains to instances of self-harm in the past, there was a 47% self-reported rate of self-harm in the 2015 dataset and 65% in 2017 dataset. In fact, 35% of the 2015 participants indicated having attempted suicide in the past. In 2017, the figure increased to 51%.

DISCUSSION

The classification of "ChINS" and the number of girls housed for this reason raises important concerns as this classification incorporates several deviant behaviors which usually occur within the family. Indeed, there are parallels internationally with the Youth Justice Board (2009) which notes that many females at juvenile homes in their study are housed mainly for status offenses such as running away from home; behaviors to which the label of ChINS can be ascribed locally. They argue that behavior such as this is an indicator of underlying issues in their lives. This was also emphasized by Phillips (2013) in her analysis of the girls at the SJIRCYFO to which she concluded that popular rhetoric holds that girls run away in order to spend time with their boyfriends. A phenomenon which she admits holds very little sympathy with the public. Phillips (2013) concluded that the girls may not be running to, but away from adverse contexts in their lives. This is consistent with Slowikowski (2010) who concludes that a girl who is detained for running away from home can be the product of victimization at home and this was a catalyst for the behavior and if left unaddressed, this can lead to greater problems in the life course and contribute to inter-generational issues in the family.

With the foregoing in mind, the label of ChINS may perhaps be a reaction to familial, educational, or peer issues which are carried out for reasons unknown and unresolved. Conversely, there may be pull factors that provide the catalyst for deviancy. It is therefore crucial to understand what might have pushed or pulled the delinquent female juveniles into deviance and delinquency. Thus, issues such as conflict between parent(s) and girl and running away from home become the behaviors that define this classification. ChINS then becomes a symptom of an underlying factor in the life of the girl. If under the law a parent brings a girl before the courts under this classification, then there may have been social factors involved in the deviancy.

The reports of the number of institutionalization episodes are important to note. The results hint at a revolving door of sorts in the lives of some of the females where they are repeatedly housed in the same home or another. Noteworthy is the fact that a significant number of the population under inquiry had also spent time in other institutions, thus making them a product of multiple instances of interactions with institutions. The results question the role of the parents and other caregivers in the lives of juvenile females and whether a lack of intervention would increase the chances of detention. Other institutions would imply noncriminal familial issues which have remained unresolved. Again, the basic institutions in the lives of the girls are brought into scrutiny and the potency in their lives is a focal point. Returning to the same familial contexts and the issues therein may be a hinderance to improved behavior and a movement away from the juvenile justice system.

The nature and extent of familial institutionalization provided some interesting findings. Firstly, though the percentages decreased between the 2 years, the majority reported having at least one immediate family with prior institutionalization in 2015 and just under half in 2017. This is consistent with Mullis et al. (2004) who correlate delinquency in girls with the institutionalization of their parents and the propensity for this to occur inter-generationally. The same holds in this study. Interestingly, the fathers of the detained females had the lowest percentage of incarceration while mothers and siblings had a higher proportion. The research did not attempt to find causation between these two variables, yet it is noteworthy that most of the female juveniles have family members with a history of prior incarceration.

In all instances, the occurrence of abuse in all spheres had increased between the two cohorts under study. In one instance, the percentage has doubled. This was the case even when self-reported combinations of abuse were measured. This is consistent with the findings of the Youth Justice Board (2009), Shepherd (2002), and Mullis et al. (2004) and is a point of concern. The issue is further amplified when one considers the percentage of the population experienced at least two of these methods of abuse. The interventions therefore must be of a nature that assists the female juvenile to deal with the implications of the abuse meted out to the female juveniles.

The increase in gang affiliation is also noteworthy as there is a need to further understand the role, purpose, and activities of juvenile females in the operation of gangs in Trinidad and Tobago. Moreover, the use of guns and knives has decreased between the two cohorts. This would further illuminate the motives of gang activity both on a theoretical and practical basis thereby facilitating meaningful interventions. The data on alcohol usage is also important, given the fact that its occurrence had increased when data from the two cohorts were analyzed. This finding is worthy of explication as there are laws geared toward the prohibition of alcohol use by minors in Trinidad and Tobago's context. Marijuana usage has also increased between the cohorts and in 2017, nearly half of the population sampled had used it. There is also a need to address the issue of personal harm and injury as well as the issue of attempting suicide. The increases in this type of behavior are indeed cause for concern and interventions would be necessary.

The analysis provides a means by which the data can derive a profile of the young female under state supervision in Trinidad and Tobago. They must first be disaggregated by the two periods. In 2015, this profile was characterized by a 15-year-old female who is a ChINS. She has spent more than one stint at the center and has at least one family member who has been incarcerated. Finally, she has already had an encounter with alcohol. Similar to the cohort in 2015, institutionalized female juvenile delinquents in 2017 had an average age of 15 years, is a ChINS, and had previously used both alcohol and marijuana. This is where the similarities between the two cohorts end and the females of 2017 take on a different persona. In 2017, institutionalized female juvenile delinquent is characterized by a history of physical abuse and had witnessed DV at least once in her home. She has been a member of a gang and has carried a concealed weapon at some time in her life. Additionally, she has harmed herself at least once in her lifetime and has also attempted suicide. Instructively, the comparison between the cohort of girls in 2015 and 2017 at the SJIRCYFO is important as the number of deviant and risky behaviors associated with those female juveniles has increased and thus is worthy of more research and analysis as well as interventions.

POLICY IMPLICATIONS

Emanating from this study are several policy implications for local policymakers. Regarding policy implications, strategy should be geared toward more short-term programs that meet the needs of girls that may be under state supervision for a few weeks or a few months, given the increase in remanded girls who may not enter the system on a long-term basis. Familial interaction is a contentious issue, given the results which found that many girls in the system have parents who either are or were incarcerated themselves. This emphasizes the role of the state as *parens patriae* with an emphasis on interventions that reconcile the role of the parent if they are also detained. Despite the decrease, repeated returns to the SJIRCYFO can be addressed under the role of the parent as it is in the family that the deviant behaviors can be addressed before they are brought before the courts.

Interventions that address girls who inflict personal harm and injury toward themselves is a key issue. Like the classification of ChINS, this behavior is a symptom of other issues which much be addressed if their quality of life is to be improved. Of great importance is the issue of ChINS juvenile females. From the findings, the data suggests that the classification is an issue worthy of further exploration. Before conclusions can be drawn about the girls under this classification, there is a need to understand the reasons for their need for supervision within the institutions that they interact. Future research can examine the reasons informing their deviancy while establishing their perspectives on the way they view their behavior subjectively. Once the underlying reasons are ascertained then measures can be taken to address the symptoms of this issue.

The challenges to achieving the aforementioned interventions are quite clear since the study revealed that nearly 30% of girls under state supervision receive no visits from family members. There is a need to gain a comprehensive understanding of substance abuse by juvenile females, given the report of use in this study. This would be geared specifically toward alcohol and marijuana use, with the aim of understanding the reasons for the use of each. There is a need for an in-depth understanding of the role of juvenile females in gang activity in Trinidad and Tobago as the results suggest their affiliation. A greater understanding of this would assist in tailoring programs geared to thwarting their affinity with gang activity. The solution may lay in replacing the satisfaction gained from gangs with that of a pro-social institution and activities. This however must be premised on research and global best practices.

CONCLUSION

Even though the percentage of female juveniles who run afoul of the law and/or those who are deemed delinquent are fewer when compared with their male juvenile counterparts in local, regional, and international contexts, the research indicates that there are adverse issues permeating their lives that are worthy of examination. Their invisibility when compared to their male counterparts is a phenomenon which must change. The analysis and subsequent findings of the current research effort indicate the need for a closer examination of the sociological factors present in the lives of the female juvenile in Trinidad and Tobago. It is submitted that the authorities in Trinidad and Tobago have made great strides in recent years with the implementation of new legislation in tandem with the UN Convention of the Rights of the Child (1989) and have taken necessary steps to increase the chances of modern practices in juvenile interventionist strategies. The implementation of the Juvenile Court is a prime example of the nation's progress in meeting the needs of juveniles who run afoul of the law are institutionalized. Despite this and based on the data analyzed in this paper, there are several interventions that can be implemented to strengthen the delivery of services to female youth.

REFERENCES

Abdulah, C. O., Moses, E. A., Shivaprasad, L., Ottley, C. R., & Mieres, H. F. (1980). *Final report of the commission appointed to enquire into the existing conditions at the prisons and to make recommendations for reform in light of modern concepts and penal practice and rehabilitation measures.* Port of Spain, Trinidad: Government of Trinidad and Tobago.

Adler, F. (1975). *Sisters in crime: The rise of the new female criminal*. New York: McGraw Hill Book Company.

Arnull, E., Eagle, S., Gammampila, A., Archer, D., Johnston, V., Miller, K., & Pitcher, J. (2005). *Persistent young offenders: A retrospective study*. London: Youth Justice Board for England and Wales.

Baptiste, C., Sylvester-Thomas, B., Mc Honey, C., Rougier, J., Husbands, G., Ali, C., Donald-Grant, E., Vallie, C., Groome-Duke, C., Brown, D., Renaud, H. (2002). *Republic of Trinidad and Tobago final report of the cabinet appointed task force on prison reform and transformation*. Port of Spain, Trinidad: Government of Trinidad and Tobago.

Bishop, D. M. (2000). Juvenile offenders in the adult criminal justice system. *Crime and Justice, 27*, 81–167.

Cain, M. (1996). Developing a juvenile justice policy: Anomalies of the theory and practice in Trinidad and Tobago. *Caribbean Quarterly, 42*, 87–100.

Carrington, K. (2013). Girls and violence: The case for a feminist theory of female violence. *International Journal for Crime, Justice and Social Democracy, 2*, 1–17.

Carrington, K., & Pereira, M. (2009). *Offending youth: Sex, crime and justice*. Sydney: Federation Press.

Cauffman, E. (2008). Understanding the female offender. *The Future of Children, 18* (2) 119–142.

Crime and Pubic Analysis Branch. (2017). Reports on persons between 11-17 years charges for serious crimes during the years 2006-2015. [Data file]. Port of Spain: Trinidad and Tobago police service.

Crime and Public Analysis Branch. (2017). Reports on persons between 11-17 years charged for minor crimes during the years 2006-2015. [Data file]. Port of Spain: Trinidad and Tobago police service.

Daly, K. (1998). Gender, crime and criminology. In M. Torny (Ed.), *The Handbook of Crime and Justice* (pp. 85–108). Oxford: Oxford University Press.

Daly, K., & Chesney-Lind, M. (2006). Feminism and criminology. *Justice Quarterly, 5* (4) 497–538.

DiNapoli, P. P. (2003). Guns and dolls: An exploration of violent behaviour in girls. *Advances in Nursing Science, 26,* 140–148.

Farrington, D., & Painter, K. (2004). *Gender differences in risk factors for offending.* London: Great Britain Home Office.

Fox, S. J. (1970). Juvenile justice reform: A Historical perspective. *Stanford Law Review, 22,* 1887.

Gadsby-Dolly, N., Mitchell, R., Jennings-Smith, G., Gayadeen-Gopeesingh, V., Moses, D., Mahabir, D., & Hosein, K. (2017). *Third report on the joint select committee on human rights, equality and diversity.* Port of Spain: Parliament of the Republic of Trinidad and Tobago.

Goodkind, S., & Sarri, R. (2006). The impact of sexual abuse in the lives of young women involved or at risk of involvement with the juvenile justice system. *Violence Against Women,* 12 (5) 456–477.

Hawkins, D. J., Cantalano, R. F., & Miller, J. Y. (1992). Risk and protective factors for alcohol and other drug problems in adolescence and early adulthood: Implications for substance abuse prevention. *Psychological Bulletin,* 112 (1) 64–105.

Judiciary of Trinidad and Tobago. (2018, September 23). *Children court system.* Trinidad and Tobago Juvenile Court Project. Retrieved from http://www.jcp.tt/children-court/system

Judiciary of Trinidad and Tobago. (2019, June 8). *Children court rules, 2018.* Court Library Services Unit. Retrieved from http://www.ttlawcourts. org/index.php/law-library/news-aalerts/new-legislation-trinidad-and-tobago/legal-notices/7810-22-children-court-rules2018

Judiciary of Trinidad and Tobago. (n.d.). Retrieved from www.ttlawcourts. org/

Kathleen, D., & Chesney-Lind, M. (1988). Feminism and criminology. *Justice Quarterly,* 5(4), 497–538.

Laurent, B., Barnes, A., Chambers, T., & Gray, S. (2011). *Caribbean basin security initiative juvenile justice assessment.* Bethesda: Democracy International Inc.

McWey, L. M., & Mullis, A. K. (2005). Improving the lives of children in foster care: The impact of supervised visitation. *Family Relations,* 53(3) 293–300.

Miller, J., & Mullins, C. W. (2009). Feminist theories of girls' delinquency. In M. Zahn (Ed.), *The delinquent girl* (pp. 30–49). Philadelphia: Temple University Press.

Moffitt, T. E. (1993). Adolescence-limited and life-course-persistent antisocial behavior: A developmental taxonomy. *Psychological Review,* 100(4), 674–701.

Moffitt, T. E., Caspi, A., Rutter, M., & Silva, P. A. (2004). *Sex differences in antisocial behavior: Conduct disorder, delinquency and violence in the Dunedin longitudinal study.* Cambridge: Cambridge University Press.

Mullis, R. L., Cornille, T. A., Cornille, T. A., Mullis, A. K., & Huber, J. (2004). Female juvenile offending: A review of characteristics and contexts. *Journal of Child and Family Studies,* 13(2), 205–218.

Office of Juvenile Justice and Delinquency. (1998). *Office of juvenile justice and delinquency prevention, National Council on Crime and Delinquency.* Washington, DC: U.S Department of Justice.

Patton, J. D. (2008). Working with female juvenile delinquents: What youth practitioners need to know. *Journal of Youth Development,* 3(2), 1–12.

Phillips, D. (2013). *Youth at risk focusses on St. Jude's School for Girls and St. Michaels School for Boys: Survey of Inmates at St. Jude's School for Girls.* Port of Spain, Trinidad: Government of Trinidad and Tobago.

Sampson, J., Salandy, R., Issac, V., Sampson-Brown, M., Phillip, D., Bishop, J., Farrell, D., Cain, M. (1994). *Report of the cabinet appointed committee to examine the juvenile delinquency & youth crime situation in Trinidad and Tobago.* Port of Spain, Trinidad: Government of Trinidad and Tobago.

Seelal, N. (2015, June 30). Charges for beaten girls. *Trinidad and Tobago Newsday.* Retrieved from http://digitaledition.newsdaytouch.co.tt/?iid=122614&startpage=page0000003#folio=1

Seepersad, R., & Williams, D. (2016). *Crime and security in Trinidad and Tobago.* Kingston, Jamaica: Ian Randle Publishers.

Shepherd, R. E. (2002). Girls in the juvenile system. *William and Mary Journal of Women and the Law*, 9(1), 31–41.

Slowikowski, J. (2010). Girls Study Group: *Understanding and responding to girls' delinquency. Causes and correlates of girls' delinquency.* U.S. Department of Justice. Office of Juvenile Justice and Delinquency Prevention. Retrieved September 23, 2018, from https://www.ncjrs.gov/pdffiles1/ojjdp/226358.pdf

Sumter, M., Monk-Turner, E., & Rougier, J. (2013). Assessing current programs and reentry needs in Trinidad and Tobago: Insights from offenders—an exploratory study. *African Journal of Criminology and Justice Studies*, 7-2(1) 118–139.

Wallace, W. C. (2013). Addressing the unmet needs of children and youth in detention in Trinidad and Tobago. *Journal of Eastern Caribbean Studies*, 79–106.

Xavier, D. (1990). *Reflections: Commemorative issue of the 100th year anniversary of St. Jude's School for Girls.* Port of Spain: Corpus Christi Carmelites.

Youth Justice Board. (2009). *Girls and offending—patterns, perceptions and interventions.* London: London South Bank University.

Zahn, M. A., Agnew, R., Fishbein, D., Miller, S., Winn, D.-M., Dakoff, G., Kruttschnitt, C., Giordano, P., Gottfredson, D., Payne, A., Feld, B., & Chensey-Lind, M. (2010). *Causes and correlates of girls' delinquency.* U.S. Department of Justice. Office of Justice Programs. Office of Juvenile Justice and Delinquency Prevention.

Conclusion

Renowned American poet Henry Wadsworth Longfellow (1807–1882) famously quipped "Great is the art of beginning, but greater is the art of ending." In light of Longfellow's postulation, Volume 1 of *Caribbean Perspectives on Criminology and Criminal Justice* is quickly and artfully approaching its end. It is my considered view (maybe a biased one) that based on the wide range of research topics that were covered in this book by the authors of regional and international orientation and repute that the book is of much utility to the readership. What makes this book so riveting and useful is that the book chapter authors have not only described the trials facing the Caribbean, but, in many instances, they have articulated clear and cogent strategies aimed at alleviating the concerns highlighted.

At this juncture, I urge the readership to temporarily cast aside my views on this book and to make a determination of the book's value and contribution to the development of new knowledge from a Caribbean perspective. In other words, did the book achieve its mandate as set out in the introductory chapter? What do you think of the book? How could it have been better structured? If you were the editor of this book, what would you have done differently to possibly enhance the book?

While those questions are being deliberated upon, it is critical to offer a brief summary of what the book entailed. The chapters contained in this book examined contemporary issues such as the Judiciary, policing (both colonial and contemporary), gangs, homicides, crime prevention, drug trafficking, money laundering, juveniles in state custody, and criminological crimes. Importantly, the issues outlined above and succinctly researched by the book chapter authors are traditional as well as contemporary issues facing the Caribbean that **MUST** be attended to. In fact, the possible consequences of not attending to the aforementioned problems are too dire for them to be left unattended.

Caribbean Perspectives on Criminology and Criminal Justice is therefore a thorough, comprehensive and contemporary reference book on traditional, modern, and regional issues affecting the citizenry in the Caribbean. Volume one of *Caribbean Perspectives on Criminology and Criminal Justice* is therefore a comprehensive reference work on issues and concerns in the field of Caribbean criminology and criminal justice. Importantly, the book provides expert analyses of a wide range of criminological and other crime related issues that pervade the Caribbean.

While summarizing the information concerning the issues and challenges facing Caribbean criminal justice systems and the people who utilize those services, it is important to note the relativity of one's perception. Surely, there are a multiplicity of issues, challenges, and nuances facing Caribbean criminal justice systems, and, thus, they can be handled in a number of ways. However, the basic social rules of engagement, research, and authorship should be remembered. Therefore, subjecting other people's academic work to humiliation cannot be justified. Indeed, while there are numerous criminological and criminal justice challenges facing the Caribbean, only those that were written in an empirically sound manner found their way into this book. Instructively, while one may conclude that most of the everyday criminological, criminal justice, and social issues can be discussed and interpreted in various ways; there cannot be any definite evaluation or limitation to the explication of these issues.

As indicated in the introductory chapter, this book was premised on an existing gap in the knowledge on Caribbean criminology and criminal justice that was quite visible to the book's editor while he was a postgraduate student at The University of the West Indies, St. Augustine campus. Additionally, this gap in the literature was also previously visible to Pryce (1976). Importantly, it should be noted that the gap in the literature consisted of: (1) a lack of specific literature, concepts, and understandings of crime and criminal justice issues in the Caribbean, and (2) a plethora of locations (journals, articles, etc.) for literature, research, and conceptualizations on crime and criminal justice issues in the Caribbean. Western dicta and existing approaches to understanding crime in developing regions, such as the Caribbean, were also critiqued by Jones (1981) and Sumner (1980) who both suggested that crime in developing countries should be viewed through the lens of the developing countries. In sum, the central thesis of this book is that there should be a body of criminological materials that operates in a manner that it aids in the development of a subfield in criminology and criminal justice, one that recognizes a Caribbean criminology. This book, *Caribbean Perspectives on Criminology and Criminal Justice,* therefore addressed the two previously mentioned gaps by creating a singular space for authors to focus on criminological and criminal justice issues in the Caribbean.

Importantly, this book does not purport to be the panacea for the ills facing the Caribbean or that it contains all of the answers. What can be gleaned from this book is that a collective body of individuals sought out the underlying causes of anarchy within our social systems and sought to support reform initiatives by providing empirical evidence as well as global best practices aimed at enhancing safety and security in the Caribbean. The chapters in this book therefore provide important information in addition to important lessons for those who are trying to understand the many challenges facing criminal justice systems in the Caribbean. The contents of the book facilitate responsiveness to Caribbean problems, acknowledgement of local initiatives (see, for example, chapters by Dore and Peters) and the development of capacity to achieve much needed change. Without a doubt, Volume 1 of this book offers much utility to students, legislators, policymakers, and the ordinary "*Caribbean person*" as the research is insightful, impactful, and significant.

While not attempting to highlight any one chapter to the detriment of others, an in-depth reading of the chapters by Mano, Katz et al., Haughton and Smith, or Isaac et al. certainly highlights the significance of the research conducted as well as the end product, *Caribbean Perspectives on Criminology and Criminal Justice.* I am certain that apart from those chapters mentioned above, that there are many other chapters and virtues that will stand out as you read this book. In spite of the list of virtues that I have espoused about this book, whatever stands out for you, the readers, is what is important and I urge you to not just read and make notes, but to apply the knowledge gained in a manner that will redound to the benefit of the Caribbean.

Instructively, Melville (1851) submitted that to produce a mighty book, *you must choose a mighty theme as no great and enduring volume can ever be written on the flea.* Indeed, there is no doubt that a mighty theme was chosen for this book as the book was not written on a flea, but on a proverbial dragon. And so, as Volume 1 of this mighty book comes to an end, be mindful that this great and enduring volume, *Caribbean Perspectives on Criminology and Criminal Justice,* will not be closed, but will continue with Volume 2 in the near future and with other volumes, long after my tenure as a scholar is over.

EDITOR'S THANK YOU

The articles contained in this book were subject to an independent double-blind peer review process by reviewers who were chosen for their diverse perspectives, experience, knowledge, and technical expertise in accordance with procedures approved by established international journals. The purpose of this independent review was to provide candid, critical, and insightful comments directed at ensuring that the finished product was of the highest academic standard. Additionally, the independent peer reviews were designed to ensure that the book is academically sound and attains established institutional standards for objectivity, evidence, and fitness for purpose as set out in the Call for Papers.

Although the reviewers listed below have provided many constructive comments and suggestions, they were not asked to or required to endorse the final product before its publication. The review of this book was overseen by Dr. Rahima Schwenkbeck and responsibility for the final content of this book rests entirely with the editor and the authors. In order to maintain reviewer confidentiality and process integrity, the reviewer's comments were revealed to the book chapter authors; however, the reviewers of specific chapters and their contents have been kept confidential.

This high quality of articles that are presented in this book would not have been possible without the contribution of the knowledgeable, professional, and articulate group of reviewers. These reviewers performed this admirable and unenviable task of peer reviewing and offering constructive critiques as well as selecting the most erudite articles for this book. They took time away from their busy professional careers as academics to proffer comments and suggestions on ways to improve the articles. In some instances, the reviews were conducted while the reviewers were in the middle of examinations, preparing students for theses defenses, conducting consultancies, and even while suffering through the death of loved ones and the excitement of the birth of new-borns.

It would be remiss of me to not offer words of gratitude to this body of men and women who performed the task as reviewers of the articles appearing in this book as well as several other articles that were not accepted, but reviewed and referred to international journals. This task of reviewing articles is an arduous one that many academicians frown upon due to its time-consuming nature; however, the reviewers mentioned below performed this task in a selfless manner and on a voluntary and pro-bono basis. Indeed, these reviewers provided yeoman and voluntary service to the editor of this book and by extension, the book chapter authors. Without them *Caribbean Perspectives on Criminology and Criminal Justice* would not have been a reality.

To the following reviewers, I owe a debt of gratitude and I proffer a sincere thank you:

Professor Anthony Harriott—Institute of Criminal Justice and Security, The University of the West Indies, Mona, Jamaica.

Professor Charles M. Katz—Center for Violence Prevention & Community Safety, Arizona State University, USA.

Professor Edward Maguire—School of Criminology and Criminal Justice, Arizona State University, USA.

Professor Kevin Haines—Institute of Criminology and Public Safety, The University of Trinidad and Tobago.

Professor Lystra Hagley-Dickinson—University of St. Mark & St. John, Plymouth, UK.

Professor Onwubiko Agozino—Virginia Tech Roanoke, Virginia, USA.

Dr. Acolla Cameron—Department of Management Studies, The University of the West Indies, St. Augustine, Trinidad and Tobago.

Dr. Allan Patenaude—The University of the West Indies, St. Augustine, Trinidad and Tobago.

Dr. Andrew Fox—Juvenile Rehabilitation, Washington State, USA.

Dr. Camille Gibson—Prairie View A&M University, USA.

Dr. Christine Descartes—Department of Behavioural Sciences, The University of the West Indies, St. Augustine, Trinidad and Tobago.

Dr. Corin Bailey—The University of the West Indies, Cave Hill, Barbados.

Dr. Danielle Watson—Faculty of Arts, Law and Education, University of the South Pacific, Laucala Campus, Fiji.

Dr. Dianne Williams—Independent Consultant, USA.

Dr. Dylan Kerrigan—School of History, Politics and International Relations, University of Leicester, UK.

Dr. Gabrielle Jamela Hosein—Institute for Gender and Development Studies (IGDS), The University of the West Indies, St. Augustine.

Dr. Hakim Mohandas Amani Williams—Gettysburg College, USA.

Dr. Kai-Ann D. Skeete—Shridath Ramphal Centre, The University of the West Indies, Cave Hill.

Dr. Laurette Bristol—Programme Manager, Human Resource Development, CARICOM Secretariat, Guyana.

Dr. Lorna Grant—North Carolina Central University, USA.

Dr. Marika Dawkins—The University of Texas Rio Grande Valley, USA.

Dr. Michael Berlin—Department of Criminal Justice and Applied Social & Political Science, College of Behavioral and Social Sciences, Coppin State University, Baltimore, MD, USA.

Dr. Mustafa Ozguler—International Police Executive Symposium, USA.

Dr. Nathan W. Pino—Texas State University, USA.

Dr. Natasha Kay Mortley—Institute for Gender and Development Studies, Regional Coordinating Office, The University of the West Indies, Mona, Jamaica.

Dr. Patrice K. Morris—Georgia Gwinnett College, Lawrenceville, Georgia, USA.

Dr. Perry Stanislas—De Montfort University, Leicester, UK.

Dr. Peter K. St. Jean—Department of Sociology and Criminal Justice, North Park University, Chicago, USA.

Dr. Sasekea Harris—Science and Engineering Branch Library (SEBL), The University of the West Indies, Mona, Jamaica.

Dr. Scott Romaniuk—China Institute, University of Alberta, Canada.

Dr. Talia R. Esnard—The University of the West Indies, St. Augustine, Trinidad and Tobago.

Dr. Tiffany R. Simmons—Department of Sociology and Criminology, Howard University, USA.

Dr. Tisa M. McGhee—Barry University School of Social Work, USA.

REFERENCES

Jones, H. (1981). *Crime, race and, and culture.* New York: Wiley.

Longfellow, H. W. (1807–1882). The Poems of Henry Wadsworth Longfellow: Complete in One Volume (Classic Reprint). London: Forgotten Books (July 20, 2012).

Melville, H. (1851). *Moby-dick; or, the whale.* New York: Harper & Brothers, Publishers. London: Richard Bentley.

Pryce, K. (1976). Towards a Caribbean criminology. *Caribbean Issues,* 11(2), 3–19.

Sumner, C. (1980). Crime, justice, and underdevelopment: Beyond modernisation theory. In C. Sumner (Ed.), *Crime, justice, and underdevelopment* (pp. 1–39). London: Heinemann.

www.ingramcontent.com/pod-product-compliance
Lightning Source LLC
Chambersburg PA
CBHW062048270326
41931CB00013B/2983